From the
TUNDRA
to the
TRENCHES

FIRST VOICES, FIRST TEXTS

SERIES EDITOR: WARREN CARIOU

First Voices, First Texts aims to reconnect contemporary readers with some of the most important Aboriginal literature of the past, much of which has been unavailable for decades. This series reveals the richness of these works by providing newly re-edited texts that are presented with particular sensitivity toward Indigenous ethics, traditions, and contemporary realities. The editors strive to indigenize the editing process by involving communities, by respecting traditional protocols, and by providing critical introductions that give readers new insights into the cultural contexts of these unjustly neglected classics.

From the

TUNDRA

to the

TRENCHES

EDDY WEETALTUK

Edited and with a foreword by Thibault Martin
Introduction by Isabelle St-Amand

UMP
University of Manitoba Press

University of Manitoba Press
Winnipeg, Manitoba
Canada R3T 2M5
uofmpress.ca

Printed in Canada
Text printed on chlorine-free, 100% post-consumer recycled paper

20 19 18 17 16   1 2 3 4 5

Cover image: Courtesy of the Weetaltuk family and Carnets Nord
Back flap image: Courtesy of Avataq Cultural Institute
Cover design: Mike Carroll
Interior design: Jess Koroscil

Library and Archives Canada Cataloguing in Publication

Weetaltuk, Eddy, 1932–2005, author
From the tundra to the trenches / Eddy Weetaltuk,
author ; Thibault Martin, editor.

(First voices, first texts ; 4)
Previously published in French translation under title: E9–422,
un Inuit, de la toundra à la guerre de Corée.
Includes bibliographical references.
Issued in print and electronic formats.
ISBN 978-0-88755-822-1 (pbk.)
ISBN 978-0-88755-536-7 (pdf)
ISBN 978-0-88755-534-3 (epub)

1. Weetaltuk, Eddy, 1932–2005. 2. Inuit—Canada—Biography.
3. Korean War, 1950–1953—Canada—Biography. 4. Soldiers—
Canada—Biography. I. Martin, Thibault, 1963–, editor II. Title.
III. Series: First voices, first texts ; 4

E99.E7W438 2016   971.004'97120092   C2016-903149-7
                                                C2016-903150-0

The University of Manitoba Press gratefully acknowledges the financial support
for its publication program provided by the Government of Canada through the Canada
Book Fund, the Canada Council for the Arts, the Manitoba Department
of Culture, Heritage, Tourism, the Manitoba Arts Council,
and the Manitoba Book Publishing Tax Credit.

Table of
CONTENTS

Note to the
READER

The story you are about to read really happened and all the people you will come across here really existed. I thank them for having contributed to my numerous adventures and I hope they will forgive me for having made public some pieces of their own life.

To protect the memory of some of my friends, I have chosen to disguise some names. For the same reason a few place names have been omitted to keep the origin of those people discreet. Still, most of the names are accurate, as I wish to acknowledge the people who have helped me throughout my life.

I wish to express my deepest gratitude to the people who helped to prepare this manuscript: Marie-Claude Prémont (McGill University) and her family, Mario Aubin and his family, Martine Breuillard, Marie-Claude Perreault, and her two daughters, Géraldine and Juliette; Stephan Wodicka and Maureen Waters, who reviewed a first version of the manuscript; Henry Strub, who took care of my manuscript thirty years ago; and Thibault Martin, who helped me to finalize this book.

My deepest gratitude goes also to the residents of Umiujaq and to the municipality office and its employees. I wish also to extend a final and special thanks to Charlie Tooktu, who supported and advised me during the preparation of this book.

—*Eddy Weetaltuk*

Note on the
ILLUSTRATIONS

Eddy Weetaltuk produced a series of pastel drawings to accompany the text of *From the Tundra to the Trenches*, a selection of which appear in this volume. All illustrations and photographs are reproduced courtesy of the Weetaltuk family. Page numbers in the captions refer to the corresponding scenes in the text.

FOREWORD

BY *Thibault Martin*

TRANSLATED FROM FRENCH BY JEREMY PATZER

Completing a manuscript and knowing that the words one has chosen to express emotions, thoughts, and dreams will soon be in print brings an enormous sense of relief and accomplishment. Unfortunately, Eddy Weetaltuk will not have the chance to experience this joy. He passed away on 2 March 2005, four days after learning that the revision of his manuscript was complete and that he would soon receive the conclusion. For his loved ones and for those who accompanied him on his journey as a writer, knowing that he will not be able to see his work published brings great sadness. Nevertheless, I think he had no regrets, happy as he was to have completed the work and confident that his community, and Canadians as a whole, would finally be able to read the story that he had yearned to tell for thirty years.

When Eddy Weetaltuk wrote the first version of this book in 1974 he was, above all, driven by the desire to express certain emotions that he could no longer confine within himself. Thirty years later, when the possibility of publishing his manuscript finally presented itself, he took to it again with a different perspective. This time, while reworking the text, he thought of the younger generation of Inuit.[1] He expressed his desire that they find in the reading of his "adventures"—for this is what he liked to call the experiences he had in his earlier life—the inspiration to lead a life of discovery, all the while taking hold of their cultural heritage. He also wanted his work to encourage Inuit to take up the pen and write their own history, just as Zacharias Kunuk took up the camera to immortalize Inuit stories.

The life of Eddy Weetaltuk is not the only adventure here; the story behind the publication of this book is itself an epic one. It began when he returned to Kuujjuarapik, after spending fifteen years in service to his country and travelling the world. Being back in his community made him realize that, as an Inuk in the Canadian Forces, the events he witnessed and the experiences he underwent were unique. He thus decided to put on paper everything that he could remember, before time erased from memory any detail of the events. "Put it on paper" is exactly what Eddy did. Not content to just put his experiences into words, Eddy preserved his most remarkable memories in images. He thus completed, alongside his writing, a series of pastel drawings.

Eddy Weetaltuk considered this work on his memoirs an extension of his duty as a soldier,[2] and it was his wish that his account be published for posterity. This is why in 1975, with the help of his friend Henry Strub, he sent the manuscript along with his drawings to the National Museum of Man in Ottawa. Strub, acting on behalf of Eddy Weetaltuk, also succeeded in piquing the interest of filmmaker Jim Hussinger, who in turn wrote a script with the intention of producing a film based on Eddy's life. Strub exchanged correspondence with authorities at the museum[3] for more than two years in the hopes of advancing Eddy Weetaltuk's project. Although Strub's contacts expressed interest, each response they provided to his requests remained vague. Strub was also asked, on different occasions, to intercede with Eddy Weetaltuk in order to convince him to create more drawings and to add to his text sections describing the traditional Inuit way of life. The goal of these requests was to make the story, according to the terms used in the museum's correspondence, "more balanced." In good faith, Eddy Weetaltuk set himself to work once again in order to satisfy the demands of the experts certified in Inuit ways of life. Despite this, no offer to publish was given. Museum authorities' lack of consideration for the gift Eddy wanted to share irritated Henry Strub who, one day, let loose a commentary that revealed his impatience: "Weetaltuk is a very important person: Canada belongs to him and we should not put ourselves in the position of appearing to act in traditional colonial overlord style."[4]

About two years later, Henry Strub, who had been searching to his wits' end for a private publisher, made the unfortunate discovery that the museum had misplaced the original photographs of Eddy's drawings. They were not found again until October 1977. Meanwhile, Strub's life had taken such a detour that he stopped exchanging letters with the museum. Eddy Weetaltuk, who had been awaiting the publication of his book for more than two years, resigned himself to seeing his manuscript, drawings, and film script archived.

In 2002, twenty-seven years later, Eddy's manuscript resurfaced at the Canadian Museum of Civilization[5] (hereafter Museum of Civilization). Maria von Finckenstein, curator of Inuit Art, learned of the existence of Eddy Weetaltuk's work and, after having realized the historical value of the text and the artistic merit of the drawings, contacted her counterparts at the Canadian War Museum (hereafter War Museum). She encouraged them to contact Eddy to acquire his manuscript and drawings. In effect, Eddy Weetaltuk had not yet ceded ownership of anything, but had simply entrusted and left his work at the museum's disposal. After examining it, the acquisition committee decided that the War Museum should proceed and make an offer to Eddy. The correspondence between Maria von Finckenstein[6] and the War Museum to which we could gain access[7] indicates that the museum had estimated the value of the drawings alone at $8,300. Despite this, the War Museum hoped Eddy Weetaltuk would relinquish his collection gratis and accept a charitable receipt in place of payment. It seems his contact at this time asked him to send the original manuscript since the document previously given to the museum was only a copy. At that point, Eddy Weetaltuk was under the impression that the War Museum was finally going to publish a book based on his manuscript and drawings. He sent the documents immediately, although no agreement had been arrived at concerning the acquisition of the work.

Time passed and Eddy had received no further news from the museum. This was when he met Marie-Claude Prémont, lawyer and professor at the Faculty of Law at McGill University. He asked her to contact the War Museum in order to know the status of his book project. In fact, Marie-Claude Prémont was not the first person Eddy Weetaltuk had approached about his manuscript; on different occasions he approached several anthropologists and civil servants for help in his project. Marie-Claude Prémont was, however, the only one to consider his request seriously enough to take the necessary time and steps to track down and "repatriate"[8] his manuscript and drawings.

Marie-Claude Prémont initiated contact with the War Museum during the summer of 2002, requesting the status of Eddy's dossier. She was told that the museum had no specific plans for the manuscript and drawings and she therefore requested that they be returned to Eddy Weetaltuk. In response to this request, Marie-Claude Prémont's contact notified her that the museum was prepared to buy the drawings for $1,000—despite the fact that their value had been estimated at around $8,300 by an employee of the same museum.[9] With Eddy Weetaltuk's goal being the publication of his work, he refused to part ways with his drawings and wished to recover them along with the original manuscript. Marie-Claude Prémont (serving as Eddy Weetaltuk's legal representation in dealing with the museum) was then notified by her museum contact that the original manuscript had never been sent to them. Eddy, who had retained an acute sense of organization since his time in the military, then sent them a copy of the Canada Post receipt that he had kept for his records. This convinced the employees of the War Museum to search more intently for the document that was so important to Eddy. It was finally located and returned to its owner at the end of 2002. Almost thirty years after he had initially sent it, Eddy was back to square one.

Once the manuscript had been returned, Marie-Claude Prémont took steps toward getting it published. The publisher that she approached found the manuscript very interesting, but felt that the writing required major revision. I met Prémont some time after she had received this response. When she found out that I knew Eddy Weetaltuk (I had stayed with him while completing research for my doctorate), she recounted the story of the manuscript and asked if I would help him revise it such that it would conform to the requirements of the publisher.

A little while later I received a typed hard copy of the text. The original manuscript had become difficult to read after so many years, thus Eddy had to have it transcribed. It had been a fairly long task, but it permitted him to take up the story again, since it was he who had dictated to the typist. After I received and familiarized myself with the manuscript, I contacted Eddy Weetaltuk's friends, Marie-Claude

Prémont and Mario Aubin, to discuss the best approach to working with him. It was decided that he would come spend some time at my place so that we could rework the text together. At the time, I was living in Winnipeg, about 3,000 kilometres from Umiujaq, his community. As his health was fragile, his friends felt it best that he not spend too long at my place. To a certain extent, the brevity of his stay shaped the nature of our collaboration.

Perhaps the reader will wonder how Eddy and I managed this undertaking and in what way my involvement might have influenced the content and introduced a certain bias—and, of course, what precautions we took to minimize this. I will try to shed some light on this in the pages that follow. My purpose was above all technical in nature, with my role consisting in reformulating and restructuring the sections that needed revision so that the original could be read without difficulty and the various dramatic and comedic situations were all presented in the proper tone.

To sum up, the work of revision consisted in the rewriting of those passages whose formulation was most problematic, as well as in the addition and elimination of certain sections. Some anecdotes were also added or removed in order to liven up the reading. Some of these changes were suggested by Eddy Weetaltuk; others were suggested by me. It should be said that his choices were motivated by several different factors. Eddy Weetaltuk wanted to send a message to Inuit youth while at the same time exorcising his past and, above all—and this might surprise the reader—he wanted to write a *bestseller*. It was not simply because he was expecting remuneration, but because he wanted as many people as possible to read the story of an Inuk, written by an Inuk. In this way, he wanted to say to the entire world that a "man of the North," an Aboriginal person, could find as brilliant a destiny as any other Canadian. He had this desire to connect with a large readership since the beginning. As he said to his friend Henry Strub, "By all means [the museum] can go ahead with my drawing and writing if they can make a success of it."[10] Eddy Weetaltuk would also say to me that he wanted the book to be published in the countries where he had travelled, especially Germany and Korea, and in the different languages that he had learned. At the time of writing these lines, this book has already been published in French and German.[11]

Here is, for the record, a more precise description of our collaboration. During Eddy Weetaltuk's stay in Winnipeg, we concentrated on a critical reading of the text. The first thing we did was organize the book, dividing it into chapters. I remember that we discussed titles a lot. As we were reading through the manuscript, we would identify passages that needed to be reworked, be it because they needed to be put into context, or because they were redundant, or had been written too hurriedly. Each time such a passage was identified, we discussed the changes that needed to be brought to it. Once the day of reading came to an end, I would work on the text to bring to it the changes that we had agreed on. The next day, Eddy Weetaltuk read the reworked pages, corrected them when necessary, and suggested other modifications that I would later add. I should specify, however, that it was often I who suggested the passages to be revised and proposed changes to the written expression, while it was Eddy who provided those elements that would help me remain true to his thinking.

On several occasions I recommended that we rewrite or change some sections that were particularly graphic—keep in mind that much of his story takes place in times of war, with all that this implies in terms of atrocity. That said, he did not follow all of my suggestions and chose to keep certain scenes that the reader may find difficult. I also suggested that certain persons might be uncomfortable seeing their name or the name of a relative appear in the book. I proposed changing names when it seemed appropriate, and the identities of several individuals have been protected by using pseudonyms. However, Eddy Weetaltuk chose to maintain others' real names. In short, Eddy Weetaltuk maintained control of the rhythm, the content, and the style of the text.

Despite all the precautions taken in order to ensure the integrity of Eddy Weetaltuk's self-expression in this book, I knew all too well that my interventions and my advice risked altering his life story and I wanted to be sure that he was conscious of and comfortable with this influence. I asked him on several occasions if he wanted to continue working with me and if he was satisfied with my advice. In essence, I was worried about the legitimacy of my role as assistant biographer, so much so that one day I even asked him why he trusted me. Without hesitating, he responded: "You and your wife, you have a daughter of your own, but you have also adopted another girl and you love her like your own. You are like Inuit.[12] You love other people's children and you raise them as your own. This is why I trust you and I know that you are going to help me write a good book."

When Eddy Weetaltuk returned to Umiujaq after several weeks of intense work, we had by then been over the entirety of the text and I had made the key modifications. However, there remained the task of doing a systematic edit of the work as a whole. I also had to finish several passages that we had not yet finalized. After his departure, I continued revising and would send him the chapters, one by one, as I completed them. He reread them, made notes on the paper, and sent them back to me. When I wanted information or further specification, I would telephone him. These exchanges lasted for about a year—until his death. Fortunately, Eddy Weetaltuk had had the time to reread and approve most of the text before leaving us. Only the last pages of the conclusion had not been reread.

Perhaps the reader will notice that the tone of the text evolves as the story progresses. In the beginning, the narrator is enthusiastic and full of humour, only to become more and more serious. This change in style is in part related to the nature of the situations recounted, however, Eddy's state of mind during the rewriting of the book intensified this effect. Indeed, when we began working together, he was passionate, energized, and keen to revisit his story in depth—he would spend a lot of time telling me about the experiences of his younger years. But the more time passed, the more pressed he was to finish the manuscript—because he wanted to complete the project, yes, but also because the summoning up of a more recent past interested him less, especially when it was a matter of reliving sad moments.

Thirty-five years ago, when the National Museum of Man received the manuscript of almost 200 pages that was the story of Private Eddy Weetaltuk, no one believed that this text, written by an Inuk, could hold any kind of literary interest. It was therefore treated as an archival document, an unrefined piece that could possibly serve as a documentary source and be used for historiographical purposes. We must not make the same mistake today and see in his story only a firsthand account that would be of interest to only anthropologists or historians. No, the text that Eddy Weetaltuk has brought us is not a historical document, but a literary work, and it should be considered as such. In effect, just because this work is autobiographical does not mean that it is any less the result of a creative process. Eddy Weetaltuk does not merely list off events in this book: he stages them. He employs powerful literary devices and makes use of dramatic and provocative situations, skillfully chosen to renew the reader's attention or to breathe life into the story. In the first pages of this book, one will discover the skill with which the narrator draws attention. Further on, one will see that Eddy Weetaltuk does not hesitate to depict scenes with an eroticism that is raw, even disturbing, in a way that is reminiscent of certain scenes from Maupassant or Bukowski. Simultaneously, he also plays on metaphors, going so far as to loosely translate his own name, "Weetaltuk," to back his words. The title, too, is chosen to attract a wide readership. In fact, Eddy knew perfectly well that in the Western imagination Inuit are lost in the middle of the barren tundra. Nevertheless, the region of his birth and his different childhood homes are not situated in the Arctic, but rather in the Subarctic, a territory characterized by taiga forest vegetation. But, no matter, he had no hesitation in modifying the tree line by several hundred kilometres in order to meet readers' expectations. One will therefore observe that this text is not a simple chronological succession of events, but a literary story that brings to the fore the emotions, fears, weaknesses, and, above all, the human desire for liberty. In short, like all literary works, Eddy Weetaltuk's story deals in the specifics of individual experience, only to confront us with the greatest of existential questions.

Moreover, the book that you are about to read is unique in that it was first thought up and written in a time when Inuit were still referred to as "Eskimos" by mainstream Canadians. For many, they were simply the last witnesses of an archaic way of life. Few saw in them peers capable of creating and building the world from their own vantage point. Nevertheless, in that era Eddy Weetaltuk wrote, taking hold of history, looking upon himself and upon the modern world with a vision that made no compromises—a vision of equality. In this sense, Eddy Weetaltuk shared the fate of many writers who were ahead of their time: his talent stayed unrecognized until his death.

In his story, Eddy Weetaltuk makes several statements that might surprise the reader. First of all, he was convinced that he had been Canada's first Inuit combatant. Is this really possible, considering that at least 12,000 Aboriginal Canadians participated in the modern wars in which Canada has taken part? In addition, he was convinced that from 1940 to 1960, the Canadian government restricted the mobility of Inuit, preventing them from leaving the North. Although the veracity of these perceptions have, in my opinion, little impact on the quality of the story, an anonymous reviewer of this book thought it was important to clarify these two points. I will turn my attention to this in the pages that follow. I will then return to the unique contribution Eddy Weetaltuk's account offers to Aboriginal and Canadian literature.

Eddy Weetaltuk believed all his life that he was the first Inuk Canadian to have participated in military combat. A certain number of clues led him to develop this belief. First of all, he had read it in a missionary periodical where he had been referred to as the "first known Inuit Canadian soldier."[13] The purpose of the article was not to relate the military history of Eddy Weetaltuk, but rather to discuss his "miracle healing." In effect, in the late 1940s, when he was a student at the Fort George residential school,[14] a contagious illness spread across the James Bay region and five children in the school died. Eddy Weetaltuk himself fell into a semi-comatose state. Hope of him surviving was all but lost when one of the Oblate brothers placed a religious symbol of

Brother Andre, founder of Saint Joseph's Oratory in Montreal, around Eddy's neck. The intervention is said to have saved his life.[15] He spoke to me on a number of occasions about this episode. He believed that he was the first Inuk soldier because it was written by a priest. He believed this idea as much as he believed that he was healed by miracle as a child.

Several other important signs had also contributed to this conviction. First of all, some soldiers he had encountered in his youth seemed to believe that Inuit could not join the army. Other occurrences then brought him to think that the few rare Inuit who, like him, had succeeded in joining the army, did not have the right to leave the country and thus could not fight on the front lines. In fact, sometime after the Korean War, while his battalion was preparing for a departure to be stationed in Germany, the other two Inuit[16] in his regiment were transferred to Churchill. For Eddy, this incident confirmed that Inuit were not authorized to leave Canada and that the government wanted them to stay in the North.

When he returned to his community, Eddy Weetaltuk tried for several years to find Inuit who participated in the Second World War or who had served, like him, in the Korean War. He tried to compile a list of all Inuit who had participated in military operations, be it in conventional armed conflicts, as Canadian Rangers during the Cold War, or, even more recently, as peacekeepers. The information that Eddy gathered showed that several Inuit had participated in a variety of peacekeeping operations, a fact of which he was quite proud. But, despite all his research, he had not been able to find any Inuit veterans of the Korean War or the Second World War. He left this world certain of having been the first Canadian Inuk to see combat.

Historians have recently taken an interest in the contribution Aboriginal Canadians made to war efforts, most notably within the context of the Royal Commission on Aboriginal Peoples (hereafter RCAP).[17] Their documentary sources show that during the First World War at least fifteen Labrador Inuit engaged in battle in Europe. At that time, the coastal area of Labrador belonged to Newfoundland—which was not yet a part of Canada—meaning, technically, that these soldiers were not Canadian. Of course, it was not for this reason that Eddy

Weetaltuk thought that he had been the first Inuit Canadian soldier, but because the Labrador Inuit's contribution to the war effort had remained unknown to the public at large. Once the First World War was over, these soldiers' sacrifices were neither recognized nor publicly honoured. Nevertheless, at least two of the fifteen Inuit soldiers made their way into military history. Frederick Frieda, of Hopedale, and lance corporal and sniper John Shiwak of Rigolet, both members of the Royal Newfoundland Regiment, died on the battlefield in France.[18]

In fact, very little is known about Inuit participation in war. Hence the historians who contributed to the RCAP—as well as those who contributed to the commemorative document published by the Minister of Veterans Affairs, *Native Soldiers, Foreign Battlefields*[19]—estimate that Inuit probably participated in both world wars: "The Aboriginal people of Canada responded whole-heartedly to the wartime emergency of 1914–1918. Status and non-status Indians, Métis and Inuit all served overseas, frequently in the front lines."[20] During the Second World War, "[Indian Affairs] would report a total of 3,090 participants—including 72 women and 7 Indians from the Yukon. However, the actual number of Native recruits was likely higher than the figure recorded, since, again, some Indians and most Métis and Inuit were excluded from Indian Affairs' tally."[21] While the participation of First Nations in the two world wars is generally well documented, data concerning non-status Indians and Metis is sparse and the only information available about the Inuit concerns the fifteen from Labrador. In fact, the national institutions that serve in the maintenance of our collective memory—Veterans Affairs, Indigenous and Northern Affairs, the Department of National Defence, and Canadian Heritage—are now limited by their past lack of interest, and can only speculate as to the Inuit contribution.

Similarly, one cannot find any information concerning Inuit participation in the Korean War in these publications. Only John Moses, in a publication by the Department of National Defence,[22] mentions the participation of an Inuk in the Korean War, and this Inuk is Eddy Weetaltuk: "Cultural and language differences made it especially difficult for Inuit to join the Forces, but one who did was Eddie Weetaltuk, born near East Main River, Quebec, who had been raised at residential schools in northern Quebec and Ontario. After working as cook and labourer in pulp and paper enterprises around Timmins, Ontario, and in various lumber camps in the upper Ottawa valley, he joined the Canadian Army Special Force under the name of Eddie Vital in 1952."[23]

From one perspective the lack of data concerning Inuit participation in Canada's war effort is quite surprising, given that during the Second World War as well as during the Cold War several military bases were located in the North and in Inuit communities.[24] However, military history is written from the perspective of mainstream society and not from that of Aboriginal Canadians, and contributes only to those topics that interest the majority. Inuit—their achievements and their stories, as well as their defence of the Arctic—were too far from the day-to-day concerns of the majority to attract attention.

In short, a number of factors made Eddy Weetaltuk believe, all his life, that he was the first Canadian Inuk to have fought in battle. Without a doubt the first factor was the impossibility of locating other Inuit who had served in war prior to him. Then, during those years that he served in the Canadian Armed Forces, the information that he received indicated that Inuit were not encouraged to participate in Canada's war efforts outside of the country. To this one must add the dearth of information available to the public concerning Inuit contributions to the defence of Canada.

When he was young, Eddy Weetaltuk was convinced that the Canadian government opposed Inuit leaving their communities and moving to the South. It was because of this that he lived a large part of his life under an assumed name. Some readers might wonder if the government actually compelled Inuit to remain in the North, and if they did not in fact have the right to enroll in the army. There are essentially two ways to respond to these questions. The first is sociological and the second historical. Sociologically, one can say that these facts were true from Eddy Weetaltuk's point of view. He did not concoct this theory for the pleasure of projecting himself as the victim of a colonial regime, but rather he deduced it from observing the practices of agents representing Canadian institutions—notably the Royal Canadian Mounted Police and Indian and Northern Affairs Canada. As we will see later on, these agencies seemed to share the common goal of controlling the movements of Inuit, forcing the sedentarization of Aboriginal populations. He had access to no other information, thus for him reality was based on what was available. In other words, these facts were real enough that they led him to make certain decisions over others. Eddy Weetaltuk's reality was the result of the sole reading of the world that he could make from the actions, tacit understandings, and half-truths Canadian institutions served to Aboriginal peoples under the guise of information.

Now, does history prove Eddy Weetaltuk right? The response is implicitly affirmative. If they do not always confirm his perception of the situation, the initiatives instigated by federal agencies since the end of the Second World War at least explain it. First of all, from the end of the 1950s, Ottawa had a policy of sedentarization in place and gathered Inuit families into permanent settlements. This policy's stated goal was to facilitate the distribution of aid to Inuit, but it also allowed for increased control over the territory and its inhabitants. Thus, hunters who would travel their territory according to a seasonal rhythm found themselves constrained to permanently settle in locations that they had not chosen, but which were imposed upon them according to the government's own considerations.[25] Then there was an increasingly marked presence of the Royal Canadian Mounted Police in the North. Each summer during the 1950s, the Eastern Arctic Patrol crossed and, sometimes by force, evacuated Inuit territory of those suffering from tuberculosis. The large numbers of Inuit that were removed from their communities in this way made for what Jetté[26] referred to as the "Great Upheaval of the Inuit"—an allusion to the British expulsion of Acadians in the eighteenth century. This left an indelible mark on the collective memory of Inuit, contributing to their sense of lost liberty, which partly explains Eddy Weetaltuk's certainty.

However, the most striking experience was that of the forced relocations—the now common description for the transfers of Inuit families organized, in the early 1950s, by federal agents.[27] Two such moves involved several families from Inukjuaq (called Port Harrison at the time) who were relocated in 1953 and 1955 to Grise Fjord and

Resolute Bay, some 3,200 kilometres farther north. Other Inuit from Pond Inlet (Nunavut) were sent to Resolute Bay. These two destinations were among the most isolated and barren places in the Canadian Arctic. It is understandable, then, that such policies might have helped convince Eddy Weetaltuk that the government wanted to "make Inuit stay in the North." The impact of these relocations was all the more significant for Eddy, since he had family that resided in Inukjuaq—and continue to live there to this day. Another relocation, concerning Nunavik again, sent Inuit from Kuujjuak (Fort Chimo) to Churchill, Manitoba, in 1955. Of course, these forced relocations took place after Eddy Weetaltuk joined the army (in 1952), but they reinforced his belief that Inuit freedom of movement was limited. Moreover, his encounters with other Inuit and his stay in Churchill contributed to his construction of a reality in which the state wanted to put Inuit under "house arrest." Eddy's impression of state intervention in Inuit life led him to remove himself from the North, where he thought himself a prisoner.

During the writing of the manuscript's initial version, Eddy Weetaltuk already had the conviction that the state sought to control the place of residence of Inuit. During our time together for the revision, however, he was even more convinced of it, since other instances of forced relocation had since taken place. The displacement of the Fort George community, where he had been a student in the residential school and spent a large part of his childhood, left the greatest impression on him. The relocation of the village, originally located on an island at the mouth of the La Grande River, was a consequence of hydroelectric development in the James Bay area. It is noteworthy that around fifty Inuit still live in Chisasibi, the village created by the relocation.

Eddy Weetaltuk's work is innovative in many respects—first of all because it offers an Inuit interpretation of history and brings a non-Western perspective to the Canadian colonial experience in the Far North. But rather than presenting Inuit as victims of history, his writing shows that, despite the hold taken by modern institutions, Inuit have never relinquished control of their individual destiny. As such, the story that he tells is of a man in pursuit of his dreams, not of a victim. All his life he considered himself accountable for his actions. From his point of view, colonialism had created certain conditions and imposed certain rules. But these, whatever their injustice, did not prevent him from living freely and equally—in the philosophical sense, if not the legal one. Eddy Weetaltuk thought it was important to bring his story to Inuit youth so that they could have access to one that broke from the tradition of anthropological works that put too much emphasis on the victimization of Inuit. He wanted to say to young Inuit that it was possible to have a life and to be its author and leading actor.

Nevertheless, Eddy Weetaltuk's reflections are not centred on the issue of Inuit relations to mainstream Canadian society. What interests him is the individual in his or her universe as a whole, be this in the North, the South, in a family setting, on the battlefield, or even in prison. Eddy, who spoke five languages and had thus developed the unique ability to understand the world from different perspectives, asked himself a number of questions on human nature and on the value of supposedly universal ideals. In this regard, the judgment that he renders on Western society, on Inuit, on war, and on himself is far from naive. Eddy demonstrates this by the manner in which he relates the story, being neither hero nor accuser, but by exposing his own weaknesses and pain as if to exorcise them. For us Western readers, Eddy Weetaltuk's story constitutes a unique experience that helps us to realize that, beyond the dichotomy that opposes "White" and "Aboriginal," we have in common a world that we build together, for better or for worse.

Eddy Weetaltuk also wanted his work to give Aboriginal veterans and their descendants an uncensored account—presenting the experiences and emotions lived by their ancestors in the name of their attachment to Canada. This is why he did not want to hide the identity of his fellow soldiers. He wanted them to be recognizable to themselves and their families. His story also reveals the emotional and cultural shock that many Aboriginal soldiers experienced upon joining the military. He presents an account that goes beyond the singular experience of an Inuit volunteer and reverberates with the experiences of so many other Aboriginal soldiers. It is noteworthy that Eddy, during all those years spent in service to his country, felt as though he shared a common circumstance with his Metis and First Nations comrades and held a particular affinity for them, although he formed bonds of friendship with soldiers of all origins.

Aboriginal soldiers' sacrifices on the battlefield earned them the respect of their brothers in arms, and they were treated as equals by the other soldiers. Despite this, the treatment that awaited the Aboriginal veterans once they were no longer in the service was particularly immoral and unjust. This is why I thought it would be interesting to append a chapter that reveals the scope of Aboriginal contribution to the defence of Canadian values (see Appendix). The chapter also takes stock of the wrongs suffered by Aboriginal soldiers and their families and of the struggles for equality that founded contemporary emancipatory movements for Canada's First Peoples. This appendix allows the reader to discover a little known aspect of Canadian history. The analysis it offers, however, cannot measure up to the account that Eddy Weetaltuk offers us. It is thus proper that I now yield to the hero of this voyage through the extremes of war.

NOTES

1. I have adopted the following rules of use: "Inuk" is the singular noun, while "Inuit" is both the plural noun and adjective. Both words are always capitalized. Given that the word Inuit means "the people," I have endeavoured to avoid redundant usages such as "the Inuit" or "the Inuit People."

2. A number of Aboriginal soldiers have, just as Eddy, wanted to leave a written account of their participation in war. Amongst them, Chief Louis Jackson relates in his book *Our Caughnawaga in Egypt* (Ottawa: W. Drydale and Co., 1885) the events that he experienced, alongside other compatriots from Kahnawake, during the Battle of the Nile. Another Aboriginal soldier, James Brody, kept a journal during his years in service. More recently, the Saskatchewan Indian Veterans Association published a work, *We Were There* (1989), to commemorate the sacrifices of Aboriginal soldiers.

3. Notably, with the ethnologist in charge of the Inuit collection and the curator of ethnographic collections.

4. Letter to Mr. Denis Alsford, Curator of Collections, National Museum of Man, Ottawa, 9 June 1976.

5. Previously known as the National Museum of Man.

6. Although museum authorities, in my opinion, could be blamed for their negligent treatment of Eddy Weetaltuk's work, it must also be said that von Finckenstein displayed a certain diligence, going so far as to contact the Avataq Cultural Institute in an attempt to trace the history of the manuscript. She then tracked down Eddy Weetaltuk and offered to give to her colleagues the name of an interpreter who spoke Inuktitut.

7. This was obtained through a request made under the Access to Information Act.

8. The question of "repatriating" creative works goes beyond the issue of Eddy Weetaltuk's manuscript, although the process of recuperating his work taken on by Marie-Claude Prémont is somewhat emblematic. In effect, it is a subject of controversy with high political stakes that has engaged academics as much in Canada as in the majority of states with Aboriginal populations, as well as in former European colonies. At issue is the return of artifacts, works of art, and even human remains that belonged to Native and Indigenous populations. For years, members of these communities have sought to repatriate the goods, religious objects, and objects of historical significance that were taken from them during the colonial era. Although several administrations have responded positively to these demands, others are resistant. In all cases, however, the process of restitution is often slow and does not garner the immediate support of all the actors in the curatorial milieu.

9. Information obtained from the internal correspondence of the museum.

10. Letter to Henry Strub, 5 October 1975.

11. Eddy Weetaltuk, with Thibault Martin, *E9-422: un Inuit de la toundra à la guerre de Corée*, translated by Marie-Claude Perreault (Paris: Carnets Nord, 2009). Eddy Weetaltuk, with Thibault Martin, *Mein Leben in die Hand nehmen: Die Odyssee des Inuk E9-422*, edited by Helga Bories-Sawala, translated by Rolf Sawala (Hamburg: DOBU Verlag, 2015).

12. Traditionally, Inuit children were often adopted, not because they had no parents, but rather to add a social kinship to biological kinship. This practice results in a significant circulation of children within the community and contributes to the reinforcement of community solidarity. The research I conducted in Kuujjuarapik and Umiujaq in 1998 shows that, still today, a significant number of children are not raised by their biological parents but by other community members.

13. I was unable, unfortunately, to locate this publication.

14. Today known as Chisasibi.

15. This episode in Eddy's life was also reported in the periodical *Catholic Missions in Canada* 22, no. 3 (Fall 2003): 16–7.

16. They were originally from the Northwest Territories.

17. RCAP (Royal Commission on Aboriginal Peoples), *Royal Commission Report on Aboriginal Peoples* (Ottawa: Canada Communication Group Publishing, 1996). Electronic version (RCAP, 2006) available at http://www.ainc-inac.gc.ca.

18. RCAP, 2006, 7.

19. Janice Summerby, *Native Soldiers, Foreign Battlefields* (Ottawa: Minister of Veterans Affairs, 2005), http://www.veterans.gc.ca/public/pages/remembrance/those-who-served/aboriginal-veterans/native-soldiers/natives_e.pdf (accessed November 2016).

20. RCAP, 2006.

21. Summerby, *Native Soldiers*, 21.

22. John Moses, Donald Graves, and Warren Sinclair, *A Sketch Account of Aboriginal Peoples in the Canadian Military* (Ottawa: Department of National Defence, 2004), http://dsp-psd.pwgsc.gc.ca/Collection/D61-16-2004E.pdf.

23. Ibid., 78.

24. I engage with this issue in more depth in the Appendix.

25. Diamond Jenness, "War Ferment," in *Eskimo Administration II: Canada* (Montreal: Arctic Institute of North America, 1964).

26. Mireille Jetté, *Et la santé des Inuit ça va? Rapport de l'enquête de Santé Québec auprès des Inuits du Nunavik* (Quebec: Government of Quebec, 1992).

27. This is examined in more detail in the Appendix. The first relocation took place in 1934. It involved the transfer of Inuit from Cape Dorset, Pond Inlet, and Pangnirtung to Devon Island.

INTRODUCTION

BY *Isabelle St-Amand*

Finally, the day came to move. Everyone was quiet except the corporals and sergeants, who were screaming out orders all day long. I suspected that my comrades were like me, too anxious to be able to talk. Like most of them, I never wanted to be a hero, I only enrolled because I needed a job. I was only nineteen years old and I still had a lot to live for. But instead I was heading to the front. I seriously thought of deserting, but I knew the punishment. I had already experienced the army detention and I wasn't going to taste it again. Thinking about what I had endured for misplacing my papers, I was sure the treatment for a deserter, especially a deserter enrolled under a fake identity, would have been unbearable. I was also thinking of my Inuit countrymen and I did not want to bring shame on my people. If I had deserted, everybody would have said that Inuit are not courageous enough for war. At that point I thought that I would rather be dead than bring shame on my family. I was probably the first Inuk to go to war. I had to be strong; I had to prove that Inuit are just as courageous as any other people. I was sad thinking I could die without seeing my family, but if my fate was to be killed, I was going to die with dignity. I was determined. I was going to show the world how an Inuk fights and dies.
—Eddy Weetaltuk, *From the Tundra to the Trenches* (83–84)

The life story of Eddy Weetaltuk, whose spirit is compellingly conveyed in this epigraph, interweaves reflections on war and settler colonialism, religion and sexuality, love and friendship, and the fundamental issue of identity. The witty and insightful narrative leads the reader along the exceptional life path of this Inuit war veteran and artist. From witnessing his childhood in the James Bay region, at a time of intense colonial encounters, the reader experiences his involvement as a combatant in the Korean War, and his later return home to Kuujjuarapik, also known as Whapmagoostui, Poste-de-la-Baleine, and Great Whale. Eddy Weetaltuk comments on the parallel between the place's many names and the false identity he took on to free himself from institutionalized racism: "But there are worse things than having too many names. Living with a borrowed name, like I had to do, as you will soon discover, is certainly more difficult to bear" (4). This personal, embodied experience of identity politics resulted in a far greater impact on his existence than he could have foreseen in 1951, the year he left James Bay for the South. Shortly thereafter, Weetaltuk, whose name means "innocent eyes" in Inuktitut, enlisted in the Canadian Armed Forces under the name of Eddy Vital. He passed himself off as the son of a French-Canadian man from Winnipeg in order to gain the freedom, mobility, and opportunities he felt deprived of as an Inuk in the mid-twentieth century. For nearly twenty years, he travelled the world in search of a better life, without being able to disclose his true identity.

Eddy Weetaltuk was born in 1932 in the James Bay region. He was the son of Mary Weetaltuk and hunter Rupert Weetaltuk, and the grandson of George Weetaltuk. His grandfather was a family leader who acted as a guide for American filmmaker Robert J. Flaherty during the shooting of the documentary film *Nanook of the North*. At the beginning of his life story, Weetaltuk identifies himself as an object of settler colonial policies and, through the events of his birth, situates himself within his family and home territory: "E9-422, Edward Weetaltuk, was a very small baby boy. Just a little bigger than a large wooden matchbox. I was born on cold snow while Mother was cutting wood to keep our family warm. My family used to travel to Strutton Island every spring for our annual arctic whale hunt. That's how I came into this world" (5). As recounted in his life story, he suffered through seven long years of famine out on the land as a child, attended the Fort George residential school, and later, against all odds, survived active service as a mortar operator on the front. As Dale Selma Blake points out, Weetaltuk's life narrative echoes other Inuit autobiographies that often emphasize the struggle for survival.[1]

Weetaltuk was a contemporary of Inuit authors Anthony Apakark Thrasher, Alice French, and Minnie Aodla Freeman, who were the first to publish autobiographies in the late 1970s—*Thrasher... Skid Row Eskimo* and *My Name is Masak,* in 1976, and *Life Among the Qallunaat* in 1978. Unlike his fellow authors, Weetaltuk was not known as a writer, but rather as a war veteran and artist. Although initially drafted in 1974, his life story would not be published before the turn of the twenty-first century, for reasons we will look at later in this introduction. In her book *Stories in a New Skin: Approaches to Inuit Literature,* Keavy Martin writes that many oral history and oral traditions projects were conducted from the 1980s through the 2010s by institutions and communities across the Arctic in order to explore "what life was like before the massive government interventions of the 1950s and 1960s."[2] Martin further emphasizes that "the pragmatic, ethnographic aspects of life writing or life telling have in fact been harnessed by Nunavummiut, as Frédéric Laugrand argues, 'to better affirm the continuity of their ancestral values, as if history had never displaced them.'"[3] Because the memories of elders act as repositories for these values, adds Martin, their life stories are often called upon to compensate for interruptions caused by colonial settlement, residential schools, and community relocation.[4] The life story of Weetaltuk falls into this context, but it also explores and makes sense exactly of those moments of upheaval.

Weetaltuk's life was exceptional. Like Freeman and Thrasher, he was among the first of his people to undertake a long journey through Canadian society and settler institutions in the South. In their respective autobiographies, Freeman and Thrasher recount their first-hand experience of the civil service and the prison system. Weetaltuk's memoirs, on the other hand, focus on his experience in the military, the avenue he followed as a young man in the hope of living the "life of adventures" he had been dreaming of. Weetaltuk's life writing evokes what Paul John Eakin defines as "a special form of reflexive consciousness," the autobiographical act being "a mode of self-invention always practised first in living and only eventually, and occasionally, in writing."[5] Weetaltuk created a new trajectory for himself, made stories of his life path and, through his autobiographical writing, made sense of these unique experiences, situations, and understandings. By exploring, inhabiting, and conceiving a present in rapid transformation, his life story expands and shores up what links the past to the future. *From the Tundra to the Trenches* weaves threads of continuity across both time and space. In many ways, it echoes the stories of the Yukon elders who, as Julie Cruikshank recollects in *The Social Life of Stories*, spoke of land "in terms of travel and mobility, frequently constructing life stories as travel narratives."[6] Weetaltuk's story provides an account of life in Inuit territory. It also ventures into new lands across Canada and makes its way to countries such as Korea, Japan, and Germany. It works hand-in-hand with a new mobility and a reflexive consciousness that connects places, peoples, and events on both the local and international levels.

The Original Manuscript: Writing and Reception

Our living link to the author, who passed away in 2005, and by extension to his family and community, is through sociologist Thibault Martin. He is a professor at the Université du Québec en Outaouais, and he collaborated with Weetaltuk on the original manuscript and edited and contributed to this volume. We therefore rely on what Martin has generously shared with us to describe and contextualize the writing and editing processes that resulted in the current critical edition.

Weetaltuk returned home in 1967 after many years of service with the Canadian Armed Forces. He first put his life story on paper in 1974. As he told Martin, writing was a way for him to make a record of his war memories before they faded away, as well as to make sense of the dramatic events he had lived through. In 1975, with the help of his friend Henry Strub, Weetaltuk sent his handwritten manuscript of about 200 pages and the twenty pastel drawings he had created to illustrate his narrative to the National Museum of Man in Ottawa (now the Canadian Museum of History). The drawings' presence in Weetaltuk's work, as complementary forms of creative expression, is certainly representative of a long tradition of illustration in Inuit writing and literature. As Robin McGrath points out, such a creative blending of text and visual imagery can be found in ancient Inuit material culture and it continues to shape contemporary works, such as Peter Pitseolak's illustrated oral biography, *Pictures Out of My Life* (1971), and Armand Tagoona's autobiography of narrated paintings, *Shadows* (1975).[7] This is also evident in more recent works such as Alootook Ipellie's book of short stories and pen-and-ink drawings, *Arctic Dreams and Nightmares* (1993). In 1975, in a note accompanying the draft of manuscript and the drawings, Weetaltuk urged the museum to disseminate his life story. He emphasized a need to recognize his unique contribution to Canadian history. He stated that he had been the first Inuk in the Canadian Armed Forces to fight in a war, had travelled the world extensively, and had written a book retracing his extraordinary life. For more than two years, Strub exchanged letters with the museum authorities on the author's behalf, but the initial interest in the manuscript never translated into concrete action.

It was not until 2002 that Weetaltuk heard back from the Canadian Museum of History, when Maria von Finckenstein, the museum's curator of Inuit Art, came across his life story and drawings. At a time marked by growing interest in Inuit art and writing[8] and by the "rising visibility of memoirs composed by common soldiers and junior officers,"[9] she recognized the historic and artistic value of Weetaltuk's work. She contacted the Canadian War Museum and suggested that they acquire his text and drawings for their institution. Although no agreement was reached concerning acquisition, Weetaltuk arranged for his work to be sent to the museum in the hope that it would be disseminated.

Once again, silence prevailed. Weetaltuk only renewed his contact with the museum following a chance encounter with Marie-Claude Prémont, a member of McGill University's Faculty of Law. At the time, Eddy Weetaltuk was living in Umiujaq, in the region of the Richmond Gulf (Tasiujaq), 160 kilometres north of Kuujjuarapik. He had relocated to that village with other Inuit from Kuujjuarapik. In response to a referendum held following the 1975 James Bay and Northern Quebec Agreement, they had "opted to create a new community where they could preserve their traditional lifestyle in an area where fish and game were not threatened"[10] by hydroelectric development. The construction of the village began in the summer of 1985 and ended in December of 1986.[11] It was there that Weetaltuk first met with Prémont. As with previous visitors to his community, mostly anthropologists and civil servants, Weetaltuk told Prémont his life story and his unsuccessful attempts to find a publisher. This time, however, he had the satisfaction of seeing his project taken further, as Prémont took action to recover the manuscript draft and drawings from the Canadian War Museum. Weetaltuk was then able to submit his newly retrieved manuscript to a leading publisher in the South. His story was considered for publication, but the publisher called for major revisions. Weetaltuk was by then already in his seventies, which raised the practical questions of how and when this would be done.

This was the situation when Prémont crossed paths with Thibault Martin at an academic conference in Europe. At that point, Weetaltuk had grown sceptical about the reliability of individuals and institutions that expressed interest in his manuscript. He had developed a close relationship with Martin when the sociologist stayed in his home while completing his doctoral fieldwork in Nunavik, and this relationship played a key role in their reaching an agreement and laying out a plan for their collaboration on Weetaltuk's book. The author dictated the content of his draft manuscript to a typist and mailed a copy of the transcript to Martin in Manitoba. He then flew from Umiujaq to Winnipeg and spent a few weeks at Martin's home to begin work on the revision. As Martin notes in the foreword, their collaboration was structured by the author's fragile health and consisted of a short visit followed by exchanges via regular mail about sections that had been revised.

Editorial Process, Collaborative Authorship

Weetaltuk's life story has finally found a home in the literary series First Voices, First Texts, published by the University of Manitoba Press. His work makes a meaningful contribution to a series of critical editions focusing on underappreciated Indigenous texts that deserve to be shared with contemporary readers. Notably, *From the Tundra to the Trenches* is the second by an Inuit author of the four titles in the series thus far, the first being the 2015 edition of Mini Aodla Freeman's autobiography. The significant presence of Inuit voices in this series responds to and helps to counter the lack of institutional support in the South for the development of Inuit literature.[12]

One of the goals of First Voices, First Texts is to produce, through a careful editing process, new versions of the texts that are true to the author's vision and the community's understanding. In that perspective, it is worth noting that the editing process of the current edition of Weetaltuk's life story differs in some ways from that of the other books in the series. With Freeman's *Life Among the Qallunaat*, for instance, the first published version of the text was compared to the original typescript as part of the revision process. A collaborative effort was undertaken by Freeman and the co-editors of her book—Keavy Martin, Julie Rak, and Norma Dunning—to identify, discuss, and alleviate traces of editorial intervention. In the case of Weetaltuk's text, there was only a draft manuscript that had not yet made its way into print. Furthermore, a typescript of that manuscript had until recently been available for consultation at the Canadian Museum of War; however, access was restricted at the request of the author's family, heirs, and their advisers, who wished to preserve the privacy of Weetaltuk's relatives and keep certain compromising passages from public scrutiny.

When asked about the impossibility of accessing the original manuscript for purposes of comparison, Thibault Martin explained that the document at the museum should be conceived of as a first draft rather than an original version, in the same way that the working versions of novels are not released to the public, even after the author's passing. Martin further pointed out that Weetaltuk's direct participation and full approval were integral to the entire rewriting process, and that, consequently, the current edition constitutes the only final version endorsed by the author. One of the peculiarities of Weetaltuk's life story is that it is no longer possible to unravel where the respective voices of the author and Martin begin and end, nor to identify, aside from Martin's accounts, portions of the draft that were cut or to what extent the style was altered. Despite our enduring curiosity regarding the extent to which the revised version differs from the original manuscript, we have to realize that it is not necessarily productive to think along those lines in situating the book and in understanding its genesis.

The editing process for the current edition involved different levels of editorial intervention. As a result, it is helpful to view it in the light of the writing practices discussed by Sophie McCall in *First Person Plural: Aboriginal Storytelling and the Ethics of Collaborative Authorship*, especially as they pertain to "the degrees of authorship and degrees of collaboration between storytellers, recorders, translators, editors, and authors."[13] In her book, McCall refutes the belief in the existence of a pure voice to be identified and retrieved. She advocates instead for the use of critical approaches that have the potential to illuminate storytelling and writing practices that "often confound traditional literary understandings of voice and authorship."[14] The texts that McCall examines are often shaped both by authorship and collaboration instead of being the product of a single author's work. It is in this perspective that McCall analyzes "the subtle shifts in the balance of power between mediators who are working within a broad range of as-told-to forms, techniques, and arenas."[15] It is also what the editing process behind *From the Tundra to the Trenches* compels us to do.

We can discern two main levels of editorial intervention at work in Weetaltuk's manuscript. On an interpersonal level, the author, an Inuit writer, artist, and war veteran, discussed and revised his original manuscript in collaboration with his editor, a settler sociologist and academic. On the chronological level, the author reviewed his own original manuscript as an elder, a few decades after he first jotted down his war memories. With this book, we are therefore neither in the presence of a non-Indigenous editor who appropriated the life story of an Indigenous author under his own name, nor are we faced with the myth of the absent editor widely used in as-told-to narratives examined by McCall.[16] Instead, upon tracking the progress of a story that was initially envisioned and written by Weetaltuk, we see the interpersonal and chronological levels of intervention mingling together through a rewriting process based on a unique form of as-told-to narrative. The author and editor first talked and sat together in a Winnipeg kitchen and then corresponded by regular mail to determine which passages to modify and how that should be accomplished.

The most obvious and potentially challenging element of intervention lies in the different and conflicting positions from which the author and editor are acting and speaking. For instance, as demonstrated by the obstacles encountered by Weetaltuk over the years, it is clear that the voice of an established academic receives a greater degree of recognition than that of a soldier-author with no formal post-secondary education. In the same way, settler voices still tend to be sought out over Indigenous voices.[17] This persistent power imbalance is explicitly acknowledged by Martin in the foreword, where he details the role he played in rewriting, reorganizing, and restructuring the author and protagonist's life story—whether it meant dividing the book into chapters, reordering the narrative, or polishing the style. Martin also shares his concerns about exerting an influence over the story, explaining how he consistently and mindfully asked Weetaltuk for validation during the editing process. It is still evident that both the author and the editor approached the process of revision with their respective objectives in mind, and contributed their particular knowledges and understandings to the current edition.

In that regard, we can sense from Weetaltuk's various efforts to publish his manuscript that the author was acutely aware of these politics of voice, and that he strategically used Prémont, Martin, and his other collaborators' privilege, knowledge, and connections in order to achieve his goal, which was to have his life story published and widely circulated. For instance, as Martin mentioned in an interview,[18] Weetaltuk saw his editor's ability to produce a prize-winning book, *De la banquise au congélateur*, as a tool to be used in ensuring the success of his own book. As Martin recounts, Weetaltuk was also ready to make certain compromises and cater to the needs of the publishers and their readers if that would bring him closer to getting the fundamental tenets of his story out there. The author, who had found in the armed forces a sense of brotherhood and much sought-after recognition of his humanity, considered the work on his memoirs to be part of his military duty. His wish was to provide Indigenous veterans and their descendants with an uncensored account of his participation in the Korean War. However, following discussion with Martin and his advisers, he elected to make certain changes to his manuscript, a decision he explains in a note to the reader at the beginning of the book: "To protect the memory of some of my friends, I have chosen to disguise some names. For the same reason a few place names have been omitted to keep the origin of the people discreet. Still, most of the names are accurate, as I wish to acknowledge the identity of the persons who have helped me throughout my life" (vii). The author's agency can be thought of as being in line with the "struggle for sovereignty" that Osage researcher Robert Warrior describes as "a process of asserting the power we possess as communities and individuals to make decisions that affect our lives."[19] In that respect, it is also telling that Weetaltuk did not publish his life story in one of the many Nunavik magazines and community newspapers that since 1959 have played an important role in the development of contemporary written literature by Nunavimmiut.[20] Clearly, Weetaltuk knew exactly what he wanted to accomplish with his life story.

As an elder looking back on his life, Weetaltuk reached into his earlier memories and combined them with his current knowledge and wisdom in order to provide the reader with an enhanced text and context. In an interview conducted at Université du Québec en Outaouais,[21] Martin spoke of the revised life story in terms of an "autobiographie compensée (compensatory autobiography)" to describe how entire passages were added after he had asked the author to expand on certain episodes of his life. As Martin recalled, Weetaltuk was more interested in bringing up his childhood memories than in remembering the war and its aftermath, so a greater amount of time was spent revising the earlier part of his life story. Conversely, sections recalling later events of the author's military service were cut back. This was to avoid weighing down the narrative with lengthy, repetitive descriptions of how the protagonist, whose life had at that point become more limited, was increasingly inebriated, imprisoned, disgraced, and discriminated against.

One result of that second level of intervention, traces of which can be found in references to the narrator's advanced age and self-reflexive attitude, is that the published life story is not as raw as the original manuscript. Yet, Weetaltuk still delivers a vivid, audacious, and captivating account of his war experience. At once critical and humorous, his life narrative draws upon "an enduring value of informal storytelling," that is, as Cruikshank explains, "its power to subvert official orthodoxies and to challenge conventional ways of thinking."[22] In fact, during the revision process, the author insisted on his freedom of speech and wanted to enjoy it, now that he was no longer bound by a military oath. His attitude towards writing fell in line with Armand Garnet Ruffo's observation: "while Native literature draws strongly on Native oral and spiritual traditions, it nevertheless looks at the impact of colonialism unflinchingly and 'is no less a call for liberation, survival and beyond to affirmation.'"[23]

In many ways this book is a legacy. In a filmed interview, while referencing the revision of his original manuscript, Weetaltuk confided to the camera: "Quand ça va être fini, je pourrai creuver (When it's finished I can die)."[24] This is precisely what happened. Eddy Weetaltuk passed away on 2 March 2005, shortly after receiving in the mail the final version of the conclusion—the only section of the book he was never able to revise. Although Weetaltuk did not intend to speak in the name of his people, nor asked his community's permission before publishing his life story, he still expressed a strong sense of responsibility towards the Inuit, through both his life and his life narrative. As an elder, he wanted to pass on his story to future generations. He hoped that his words would be able to empower Inuit youth. In the last chapter of the book, he declares: "I wish to tell them: your life belongs to you. You are the ultimate master of your destiny, so don't let despair, alcohol, or drugs control you. Be yourself, be proud. Be proud of being Inuit and always remember that our ancestors had to fight every single day of their lives to survive. It is now your turn to be strong and courageous" (155–56). Weetaltuk envisioned his story as a way to alert Inuit youth to the dangers of internalizing colonial settler violence. Above all, he wanted his story to act as a reminder of the strength to be drawn from Inuit knowledge, and to serve as an inspiration to Inuit youth to pursue their dreams despite the obstacles they would inevitably have to overcome.

Since "literature and criticism are continuously responding to larger public discourses,"[25] Weetaltuk and Martin made various editorial choices. On the one hand, they were restrained by publishers' demands for a certain type of story, legal aspects imposing a certain form of censorship, and consideration for the author's relatives, friends, and comrades, whom the author wanted to acknowledge or protect. On the other, the author wanted to share his enthralling life experience with the various audiences the book addressed and bear witness to the war and its indescribable nature. Always central to the writing and editing process was the author's objective—to produce a bestseller.

A Maverick Approach

From the moment he first submitted his original manuscript in the 1970s until he completed its rewriting at the turn of the twenty-first century, Weetaltuk repeatedly stated his desire to publish an entertaining book that would sell in very large numbers and reach a dual audience of Indigenous and non-Indigenous readers. Maintaining this ambition at a time when Inuit literary writing was only just emerging reflects his maverick approach as well as the innovative nature of his project. Indeed, as late as 2008, Inuit writer and translator Zebedee Nungak observed that "for a long time, it seemed that Inuit were neither meant, nor expected to be, writers. That is, in the way that Qallunaat (white people) have been authors, poets, and producers of written works for centuries."[26] Nungak went on to say that, despite their significant literary accomplishments from the 1950s onward, "Inuit writers have yet to attain such 'firsts' as making the bestseller lists, or winning mainline literary prizes for written works."[27] This was precisely the kind of groundbreaking success Weetaltuk hoped to achieve with his life story.

In this regard, it is worth noting that Weetaltuk was adamant in his refusal to write an academic text that would cater to an audience of anthropologists and ethnographers. His insistence was not unjustified; just the opposite: it constituted an informed resistance to the combined advances of settler colonialism and academic research in the North. The creation of his original manuscript and drawings followed closely the process of sedentarization that coincided with the unprecedented proliferation of "les études anthropologiques, ethnologiques et socioculturelles sur les Inuit du Canada (anthropological, ethnological and sociocultural studies of Canada's Inuit)."[28] In addition, he asserted himself as a writer when in Inuit literary history "most early autobiographical texts were solicited by outside agents, such as anthropologists, art enthusiasts, and missionaries."[29] Not surprisingly, when Weetaltuk submitted his original manuscript to the National Museum of Man, his life story was treated as an archival document and considered for its ethnographic and historical, rather than literary, value.

It is conceivable that his manuscript, like the writing of other Inuit authors, did not meet the expectations of Canadian publishers and readers looking for ethnographic material or stories such as traditional Inuit tales and children's literature.[30] To this effect, Daniel Chartier observed that Markoosie Patsauq's novel *The Harpoon of the Hunter*, set in the pre-contact era, was translated and published by McGill-Queen's University Press in 1970, while his second novel, *Wings of Mercy*, which "a été interprétée comme une illustration de la volonté de concilier le monde inuit et le monde allochtone (was interpreted as an illustration of the will to reconcile the Inuit and non-native worlds),"[31] received less attention from major publishers.[32] A similar desire for pre-contact narratives rather than for twentieth-century war memoirs might have hindered the reception of Weetaltuk's daring tale of adventures. Although we do not have access to the deliberations of the National Museum of Man regarding Weetaltuk's life story and pastel drawings, we can imagine that similar expectations are behind the museum's request that the author create more drawings illustrating traditional Inuit life, to make the story "more balanced."

The publication of Weetaltuk's life story in the series First Voices, First Texts supports the author's vision in that it invites a literary approach to his writing. Regarding the relevance of such an approach, Keavy Martin explains, "Reading Indigenous autobiographies as literary texts, then, has an important strategic function: it aims to liberate Indigenous authors from ethnocentric assumptions regarding their choice of genre and from ethnographic readings that diminish readerly appreciation of their skill."[33] Weetaltuk's determination to situate his autobiography outside the realm of expectations projected onto Inuit authors is consistent with his challenging of a set of expectations that nonetheless continued to haunt him.

From the Tundra to the Trenches explores and reflects on what was possible for the Inuit to do and achieve in a rapidly changing world. Contrary to colonial representations of Inuit men "as poor, and defenceless creatures,"[34] Weetaltuk depicted himself as a free thinker and a hero. In his life story, he comes across as a curious and joyful world traveller, a skilful and compassionate fighter, and a charming and charismatic young man who is proud of his success with women.[35] His story also highlights the ways in which Inuit values and knowledge were put to use in entirely new contexts, showing how the author's quest for freedom and discovery went hand in hand with a deep appreciation and respect for his family, community, and culture. With the author's stated desire to reclaim his freedom and to give back to the Inuit youth and communities, this book is similar to the autobiography of Taamusi Qumaq, *Je veux que les Inuits soient libres de nouveau* (I want the Inuit to be free once more). In a way, Weetaltuk's life story also enacts what Philip Joseph Deloria advocates in *Indians in Unexpected Places*, that is, "to put the making of non-Indian expectations in dialogue with the lived experiences of certain Native people, those whose actions were, at that very moment, being defined as unexpected."[36] One of the driving forces behind Weetaltuk's autobiographical impulse is a desire to share his pride in having done precisely what was unexpected.

Circulating the Story: Across Languages and Generations

The borrowed identity Weetaltuk used to liberate himself created unique opportunities. It also became a constant source of constraint and frustration. A painful and enduring form of negation and erasure, the impossibility of presenting himself in his true identity, kept him alienated and uprooted, gradually transforming his enthusiastic exploration of the world into a gruelling state of exile. In the larger context of invisibility for the Inuit, and more specifically for the author, this book accomplishes something important. As Stó:lō author Lee Maracle writes in *I Am Woman*, "The result of being colonized is the internalization of the need to remain invisible. The colonizers erase you, not easily, but with shame and brutality. Eventually you want to stay that way. Being a writer is getting up there and writing yourself onto everyone's blackboard."[37] It is significant, then, that Weetaltuk insisted on producing a bestseller and that, towards the end of his life, he redoubled his efforts and intensified his collaborations to get his story circulated. Like the Yukon elders interviewed by Cruikshank, he demonstrated "a strong commitment to extend communication in whatever forms possible,"[38] although for Weetaltuk writing remained a priority.

Even so, Weetaltuk's life story was conveyed through documentary films and public speaking, and it also made its way into the international world of translation. In part, this fulfilled Weetaltuk's wish to see his book published in the languages he had mastered or learned over the course of his life—Inuktitut, English, Cree, French, and, later on, German and Korean. During his stay at Martin's house in Winnipeg, Weetaltuk was approached by Martine Breuillaud with the proposal to turn his life story into a documentary film. Released in Quebec in 2006, *Born on Snow* traces the collaborative process of uncovering, revising, and publishing Weetaltuk's original manuscript. It features excerpts from the manuscript on screen and in voiceover. As "a meeting ground for multiple voices,"[39] the documentary brings to light some of the dynamics at work in the editing process. Importantly, it also reflects Weetaltuk's readiness to explore new ground and engage in conversation with various peoples, in different situations, and through diverse media, including in lectures at the University of Winnipeg.

This unique turn of events meant that Weetaltuk's life story was first published in translation rather than in an English-language version. As Martin recalls, the original manuscript's revision in Winnipeg made it possible to foresee a French-language version. Weetaltuk agreed to work with Marie-Claude Perreault, Martin's wife and a translator by trade, with whom he discussed some of the issues involved in the linguistic transfer. With Martin's assistance, the translated manuscript was later submitted to a number of French-language publishers.

In 2009, four years after Weetaltuk's death, his work was published by Carnets Nord, a Paris-based publisher specializing in exceptional life stories, under the title *E9-422: Un Inuit, de la toundra à la guerre de Corée*. It was positively received in France, and Martin was invited to French literary fairs and events to discuss the life story and share his perspective as an editor and collaborator. In 2015, a German translation was produced by historian Helga Bories-Sawala and published by DOBU under the title *Mein Leben in die Hand nehmen: Die Odyssee des Inuk E9-422*. Thanks to Martin's support, the twenty pastel drawings that accompanied the original manuscript were published alongside the German text. This circulation of the text in other languages says much about the trajectories, networks, and relationships the author had made over the course of his life. Like its author, the story had to travel abroad before finally coming home.

This publication of the original English-language version is significant for many reasons, one of them being the possibility of accessing the text in its source language. This is especially meaningful for the author's family and relatives. They can now read the work of a close relative and outstanding local figure—something that had not necessarily been possible for them until now because of the particular configuration of languages at play. Furthermore, given the current prevalence of the English language, *From the Tundra to the Trenches* has been given the potential to reach the wider readership the author always wished for. It now also allows anglophone scholars and students to take account of this distinctive piece of writing and include it in the scholarly dialogue within the growing field of Indigenous literary studies across North America. In this respect, the book is called upon to perform a function similar to that of the English-language translation of Mitiarjuk Nappaaluk's novel *Sanaaq,* which was published by the University of Manitoba Press in 2014.[40] As Keavy Martin has pointed out, the publication of Nappaaluk's work in English made it possible for the first Inuit novel—which had until then remained "almost entirely unknown outside Quebec"[41]—to be anthologized and taught in courses of Indigenous literature, which previously was not the case.[42] It is our hope that this current critical edition will provide the same opportunities for Weetaltuk's life story, and allow the book to assert its presence in that rich and powerful sphere of discourse and knowledge.

Weetaltuk embodied a trying paradox that created tension throughout his life. On the one hand, he wanted to have his humanity and his unique achievements widely recognized, together with those of the other Inuit. On the other hand, he felt a strong pressure to hide his true identity, passing as a French-Canadian man in order to ful-fill his dreams in a colonial settler society. The inherent contradiction between these two powerful imperatives kept him at an impasse—for how could his determination "to show the world how an Inuk fights and dies" possibly be reconciled with the obligation to keep on "living under a fake identity"? The intensity with which Weetaltuk worked towards the publication and dissemination of his life story makes us think that a partial solution to this debilitating paradox did lie pre-cisely in that endeavour. Publishing his book, at last, enables Weetaltuk to be heard by a large audience, to whom he can present himself as he is, as a man and as an Inuk.

NOTES

1. Dale Selma Blake, "Inuit Autobiography: Challenging the Stereotypes" (PhD diss., University of Alberta, 2000), 124.

2. Keavy Martin, *Stories in a New Skin: Approaches to Inuit Literature* (Winnipeg: University of Manitoba Press, 2012), 105.

3. Ibid.

4. Ibid.

5. Paul John Eakin, *Fictions in Autobiography: Studies in the Art of Self-Invention* (Princeton, NJ: Princeton University Press, 1985), back cover.

6. Julie Cruikshank, *The Social Life of Stories: Narrative and Knowledge in the Yukon Territory* (Vancouver: UBC Press, 1998), 16.

7. Robin McGrath, "Canadian Eskimo Literature: The Development of A Tradition" (PhD diss., University of Western Ontario, 1983), 29–38.

8. Nelly Duvicq, "Les écrits du Nunavik depuis 1959: Problématiques et conditions d'émergence d'une littérature inuit" (PhD diss., Université du Québec à Montréal, 2015), 268–352.

9. Yuval Noah Harari, "Military Memoirs: A Historical Overview of the Genre from the Middle Ages to the Late Modern Era," *War in History* 14, no.3 (2007): 289.

10. "Umiujaq." Accessed 23 April 2016. http://www.nunavik-tourism.com/Umiujaq. aspx.

11. Ibid.

12. On this topic, see for instance Nelly Duvicq's PhD diss. "Les écrits du Nunavik depuis 1959," 268–352, and Keavy Martin's article "Arctic Solitude: Mitiarjuk Nappaaluk's *Sanaaq* and the Politics of Translation in Inuit Literature," *Studies in Canadian Literature* 35, no. 2 (2010): 13–29, 17–22, as well as Zebedee Nungak's seminal text "Contemplating Inuit Presence in Literature/Réflexion sur la présence inuite en littérature," *Inuktitut Magazine* 102 (2008). Nungak's article, which was cited by both Duvicq and Martin, was published in *Windspeaker* magazine in 2004 and in an augmented edition in 2008 in *Inuktitut* magazine.

13. Sophie McCall, *First Person Plural: Aboriginal Storytelling and the Ethics of Collaborative Authorship* (Vancouver: UBC Press, 2011), 2.

14. McCall, *First Person Plural*, back cover.

15. Ibid.

16. Ibid.

17. This was sadly illustrated by the recent reception of the film *Of the North* by Dominic Gagnon, when established and privileged voices from the Québécois film institutions and academic milieu insistently dismissed criticism of the film articulated by Inuit and other Indigenous artists and cultural actors. For more on these critiques and the resulting settler-colonial dismissal, see the interview "Curating the North" with Inuit filmmaker Alethea Arnaquq-Baril, the article "*Of the North*" by Innu cultural actor André Dudemaine, founder and director of Terres en vues, and the *Tillutarniit* (pulses) film screening series curated by Inuit filmmaker Isabella-Rose Weetaluktuk and Inuit visual artist and radio show producer Stephen Agluvak Puskas, as part of the 2016 First Peoples Présence autochtone Festival in response to Gagnon's film and against the exclusion of Inuit voices from the Québécois film milieu. Finally, see the scathing and ironic reply "Un peu à l'Ouest" by Québécois film critic Simon Galiero in answer to the reading of Gagnon's film and ensuing public debate with Québécois scholar and film critic André Habib, especially as it pertains to Habib's settler colonial framing of the interpretation and reception of the film and the very terms of debate.

18. Thibault Martin, personal interview, Gatineau, Quebec, 26 June 2015.

19. Quoted by Deanna Reder, "Writing Autobiographically: A Neglected Indigenous Intellectual Tradition," in *Across Cultures/ Across Borders: Canadian Aboriginal and Native American Literatures*, edited by Paul W. DePasquale, Renate Eigenbrod, and Emma LaRocque (Peterborough, ON; Buffalo, NY: Broadview Press, 2009), 158.

20. Duvicq, "Les écrits du Nunavik depuis 1959," 84–99.

21. Thibault Martin, Personal Interview, 23 July 2015.

22. Cruikshank, *The Social Life of Stories*, xiii.

23. Armand Garnet Ruffo, "Introduction," in *An Anthology of Canadian Native Literature in English*, edited by Daniel David Moses, Terry Goldie, and Armand Garnet Ruffo, 4th ed. (Toronto: Oxford University Press, 2013), xxxii.

24. Martine Breuillaud, *Né dans la neige*/Born on Snow. TV documentary produced by Vic Pelletier. Canada: QC, 2006

25. McCall, *First Person Plural*, 3.

26. Nungak quoted by Martin, "Arctic Solitude," 18.

27. Ibid.

28. Duvicq, "Les écrits du Nunavik depuis 1959," 101.

29. William H. New. ed., *Encyclopedia of Literature in Canada* (Toronto, ON: University of Toronto Press, 2002), 536. With an additional focus on gender, in "Circumventing the Taboos: Inuit Women's Autobiographies," in *Undisciplined Women: Tradition and Culture in Canada*, edited by Pauline Greenhill and Diane Tye (Montreal: McGill-Queen's University Press, 1997), Robin McGrath mentioned that "the majority of non-Inuit who recorded Inuit oral literature were male missionaries and male anthropologists who had no interest in or access to the female domain," 226.

30. Daniel Chartier, "Introduction," in *Le harpon du chasseur* by Pasauq Markoosie (QC: Presses de l'Université du Québec, Jartin de givre Series, 2011), 8–15.

31. Chartier, "Introduction," 14.

32. Instead, *Wings of Mercy* appeared in five instalments in the *Inuktitut* magazine over the years 1972 and 1973, before it was published as a single narrative by the Kativik School Board in 1984. Duvicq, "Les écrits du Nunavik depuis 1959," 112 and 122.

33. Martin, *Stories in a New Skin*, 104.

34. Renée Hulan, "'Everybody likes the Inuit' : Inuit Revision and Representations of the North," in *Introduction to Indigenous Literary Criticism in Canada*, edited by Heather Macfarlane and Armand Garnet Ruffo (Peterborough, ON: Broadview Press, 2015 [2002]), 202.

35. The adventurous spirit and the refusal to be constrained embodied and expressed by Weetaltuk evoke the kivioc-inspired attitude that Blake identified in the autobiographical work of Thrasher, "Inuit Autobiography," 110–119.

36. Philip Joseph Deloria, *Indians in Unexpected Places* (Lawrence, Kan.: University Press of Kansas, 2004), 7.

37. Quoted in Sam McKegney, "Writer-Reader Reciprocity and the Pursuit of Alliance Through Indigenous Poetry," in *Indigenous Poetics in Canada*, edited by Neil McLeod (Waterloo, ON: Wilfrid Laurier University Press, 2014), 45. Lee Maracle, *I Am Woman: A Native Perspective on Sociology and Feminism* (Richmond, BC: Press Gang Publishers, 1996), 8.

38. Cruikshank, *The Social Life of Stories*, 16.

39. McCall, *First Person Plural*, 5.

40. Mitiarjuk Nappaaluk, *Sanaaq: An Inuit Novel.* Translated by Bernard Saladin d'Anglure (Winnipeg: University of Manitoba Press, 2014).

41. Martin, "Arctic Solitude," 14. Martin specified that *Sanaaq* "was published in 1984 [in syllabic Inuktitut] by the Association Inuksiutiit Katimajiit of the Department of Anthropology at Université Laval. In 2002, the French translation by Bernard Saladin d'Anglure was published in France" by Stanké. Ibid.

42. Keavy Martin mentions that *Sanaaq* is absent from crucial publications in the field, such as Penny Petrone's 1988 anthology *Northern Voices: Inuit Writing in English* (Toronto: University of Toronto Press, 1988), Robin McGrath's *Canadian Inuit Literature: The Development of a Tradition* (Ottawa: National Museums of Canada, 1984), and Daniel David Moses and Terry Goldie's highly influential *Anthology of Canadian Native Literature in English* (now in its third edition), "Arctic Solitude," 24 and 18.

BIBLIOGRAPHY

Arnaquq-Baril, Alethea. "Curating the North. Documentary Screening Ethics and Inuit Representation in (Festival) Cinema." Interview by Ezra Winton. *Art Threat*. December 2015. Accessed 8 September 2016. http://artthreat.net/2015/12/alethea-arnaquq-baril.

Avataq Cultural Institute. "Eddy Weetaltuk: An Inuit veteran from the Korean War." 2012. Accessed 23 April 2016. http://www.avataq.qc.ca/en/News/Eddy-Weetaltuk-An-Inuit-veteran-from-the-Korean-War.

Blake, Dale Selma. "Inuit Autobiography: Challenging the Stereotypes." PhD diss., University of Alberta, 2000.

Breuillaud, Martine. *Né dans la neige/Born on Snow*. TV documentary produced by Vic Pelletier. Canada: QC, 2006.

Canadian War Museum. Musée canadien de la guerre. "About." Accessed 23 April 2016. www.warmuseum.ca/about-us/.

Chartier, Daniel. "Introduction." In *Le harpon du chasseur*, by Pasauq Markoosie, 1–34. Translated by Catherine Ego from *Harpoon of the Hunter*. Quebec, QC: Presses de l'Université du Québec, Jartin de givre Series, 2011.

Cruikshank, Julie. *The Social Life of Stories: Narrative and Knowledge in the Yukon Territory*. Vancouver: UBC Press, 1998.

Deloria, Philip Joseph. *Indians in Unexpected Places*. Lawrence, Kan.: University Press of Kansas, 2004.

Dudemaine, André. "Of the North: Inventer l'Inuit pour mieux l'asservir: Le cinéma colonialiste et ses fantômes." *Hors Champ*. Février 2016. Accessed 8 September 2016. http://horschamp.qc.ca/spip.php?article620.

Duvicq, Nelly. "Les écrits du Nunavik depuis 1959: Problématiques et conditions d'émergence d'une littérature inuit." PhD diss., Université du Québec à Montréal, 2015.

Eakin, Paul John. *Fictions in Autobiography: Studies in the Art of Self-Invention*. Princeton, N.J.: Princeton University Press, 1985.

Freeman, Mini Aodla. *Life Among the Qallunaat*, edited by Keavy Martin, Julie Rak, and Norma Dunning. Winnipeg: University of Manitoba Press, First Voices, First Texts Series, 2015.

French, Alice. *My Name Is Masak*. Winnipeg: Peguis Publishers, 1976.

Galiero, Simon. "Un peu à l'Ouest (1 et 2)." *Panorama-Cinéma*. March 2016. Accessed 8 September 2016. http://www.panorama-cinema.com/V2/article.php?categorie=9&id=436.

George, Jane. "Nov. 8: National Aboriginal Veterans Day. Remember the late Eddy Weetaltuk, Canada's first Inuk soldier." *Nunatsiaq News*, 8 November 2012. Accessed 23 April 2016. http://www.nunatsiaqonline.ca/stories/article/65674nov._8_national_aboriginal_veterans_day/.

Grenier, Alain A. Book Review of *E9-422: Un Inuit, de la toundra à la guerre de Corée* by Eddy Weetaltuk and Thibault Martin. *Téoros. Revue de recherché en tourisme* 31-1 (2012). Gouvernance des parcs au Nunavik. Accessed 23 April 2016. https://teoros.revues.org/2204.

Habib, André. "Of the North: Positions." *Hors Champ*. January-February 2016. Accessed 8 September 2016. http://horschamp.qc.ca/spip.php?article621.

Harari, Yuval Noah. "Military Memoirs: A Historical Overview of the Genre from the Middle Ages to the Late Modern Era." *War in History* 14, no.3 (2007): 289–309.

Hulan, Renée. "'Everybody likes the Inuit': Inuit Revision and Representations of the North." In *Introduction to Indigenous Literary Criticism in Canada*, edited by Heather Macfarlane and Armand Garnet Ruffo, 202–20. Peterborough, ON: Broadview Press, 2015 [2002].

Ipellie, Alootook. *Arctic Dreams and Nightmares*. Penticton, BC: Theytus Books, 1993.

Maracle, Lee. *I Am Woman: A Native Perspective on Sociology and Feminism*. Richmond, BC: Press Gang Publishers, 1996.

Martin, Keavy. "Arctic Solitude: Mitiarjuk Nappaaluk's *Sanaaq* and the Politics of Translation in Inuit Literature." *Studies in Canadian Literature* 35, no. 2 (2010): 13–29.

———. *Stories in a New Skin: Approaches to Inuit Literature*. Winnipeg: University of Manitoba Press, 2012.

Martin, Thibault. *De la banquise au congélateur: Mondialisation et culture au Nunavik*. Quebec: Presses de l'Université Laval, Sociologie contemporaine Series, 2003.

———. "Feature: From the Tundra to the Korean War: Eddy Weetaltuk's Story." *Nunatsiaq News,* 16 July 2009. Accessed 23 April 2016. http://www.nunatsiaqonline.ca/stories/article/feature_from_the_tundra_to_the_korean_war_eddy_weetaltuks_story/.

———. "Le monde de vu du haut, ou les aventures à travers le vaste monde d'Eddy Weetaltuk." *L'Autre voie*, no. 6 (n.d.). Accessed 23 April 2016. http://www.deroutes.com/AV6/canada6.htm.

McCall, Sophie. *First Person Plural: Aboriginal Storytelling and the Ethics of Collaborative Authorship*. Vancouver: UBC Press, 2011.

McGrath, Robin. "Canadian Eskimo Literature: The Development of a Tradition." Digitized Theses. PhD diss., University of Western Ontario, 1983.

———. *Canadian Inuit Literature: The Development of a Tradition*. Ottawa: National Museums of Canada, 1984.

———. "Inuit Literature in the South." *Canadian Review of Comparative Literature/ Revue canadienne de littérature comparée* 16, no.3-4 (1989): 700–706.

———. "Circumventing the Taboos: Inuit Women's Autobiographies." In *Undisciplined Women: Tradition and Culture in Canada*, edited by Pauline Greenhill and Diane Tye, 223–33. Montreal: McGill-Queen's University Press, 1997.

Moses, Daniel David, Terry Goldie, and Armand Garnet Ruffo, eds. *An Anthology of Canadian Native Literature in English*, 3rd edition. Toronto: Oxford University Press, 2005.

Nagy, Murielle. Review of *E9-422: Un Inuit, de la toundra à la guerre de Corée* by Eddy Weetaltuk. *Études/Inuit/Studies* 35, no. 1/2 (2011): 307–10. Accessed 23 April 2016. Stable URL: http://www.jstor.org/stable/42870333.

Nappaaluk, Mitiarjuk. *Sanaaq: An Inuit Novel*. Translated by Bernard Saladin d'Anglure. Winnipeg: University of Manitoba Press, 2014.

———. *Sanaaq*. Translated by Bernard Saladin d'Anglure. Paris: Stanké, 2002.

———. *Sanaaq: Sanaakkut Piusiviningita Unikkausinnguangat*. Edited by Bernard Saladin d'Anglure. Quebec: Association Inuksiutiit Katimajiit, 1984.

New, William H., ed. *Encyclopedia of Literature in Canada*. Toronto: University of Toronto Press, 2002.

Nunavik Tourism. "Umiujaq." Accessed 23 April 2016. http://www.nunavik-tourism.com/Umiujaq.aspx.

Nungak, Zebedee. "Contemplating Inuit Presence in Literature/Réflexion sur la présence inuite en literature." *Inuktitut Magazine* 102 (2008): 62–66.

Petrone, Penny, ed. *Northern Voices: Inuit Writing in English*. Toronto: University of Toronto Press, 1988.

Pitseolak, Ashoona. *Pictures Out of My Life*. Ed. Dorothy Eber. Montreal: Design Collaborative Books, 1971.

Qumaq, Taamusi. *Je veux que les Inuit soient libres de nouveau: Autobiographie (1914–1993)*. Quebec: Presses de l'Université du Québec, Jardin de givre Series, 2010.

Reder, Deanna. "Writing Autobiographically: A Neglected Indigenous Intellectual Tradition." In *Across Cultures/ Across Borders: Canadian Aboriginal and Native American Literatures*, edited by Paul W. DePasquale, Renate Eigenbrod, and Emma LaRocque, 153–69. Peterborough, ON; Buffalo, NY: Broadview Press, 2009.

Ruffo, Armand Garnet, "Introduction." In *An Anthology of Canadian Native Literature in English*, edited by Daniel David Moses, Terry Goldie, and Armand Garnet Ruffo, 4th edition, xxi-xxxv. Toronto: Oxford University Press, 2013.

Tagoona, Armand. *Shadows*. Ottawa: Oberon, 1975.

Thrasher, Anthony Apakark. *Thrasher... Skid Row Eskimo*. Edited by Gerard Deagle and Alan Mettrick. Toronto: Griffin House, 1976.

Weetaltuk, Eddy. *E9-422. Un Inuit, de la toundra à la guerre de Corée*. Edited by Thibault Martin and translated by Marie-Claude Perreault. Paris: Carnets-Nord, 2009.

——. *Mein Leben in die Hand nehmen. Die Odyssee des Inuk E9-422*. Edited by Helga Bories-Sawala. Translated by Rolf Sawala. Illustrated by Eddy Weetaltuk. Hamburg: DOBU Verlag, 2015.

1. Eddy was born on cold snow while his mother was cutting wood to keep their family warm. His birth occurred during the family's visit to Stratton Island for the annual arctic whale hunt. While Eddy's mother recounted Eddy's birthdate as 19 March 1932, his father claimed it was on 19 April (p. 5).

2. Eddy's father, Rupert Weetaltuk, and uncles hunting a young whale caught in a fishing net (p. 11).

3. The village of Kuujjuarapik and the small matchbox government houses Eddy's mother, Mary Weetaltuk, and family lived in after Eddy's father died in 1965 (p. 4).

4. Eddy's first encounter with a missionary, Father Belleau, at his Aunt Maala's. Because his mother used missionaries to frighten him, Eddy was in tears, even though the priest gave him cake (pp. 16–17).

5. Father Belleau's beard impressed Eddy, as it was the first time he saw a man with facial hair (p. 16).

6. Eddy's father punished a raven for stealing from his traps by plucking its feathers and sending it off into the severe winter cold. When the RCMP found out, they imprisoned him for ninety days for cruelty to animals. This left Eddy's mother and family with no one to provide for them for three months (pp. 12–13).

7. In September 1939, Father Éthier and Brother Martin arrived on the boat *St. Joseph* to pick up students from Old Factory for their boarding school in Fort George (p. 24).

8. With the permission of their parents, the priests enrolled Eddy and his brother David in the school. The boys were very homesick during their 100-mile boat journey to Fort George (p. 25).

9. The first time David Weetaltuk saw a bull he was frightened by its "way of moving a bit like an automat" rather than its size (pp. 25–26).

10. The first English word that Eddy learned from Sister Louise Martin was "dog" (p. 28).

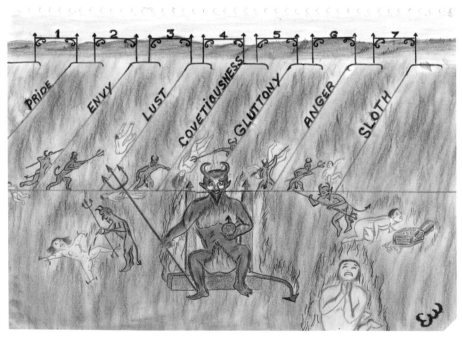

11. During catechism with Father Couture, Eddy learned about the seven capital sins and seven gates of hell. He was impressed by the father's picture of Lucifer and the demons forking sinners with pitchforks (p. 30).

12. After finishing grade 8 and turning sixteen, Eddy stayed in Fort George and worked in the mission's barn with Brother Martin, who taught him French and how to feed, breed, and keep chickens, as well as how to slaughter pigs (p. 43).

13. With Brother Martin teaching him how to slaughter a pig, Eddy was able to impress the young nun who replaced Sister Alexis. According to Eddy, Brother Martin had wanted Eddy to inherit his farm in southern Canada and encouraged Eddy to go south before he himself left the North (possibly to be confined to a mental hospital) (pp. 44–45).

14. At Old Factory, Eddy's mother cried as she said goodbye to Eddy. His friends waited in a canoe on the way to the seaplane that took them and Eddy south to Moosonee (p. 49).

15. On the train ride from Moosonee to Cochrane, Eddy was not stopped or asked for ID by a policeman because he was in the company of his white friends (p. 50).

16. In January 1952, Eddy went to the army recruiting office in Ottawa. Because of his grade-8 education with the Oblates in Fort George, Eddy was able to pass the tests while his white friend Brian was not. To see western Canada, Eddy joined the Princess Patricia regiment stationed at Wainwright, Alberta (pp. 59–60).

17. A memory of the end of war in 1945, when the Oblates and the children at the mission school celebrated Hitler's death (p. 61).

18. On his first assignment in Korea, Eddy acted as No. 1 on a team of three soldiers operating a 60-mm mortar gun. During their first few hours on the Korean front, Eddy and another soldier, Doyle, had to dig a six-foot trench while the artillery was firing (p. 94).

19. The fighting took place at night and in the mornings Eddy witnessed American fighter jets using napalm on the North Koreans. When the napalm hit enemy positions, there was a great blast and Eddy could feel the heat back in his own trench (p. 95).

20. After the atomic bombings and the defeat in the Second World War, Japanese people catered to American and Canadian soldiers fighting in Korea, who often went on shore leave in Japan. On the Japanese ship *E Sang*, a Japanese man wearing a long trench coat sold Eddy and his Metis friend Racette whisky and other items from his coat pockets (pp. 105–6).

21. On their shore leave, Eddy and Racette tried out rickshaws pulled by Japanese men. Eddy used the whip and shouted at the driver in Inuktitut as if riding a dog team. The experience reminded him of his childhood in the North (p. 106–7).

22. A North Korean attack on 1 May 1953 was particularly brutal. While Eddy and his team kept firing to keep the enemy from moving forward, many shells fell close to their mortar pit. The barrel of their gun began to smoke and they fired all of their ammunition as shells kept falling around them. Their company had to withdraw (pp. 114–15).

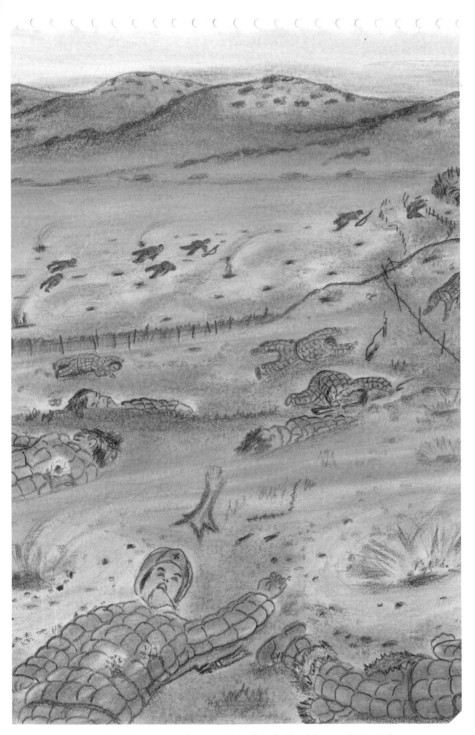

23. During the 1 May 1953 attack, two soldiers, Schofield and Sergeant Major Cole, went to retrieve the wounded from no man's land. They mostly found dead bodies. Schofield, in his blood-stained uniform, recounted the experience to Eddy (p. 116).

24. After a telephone call on 27 July 1953, in which Eddy's company got the news that the Korean War was over, Gauthier, a French Canadian soldier, celebrated by stomping on his jacket and yelling obscenities in French that only Eddy understood (p. 122).

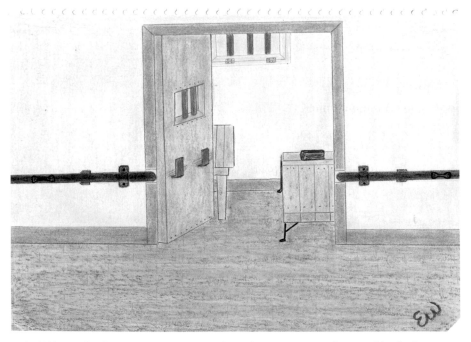

25. Eddy was placed in a Canadian army prison during his tour in Germany because of drunkenly trying to escape Camp Fort MacLeod to meet Clara, a German girl he had fallen in love with (pp. 140–41).

26. Eddy Weetaltuk in a family circle at the Eastmain River in the late 1930s. Eddy's father hunted with Cree Kitchikapoo and Tamotuk families and they gathered at this settlement, as did other Cree families throughout the year. Eastmain River had both an Anglican mission and an HBC store (p. 20).

27. Eddy's mortar gun. Later in the Korean campaign Eddy was assigned to the 81-mm mortar gun, where his skill firing the weapon garnered him compliments from his superiors (pp. 117–18).

28. Eddy's grandfather George Weetaltuk in a family circle at the beginning of 1930s. He was renowned in the region because of his many talents. In the book, Eddy discusses his skills in making canoes and boats. George Weetaltuk also produced drawings and carvings and was one of the first recognized Inuit artists (p. 36).

From the
TUNDRA
to the
TRENCHES

CHAPTER 1

WEETALTUK
or the Times of Innocence

My name is Weetaltuk; Eddy Weetaltuk. My Eskimo tag name is E9-422.

I was born in 1932 on a small island called Strutton Island, thirty miles offshore in the middle of the James Bay. At that time there was no permanent village on the island, only a few Inuit families would come there at specific times in the year. East Main,[1] located on the mainland on the Quebec side of the James Bay, was the closest trading post. It is where my father, Rupert Weetaltuk, used to sell his furs. Weetaltuk, my last name, means "innocent eyes" in Inuktitut. Although it qualified pretty well my childhood, you will soon read how I came to lose that innocence. People used to call us Eskimos. I learned later that it is a derogatory name, but back then it was just our name.

My father had been attributed the disc number E9-406 and he wore it until his death. He passed away on 14 May 1965. At that time the government of Canada numbered every Eskimo to keep track of them and we had to keep our tag number always with us. That was the way things were then. If you were to visit Great Whale today, you would be able to see for yourself proof of that old time, since a couple of houses still bear these letters.

Mother, Mary Weetaltuk, bore the disc number E9-407. She gave birth to twelve children. She spent most of her life travelling with my

---

1. East Main (sometimes East Main House), trading post of the Hudson Bay's Company, first opened in 1690. After moving to a few different locations, it was established permanently on the coast at the mouth of the Eastmain River around 1723.

father from camp to camp. After he passed away, she lived in the village of Great Whale, waiting to be reunited with him. Great Whale, 400 kilometres north of East Main trading post was the only permanent village where she had really lived. It was in Great Whale where she had a real house for the first time. Although it was a tiny and crowded house, it was still a house. We used to call those types of houses "matchboxes" because they were very basic, made of four walls and a roof and were so small that we were packed in them like matches in a matchbox. They were the first houses given to us by the government. They would come by boat, ready to build, and could be assembled easily in a few hours, like Meccano pieces. They were not really adapted to northern conditions, and we were more often cold than warm, but we didn't refuse them because they were gifts.

Great Whale was at that time—and still is—a two-community town. The communities were separated by the landing strip; on one side you had the Inuit and on the other side the Crees, whom we called the Indians. Things change and today new houses replace old ones and now Native villages are called by their traditional names. I think it is a good thing that we are coming back to our old names. The only problem is that it makes reading maps difficult for an old man like me who used to know the villages by their trading post names. Today the Inuit community of Great Whale is called Kuujjuarapik. The Cree village is named Wapmagoostui. But many people still call it Great Whale and to make it even more complex the French Canadians have their own name: Poste-de-la-Baleine. That is a lot of names for a town with a population of just about 1,000 inhabitants. But there are worse things than having too many names. Living with a borrowed name, like I had to do, as you will soon discover, is certainly more difficult to bear.

My brother David, E9-408, lived for many years with his wife and four children in a tent connected to Mother's crowded matchbox. My youngest sister, Jeannie,[2] along with her husband, Lucassie Alaku, and her daughter Lilly, born in December 1967, also lived with Mother. Her little shack was packed to its maximum capacity. Any more people

---

2. Eddy's sister Jeannie's and others' tag numbers are not provided because they were supposedly lost.

to accommodate and it would have burst. One good thing is that Inuit families visit each other like crazy. Thanks to that habit Mother was able to enjoy a few moments of silence and peace. The rest of the time they were piled up in the house like sardines, or should I say matches in their box.

My eldest sister, Ann Weetaltuk-Shields, E9-423, married a White man and moved to Quebec City, where she worked for a long time with the provincial government. She really enjoyed her job. Her husband, Bill Shields, also had a good paying job with the Tuna Fishing Ships Company. I also have a sister Minnie, who married a Cree fur trapper, Edward Gilpin from Eastmain.³ They have children and are happy, which counts for a lot. My other sister, Louise Dook, was a happy housewife to John Dook, a manager of the Great Whale River Hudson's Bay Company (HBC) trading post. They had three daughters, Lisa, Maggie, and Jackie, and a boy named Rupert.

As for me, you are going to read about my long, agonizing struggle to find a better way of life. You should know that I wrote this book to try to understand why and how I have put myself in situations where I came to commit so many unchristian acts, as Brother Couture—whom you will soon read about—would often say. Most of these situations occurred while I was "enjoying" my adventures in the Canadian Armed Services. But I don't want to kill the suspense and ruin your pleasure by getting to my story too fast. Rather, let's start slowly from the beginning.

E9-422, Edward Weetaltuk, was a very small baby boy. Just a little bigger than a large wooden matchbox. I was born on cold snow while Mother was cutting wood to keep our family warm. My family used to travel to Strutton Island every spring for our annual arctic whale hunt. That's how I came into this world. According to Mother I was born on March 19, but Father always said it was on April 19. Like I used to say to my comrades from the South, a husband's memory is quite unfaithful no matter where you live in the world. However, Father had a good excuse for not remembering my birthday, we had no calendar

---

3. Eastmain refers to the modern Cree community that started around the East Main trading post.

at that time. Like wives say in many places, husbands always have good excuses. Maybe this is why I did not stay married for long.

Mother passed away in 1969, but I still remember her beautiful wrinkled face and how she would show affection with a little smile to all who were listening to her. I thank God she lived as long as she did. Though, I am so sorry that during her life she had to endure so much sorrow. Now that I am an old man, I realize that I contributed greatly to that sorrow and I know I broke her heart the day I left our James Bay. It is unbelievable how hard on a mother's heart a son can be. Since I have begun to recall past memories, the puzzle of past events becomes clearer and my responsibility in her suffering is apparent to me. At one point she was sent to a sanatorium in Hamilton, Ontario. They told me, back then, that she had tuberculosis, but what really sent her to the hospital—and almost killed her—was the pain she felt when someone wrongly told her that I had been killed in the Korean War.

As far back as I can remember I always cherished my brothers and sisters. My oldest memory is an episode that happened when I was only three years old and my sister Ann, who was just two, was playing by a hot burning stove. She suddenly slipped and fell on the floor. While falling, the side of her cheek touched the stove and she burned herself badly. She cried in pain and it was like she was never going to stop. Seeing her suffering made me cry as if I was also in pain. That was the first time that I felt love could hurt. Sometimes I would also cry when my brother David was sad. My brother, my sister, and I were very close. We always shared the little we had, and we really had nothing. Today I am old and during my life I have had a lot of good and bad experiences, but I still feel the pain I experienced in my childhood. Now that I look back, I know that the way we were taught by my mother, to love everyone and to be compassionate, really influenced my personality and helped me to endure suffering while being able to enjoy every little happy moment.

For fun and because we were hungry, my brother and I would trap whisky jacks (some call them grey jays). They are pretty eatable and when hunters would come home with nothing—which happened quite often some years—we were happy to have them. Even a small catch would make us happy. It was not rare that tears came to our mother's eyes when she saw us happy. Actually, we were really happy at Strutton Island, as we were not often hungry because there were many arctic whales, at least during the first years of my childhood. It's only when the European whalers arrived that the whales started to become scarce and our life began to feel miserable. But before getting there, I have to explain how the Inuit hunted whales in wintertime. Arctic whales keep an opening in the middle of the ice that almost never freezes over so that they can breathe all winter long. They maintain their opening in the same manner as the seals keep a breathing hole. They always choose a place where they know they can feed. Hunters know that and they wait for them at the breathing hole. When a whale comes up for air, they shoot. Of course it is easier to write about it than to do it, as you have to wait in the cold for hours, sometimes days, before a whale comes. You can even wait for nothing. But if the whale shows up and if you shoot properly, you will kill the animal. If it is a fat one, it will not sink. While the whale is afloat, all the men from the camp hurry over in their kayaks or canoes and harpoon it, and then they pull the whale to the ice ridge. At night everyone will feast, even the dogs will have their share. Unfortunately, if the whale is thin, it will sink and nobody will feast that night.

When my fourth spring arrived, my mother fell ill while on the way back to Cape Hope Islands. Father was very worried. He harnessed eight dogs and put a female dog as the leader so the dogs would pull harder and faster and we would arrive quickly. Because the female dog was in heat, you can imagine how fast we were travelling over the bumps of ice. At one point our speed was so fast that one would have thought we were flying. It was like we had succeeded in freeing ourselves from the laws of Mother Nature. But that was just an illusion. We were still bound to earth, and when the harness strap broke, reality caught up with us. Once freed from the sled, the dogs kept on running after the female dog. Father tried to call them back but with no success. As we used to say, one might just as well howl at the moon rather than try to stop a bitch in heat. We had to face it. We were alone with no more dogs to get us to Cape Hope Islands.

That day the sun was blaring hot. The snow was melting away and we could see many holes in the middle of the frozen sea. Silence settled once the dogs' howls faded away in the emptiness. We were alone in the cold desert.

Father harnessed himself to pull the sleigh with Mother and baby Ann on it. My brother and I wanted to walk to lighten Father's burden, but for most of the trip we had to sit on the sleigh, because Father thought it was too dangerous to walk by ourselves. Father was being very careful. His loved ones were in danger and he was even more cautious than usual. Today I realize that everything I know about nature, especially about the ice floe, I learned it from my father. It is from watching him that I learned how to always look for hidden danger. Even if the ice seems flat and deeply frozen, a crack can always surprise you and in the frozen desert a simple mistake will cause your death. The biggest threat is snow blindness that strikes hunters who don't wear their goggles. The reflection of sun burns their eyes and they cannot see the dangers anymore. That day my brother and I felt very bad for not being able to help our father. We were still too young and we didn't know all the rules and dangers. That is why Father had to pull us on the sleigh. The weight of the sleigh must have been so heavy with Mother, little Ann, my brother and me on it, plus the food. Like every little boy, I believed my dad was invincible, but that day I realized that a human being cannot survive on the ice floe without his dog team, even the strongest Inuit dad. That is why I feared the worst would happen.

When Father got exhausted, he took a break, drank some cold tea, and ate a piece of bannock. While eating, Father saw a black spot moving in the distance. For a moment we thought it was a seal, sunning itself on the ice. Then we realized it was swaying back and forth and was getting bigger and bigger as if it was approaching. Father stood up on the sleigh for a better view. He smiled and yelled:

—A dog team! It's a dog team. We are saved, a dog team!

One of the dogs must have had found his way back to our camp at Cape Hope Islands. When Grandfather saw the dog still wearing his harness, he knew we were in danger and sent uncle Billy to our rescue. We were all happy to see him, even Mother as sick as she was managed to share a smile with us. In no time we were on the move again, heading towards Cape Hope Islands, riding in style. On arrival, Grandpa was waiting to greet us with the rest of the Weetaltuk family.

This lucky episode happened during a sad period that we called later the "seven years of famine." Of course we didn't know back then that the starvation would last for seven years. Actually, it is probably a good thing that we didn't know, for it would have made the pain ever deeper. The food shortage lasted almost all of my childhood but I don't complain and I am grateful that I was lucky enough to survive. I still thank God for letting me live through it. Unfortunately not everybody was that lucky and the lack of food was so serious that the Inuit were getting many kinds of diseases and many of them died. The worst of all of them was tuberculosis. It killed so many of us. Three of my sisters died during that famine. Those were sad times for my family. Mother and Father were so desperate seeing their children suffering and being unable to do anything about it. This is when I first experienced hunger and found a way of not showing it, to spare Mother the despair.

These memories are deep inside of my mind and my body. It is likely that my long adventures around the world are the result of my desire to free myself from the risk of starvation and poverty. I remember one summer in particular when we were very hungry. I do not remember the year, but I recall that we would go as long as three days with no food at all. Because there was nothing to hunt, Father set up nets for fish, but even fishing was bad. We were lucky the day he could net two or three fishes. For a large family this is not a miraculous catch. In fact, we managed to survive by picking up all sorts of small animals. I still remember we'd wander for days along the seashore looking for starfish, mussels, and sharp or round urchins that were as hairy as porcupine needles. Inside the urchins there was a yellow substance that one can either eat or drink. Those animals were rather good to eat, and I learned later that they are served in chic restaurants around the world. But an Inuk[4] can hardly survive on them. They were not our first choice, I can tell you!

---

4. Inuk is the singular of Inuit, in Inuktitut, our language.

One spring during the seven years of famine and before the ice broke up, Grandpa gave to Father some boards and fifty pounds of oatmeal. Normally oatmeal was mixed with seal fat to make a big stew to feed dogs. But we were so hungry that we ended up eating the fifty pounds of oatmeal ourselves. Mother would mix it with mussels to give it flavour. Now that I know pancakes, I would say that's what it tasted like. I do not remember what happened to the dogs, but my dad did not keep them. One thing is sure: we couldn't afford to keep them. We had hardly enough food for us; it would have been a waste to try to share the little we had with them. Dogs eat a lot, and when I say a lot, it is much more than what we could have spared. Hence, dogs can survive many days, even weeks, with nothing or almost nothing but if you want them to be useful they must eat at one point. I remember that some years during the summer when we had less use of them, men put the dogs on small islands. They were left alone and hunted small game to survive. At one point the fiercest animals would eat the weakest. When hunters would come back months later, only the strongest dogs had survived. Those survivors would make the best dog team.

With the boards given to him by Grandpa, Dad began to build a boat. It took him a lot longer than he had anticipated and I remember him saying days after days:

—It won't be long now 'til I finish the boat.

Then, after a pause, he would add:

—Once it is finished I'll take you along for a duck hunt and we'll stop on our way to pick up seagull eggs. I promise, we'll soon feast on roasted ducks and seagull eggs.

I guess he was saying that so we would not think of hunger while he was still working on the boat. Eventually, after days of work, it was ready. The next morning we set out for the seagull eggs and the duck hunt.

All day long we checked every little island surrounding Cape Hope, but we found nothing, no duck, and no seagull's nest. Nothing! It was a real nightmare. I was so sad, for we had built up so much hope for that hunting trip. At one point Father decided it was time to return to our camp. That was it! He had given up hope and we were heading back home. Then, suddenly a small tern dived at me with a loud screech. I stopped in my tracks. Father yelled at me:

—Eddy, don't move!

Then he ran to join me and looked all around. Dad smiled. On the grey sand there were three little spotted rocks:

—Look at that. Tern eggs! We found them!

Indeed, there were the eggs we were looking for! But it was only three tiny tern eggs, just enough for an appetizer. Dad got his little teapot filled up with salty seawater and gathered twigs and dry moss to boil them over an open fire. Suddenly, I realized we did not have any matches. No matter, Dad emptied a 12-gauge cartridge and banged the black gunpowder with a rock until it sparked. In no time we had good boiled eggs, one each for the three of us. Then Dad led us back to our settlement, empty-handed. We had nothing for Mother.

Now that I look back, I realize that without luck and my father's experience and knowledge of the land our family might not have survived that famine. One example of that luck is the story of a young beluga that got caught in my dad's fishnet, that same net that Dad was using to catch fish with almost no success. I will never forget the morning when my father arrived at the shore to check on the net and got the best possible surprise. A young beluga was stuck in it. The poor animal was struggling to free itself from the net but was getting exhausted and could not escape. My dad went to get my uncles who were staying with us at our camp. The four men ran down like crazy with their rifles. In no time everybody was shooting at the young whale. When it was dead, they dragged it on the shore and everyone gathered by the sea to feast. That day even the dogs were invited to lunch. We all got together by the campfire and talked for hours about the way the whale had been caught. That night our hunger was forgotten and finally, for the first time in weeks, we all had a good sleep. The whale provided us with food for several days and, as long as the food lasted, I was enjoying a good night's sleep with my stomach full of that delicious meat. Of course, one day we ran out of the beluga's meat and the hunger came back. This miraculous fishing remained engraved in our memories, and we talked about it for many years. Each time we would recall these memories, tears of joy and laughter rolled down my cheeks.

After a difficult winter and a not so easy spring, the summer arrived. With it came the Royal Canadian Mounted Police (RCMP). They were travelling around the Canadian North to make a census of the Eskimos. They stopped on Cape Hope Islands and took pictures of everyone staying at our camp. Two RCMP officers in red uniforms stood before the camera with each family. Mother told us that if we were bad, they would take us with them. I can assure you that I did believe her. They looked so official, so governmental, that I was sure they could do anything, even take us away from Mother! This was one of my first experiences with government officials. Seeing them so well dressed, so colourful, was quite impressive and contributed to the respect I long pledged to Canadian authorities.

The Mounties, seeing our misery, told us that the HBC was giving a very high price for silver fox furs. I still remember that the price they mentioned was so amazing that Dad, upon hearing it, decided to set fox traps right away. Unfortunately, Father was unlucky and for many days he came back with no fox. One morning, while checking his trapline, he saw many fox tracks and got excited. It was his day. But he soon found a raven, which had gotten trapped while trying to get a piece of meat from under the snare. Dad realized it had been stealing his baits from the beginning.

He was so angered by the ravens that he felt the urge to get revenge. The poor thing stuck in his trap was still alive. It was going to pay for all the other stealing ravens. He plucked its feathers off its body, leaving only its wings and tail, and then let it fly away in fifty-two-degree-below zero weather, assuming it would surely freeze to death pretty fast. When summer arrived, Dad bragged about his prank to some Cree hunters he had met. No doubt it was a good joke and Dad was pretty fond of telling it. But it turned out to be a bad idea, as Dad later realized when the RCMP came to our camp to arrest him. He was driven to Moose Factory in Ontario, on the west coast of James Bay. There he was judged and convicted to serve a prison sentence of ninety days for cruelty against animals. The story had travelled mouth to mouth from East Main, where Father first told it, all the way to Moose Factory. When the Mounties heard it, they apparently thought they had no other option but to arrest and try him. This is true. I am not making it up; my dad was really put behind bars for plucking a raven. I do not remember if the officers travelled all that way to arrest him, or if they asked their colleagues from Quebec to pick him up during one of their patrols in the region. I was just a kid at that time and I do not remember all the details. I was simply astounded, as I could not understand why my father was taken away for three months while we needed him to hunt and feed us. Now, each time I make a joke, I can't help but think of the three months of fasting my father made us go through, in spite of himself.

After serving his time, Dad was sent back to Cape Hope Islands. He came back on a small freight boat named *Venture* that belonged to Jack Palmquist, a fur trader. Jack was both the owner and the pilot of the boat. Though I do not question his ability as a businessman, his ability as a pilot was another story. The worst was that Jack thought he knew the Bay because he had studied the maps and thought he knew its numerous dangers. But he was indeed piloting with no real experience. Believe me, travelling with him was scary, even for an Inuk like my father, used to all the tricks that Mother Nature can put in the way of a self-confident adventurer. Nevertheless, God must have been with them that day, as they made it back safe.

Father had brought back from the South some law books, which none of us could read. But there were pictures in the books to teach the Inuit and also the Cree about the Canadian laws that we had no knowledge of. One of those pictures showed a man on top of a woman, both were smiling. In the background one could see an RCMP officer pushing back the bushes, a pistol in the right hand. I asked Mother what they were doing wrong and why the officer was going to arrest them. She answered looking at the drawing that they were making love and that love was a good thing. However, after a silence she added:

—But, Edward, you will learn later that there is good love and bad love. The police officer is probably arresting them because they are making bad love.

But she didn't specify what making love meant and what bad love was. Unfortunately, I didn't dare to ask.

That picture stayed in my mind for months, and I kept wondering what they were doing wrong. Later when I was in school, a missionary gave us a lecture about love and sex. Although I had the feeling that the answer to my question was to come, his explanation was so vague that I couldn't really get a good grasp on the issue. I stayed in the dark for a couple more months until I came to see a girl urinating. That was when I realized that boys and girls were quite different, but also pretty complementary. This gave me the idea to try with one of the schoolgirls what I had seen in the picture of the law book. I was quite surprised about the sensation I got from it, so was the girl. We liked it, and we would hide every now and then to do it again. I got the feeling that what we were doing was not the good love Mother was talking about. I expressed my fear to the girl with little result; she was not that knowledgeable about good and bad love.

However, this is not yet the time to speak of my experience in school. I am not yet finished with the period of my life where I was still innocent. So, to continue, let's go back to my father. Back from jail, Dad was still thinking about the good money he could make by selling furs to the HBC. He convinced his brother Willy to join him in his attempt to trap those valuable animals. Just before Christmas, after days of unsuccessful tries, they finally got lucky. Willy caught a silver fox, and Dad got a red and a silver fox. We were all expecting a lot from those catches. Since money was hardly known in the 1930s, we didn't have a specific idea of how rich we would be after the sale. But we were definitely going to be rich. Actually, being rich for us was not exactly what it means for people today. At that time we had almost no personal belongings and, of course, no bank accounts. Being rich was not a question of having a lot of cash but rather being able to get what we needed from the HBC store.

Let me explain how the trading companies were operating in the North back then. Trappers were not actually paid in money for the furs they were selling, but rather were given a credit that they could spend in the store. We could say that the only money we knew at that time was the fur. Of course business was very profitable for the HBC since they didn't have to spend money to get fur and they would always make a sale when they were buying fur from the Inuit. Those were the years when the HBC made a killing on the Cree and the Inuit, as I learned later in reading a history book. That is why we created the Inuit co-op in the 1960s, in order to have our own stores operated by our own people. These co-ops still exist today and help to share the profit between everyone in the community. Sharing, that's always been the Inuit way and hopefully it will continue to be our way.

When Father and Willy brought their furs to East Main's trading post, they were paid $150 for the red fox, and they got $300 for each silver fox. It seemed like they could buy the whole HBC store with that fortune. Although it was a lot of money for us, it was nothing compared to the price that furs were sold at in the South. I was told that once tanned and mounted silver fox furs could be worth up to $3,000[5] in Winnipeg, and that rich old ladies would wear them around their necks, not in the same fashion we wear them to keep us warm, but with a lot of distinction. This was in the 1930s, and wearing fur collars and feathers, like we see in the old photographs in the days of Al Capone, was only a privilege for rich people.

Brother and I waited two days for Dad's dog teams to return from the HBC trading post. We were very excited about what he would bring back from the store. So that we could see better, Brother and I stood watching in front of a small window on a trunk box where Mother kept her belongings. It was not a real window but rather a small opening in the wooden logs that Grandpa had carved so that Mum had light to sew the kamiks.[6] While standing on the trunk, I pushed my brother off so that I could watch all by myself. Mother shook me for being selfish. I fell and hit my nose on the trunk and started to bleed. I was crying really loud. Mum put a basin on the floor so I could bleed into it. My nose was bleeding so hard that it seemed I was going to fill up the basin. Dad arrived in the meantime. When he walked in, I cried harder.

---

5. Prices were perhaps lower but I remember it was said that the furs in the city were sold for ten times more than what the HBC used to pay for them.

6. Kamiks are Inuit boots; they are made from sealskins. Making kamiks takes a long time and a lot of skill. Little girls used to learn from their mothers how to prepare and dry skins before sewing them. A good kamik stays warm and dry, which is very important for the Inuit who spend hours and hours travelling and hunting in the cold.

Father asked what happened and why I was crying. Mum told him that I was a bad boy. Dad just laughed and took out some chocolates, candies, and gum from his paper bags. I stopped crying immediately and felt happy. This was the first time I had candies. The taste was so great that I almost made myself sick eating so many sweets. When I realized that my brother got more than me, I cried again in despair but I was told to be quiet. He was getting more because he was older. Such a treatment made me wish I were a giant.

Besides sweets, Father had brought back enough flour, sugar, bacon, and lard for the rest of the year. Things started to get better for the whole family. My brother and I would play in the snow all day without being hungry. Sometimes we were so happy and innocent that we became mischievous and threw snowballs at our auntie's bloomers hanging on the laundry line to dry in the wind. I was the instigator of that prank. Eventually I got caught and Mum grounded me. As punishment, I was sent inside our shack to remove all my clothes and to come back outside totally naked. She made me stand in the cold for fifteen minutes. It was freezing. I wished to be wearing anything, even underwear. I remember Mother telling me that next time I should think twice before making fun of Auntie's panties. I can still picture myself weeping from being so cold while my brother was also crying, feeling sorry for me.

Those were the years of happiness and innocence. I wish they had lasted forever!

In February 1938, the year of my sixth birthday, a team of huskies owned by the Roman Catholic Mission at Fort George stopped by our settlement. It was around noon and they stopped to have lunch. Among the travellers was Father Belleau, an Oblate of Mary Immaculate, who later became bishop. He was accompanied by another brother Oblate, whose name I have since forgotten. The two of them were missionaries at the St. Theresa School in Fort George. Father Belleau had a long beard; it was the first time I saw a man with hair on the face. Mother told me that if I wasn't quiet, they would take me away. I was so scared that I ran next door to Aunt Maala's. From a hole in the wall I watched in silence, afraid that they were going to realize that I was spying on them. Aunt Maala was doing some washing with a tub and a scrub board. I was too busy looking at the missionaries eating that I never noticed Father Belleau walking out. He had some cake and cookies he wanted to give to the children. With my aunt scrubbing so hard on her scrub board, I could not hear him approaching until he touched me on my back. I screamed with fear and was sure he was going to take me away. Aunt Maala calmed me down and said:

—Don't be silly. Father Belleau is a nice person. He is a priest. Besides, look, he brought you a gift. Take it. Yes... Go ahead, it's for you.

The priest gave me a couple of cookies and a cake. They looked so big that I was afraid my hands would be too small to hold them all. Aunt Maala told me to thank him, in English. This was the first time she spoke to me in English. Even though I didn't know what it meant and why I had to say it, I repeated after her:

—Thank you, Father Belleau.

The Oblate gave me a big smile. With that smile plus the goodies I wasn't scared anymore. Then the father walked out to his dog team. They were ready to move on towards Strutton and Charlton Islands, to visit some other camps.

By March our family was ready to move back to Strutton Island for the whale-hunting season, which lasted until the snow started melting. Earlier that year Father had met two Cree families, the Tamotuk and the Kitchikapoo. They had invited him to spend the beginning of spring with them and Dad had agreed. They wanted to learn from him how the Inuit hunt arctic whales by harpoon. The Tamotuk and Kitchikapoo were trappers and didn't know much about whaling. When we arrived at Tamotuk's hunting grounds, the geese were already flying north over their encampment. The two Cree families were waiting for us, and had all the food ready in their wigwam to treat us on our arrival: fish, and goose, beaver, and muskrat meat. We had such a feast!

Later, during our stay at the Cree settlement, Jacob Kitchikapoo's sons taught my brother and me how to set up muskrat traps. Every morning we would go out to check on the snares. We spent a lot of time together, with the result that we were learning the rudiments of Cree language without noticing it. I remember every time they found a muskrat caught in a trap they would say "OT'S K"[7] meaning "rat" in Cree. We were kids and we were having so much fun making new friends and learning new things.

Each morning, the settlement would wake up to the sound of the honking flocks of Canada geese flying over us. What a nice way to wake up. It makes you want to stay out all day. That's when I learned that Canada geese's squawking makes real hunters' hair stand right up, at least that's what the grown-ups told me. I was anxious to get skin hair, to know if I could also become a hunter like my Cree friends. By late spring, around the breakup of ice, Dad and Tamotuk set out fishnets, and every morning they would return with two large tubs full of fish. The women of the camp would spend the rest of the day cleaning them. Later they would smoke them with cedar logs that had been collected during summertime.

Not far from Tamotuk's hunting ground, there was a small island where whales used to come. Tamotuk had many opportunities to watch them, but didn't know how to hunt them. When food was scarce, he would go to the island hoping that a miracle would occur and that a whale would appear before him. But nothing would ever happen. That's why he wanted my father to teach him the Inuit way. My father was in no hurry and Tamotuk was constantly asking him when he would take him. Dad always replied:

—Be patient. The secret to whale hunting is patience. It often happens that one has to wait many days, at the same spot, before anything happens, but don't worry. They always end up coming and your turn will soon come.

Dad and Tamotuk waited many days for a whale. Finally, not one but two arctic whales came and the men killed both of them. For his first experience Tamotuk was blessed. There are days like that when everything seems to come all at once. When people at the camp heard about the big catch, everyone canoed to the small island and we feasted for hours. That day everything seemed nice and calm. The snow was

---

7. The Cree term for muskrat is "wacask."

shining like a mirror. The sky was blue, a kind of deep blue that penetrates your mind. That day everyone seemed to be friendly, as if Mother Nature had brought us everything and our only responsibility was to enjoy it. For the first time these Cree families tasted whale blubber. They told us that they prefer it boiled in sea-salted water. Mother cut up parts of the whale and hung them to dry. She also prepared pieces to be smoked in burned cedar wood. Not a single piece of the beluga was wasted. Even the dogs got their share.

In June, time came to leave for East Main. There was a large settlement at the mouth of the Eastmain River where many Cree used to gather at different times in the year. They would have celebrations and also traded with the HBC post there. When it was decided to leave, everyone got busy packing their muskrat pelts and smoked meats. Dad and Tamotuk used melted tar to patch up the small holes in our canoes made by sharp rocks on shallow waters. Before leaving for the trip, the dogs were abandoned on a small island to run around free for the summer. There was no drinking water on those islands, but the dogs would manage to survive by drinking rainwater. Their instinct tells them they cannot drink the salty water of the Bay. Even if they were very thirsty, they would not drink it. Nature takes care of itself.

After a couple of days of packing, the time came to pull down the wigwams and to load everything into the canoes. We had three canoes; each of them was about twenty-three feet long and large enough to hold a small family. The boats had blankets for sails. It wasn't the best possible sail, but it was handy and quite cheap. As we passed by the little island where the dogs had been left, they all ran by the shore, barking at us, as we sailed away. In my kid's mind, the dogs were trying to tell us that they wanted to come along. Maybe they knew we were leaving them behind for a long time with no other recourse than the laws of Nature; laws that were merciless to the weakest. Maybe they were begging for a last chance, unless they were simply telling us goodbye. Anyway, I didn't worry about them for long, as pretty soon their barking faded away and the wind was pushing our boats offshore. Once we lost sight of the shore, all we could hear was the wind.

During that trip I noticed Tamotuk's amputated right hand. He could only use his left arm and hand. Despite his handicap, Tamotuk was still able to paddle as a strong man. Dad noticed me watching him.

—When he was young, he played with a 10-calibre. The gun fired on its own, and ripped his hand off. That's what happens when one plays with a rifle, he said.

Although this warning quite scared me, I was still pretty amazed by Tamotuk's strength and couldn't stop peeking at him. I later learned what a 10-gauge is. To a kid it looks like a cannon and my admiration for Tamotuk became even bigger.

The wind started to blow harder. From the rear of our canoe where I sat, I could watch the other canoes. They were all made the same. The three of them had a similar blanket hanging over a wooden mast. All sails were up, that way the men didn't have to paddle, except to steer the canoe. Suddenly, my baby sister Ann started to cry from hunger. Mum, who was still breastfeeding her, took care of her right away. Everything was under control and we travelled with no incidents all day. I slept most of it, the canoe swaying back and forth like a swing.

When I woke up, we were entering the mouth of the Eastmain River. The canoes were scattered. We arrived last. Many people were waiting to greet us on the shore. I had never seen so many people all at once, and I was quite scared and uneasy when they all came to welcome the Kitchikapoo and Tamotuk families along with us, their Eskimo friends, whom they had never met before. All eyes were on Mother for they had never seen an "amauti," the parka worn by Eskimo women. Apparently, no Eskimo woman had ever set foot on that part of the Cree territory. Everyone was amazed to see the way Mother was carrying baby Ann on her back inside her parka's hood that we call "amaut." The very curious ones had their mouths wide open, staring at Mum. They stooped over one another to get a better look. They all stopped to scrutinize her when Reverend Sam Iseroff came to greet us. Sam Iseroff was the Anglican minister in service at East Main's mission. He shook each one of our hands, which was the custom in early days, and he welcomed us to his parish. In the meantime, Dad went to the HBC store to buy a white tent to put up by the river down below the Anglican Church. It was a sign: we were going to spend several weeks here.

We stayed all summer in East Main. Sam Iseroff had two daughters, one of them used to play with us by the river and we got to know her. She used to bring candies with her, showing off her respect and friendliness. As young as she was, she had a loud girlish laugh. She already knew how to flirt with boys, and had me chasing after her. We also used to play a game I thought was very special called "tag." At that time I thought it was invented by East Main's children. That summer too, I attended, with all the other kids, the mission's kindergarten. There I learned the ABCs. I was the smallest in the class, but still I learned pretty well. Our teacher was a White man from the South. I remember that he always said the Lord's Prayer with his eyes closed, loud enough for all to hear. He would open an eye now and then to check if we were praying or having fun. Kindergarten only lasted a month. At the end of the summer a doctor vaccinated us.

The doctor's arrival is one of those episodes of my childhood that I will never forget for it gave me my first glimpse of the big world that I figured was out there, far away from the Inuit and Cree hunting grounds, but which I could not fathom. The doctor came in on one of those early seaplanes that I had never heard of before and that were used to bring mail to northern villages and settlements. When the plane first arrived, I was with Mum. She had baby sister Ann on her back. We were walking on the trails in the settlement when we heard a loud roaring noise from the sky. We both looked up and we saw a big black bird with red wings, flying over our head. Mother told me with fear in her voice:

—It is the Devil. Be careful. He will take us away....

I was so scared that I ran into the bushes to hide. Mother burst out laughing. It was a joke.

—Don't worry, I am just kidding you. It's a plane landing on the river. Come with me, we'll have a look at it. You'll see it is just a noisy machine, nothing to be scared of.

Despite my mother's words I was still scared. I only began to calm down when I saw several children running down to the river to greet the pilot and its passengers. They were calling them White men! I wasn't scared anymore. They were not devils but only White men, like Father Belleau and the Reverend Iseroff and his lovely girls. I began thinking that the world was bigger than Strutton Island. It was really something for me to realize that people from other worlds had come to visit us. I was also impressed to see that people had taken the risk of flying in a strange machine just to visit us. We must have been very important to them. I was proud, but also a little envious because looking at the seaplane made me wish I could also fly to visit other foreign worlds.

In late summer, Dad decided to go to another Cree settlement, Old Factory, thirty miles north of East Main. We were going to travel in the canoe that Tamotuk had given to Dad to thank him for his hunting lessons. I was sad to leave my friends behind us but it was time to get on the move. On our way, we stopped to see Grandpa at Cape Hope Islands. Dad told him that he was going to Old Factory because he was looking for a job. Grandpa advised Dad to apply for a boat-pilot position with the fur trader Jack Palmquis; he was looking for a crew for his freight boat named *Venture* that he used to ship merchandise to the different settlements along the shore of the James Bay. We did not stay long at Grandpa's. Father was eager to arrive at Old Factory to find out if he could get the job. When we finally arrived, we were surprised to see that uncle Alaku Weetaltuk already had a job as a mechanic for the boat *Venture*.

That year there were plenty of fish in Maquatua River, near Old Factory. The Cree would set fishnets at high tide, and when the tide was out, they came back to pick up the fish. Trout and whitefish were abundant. It was quite a sight to see. There was a Roman Catholic Mission of the Oblates at Old Factory. There were only two missionaries there: Father Labreche and Brother Lavoie and later Father Éthier, a very good singer. It was a really small mission. You should know that the Catholic missions were not very popular at that time in James Bay because Anglican missionaries had already converted the Cree and the Inuit. Actually, I was born Anglican, as the Weetaltuk family had embraced that faith. But getting involved with the Oblates and learning their religion gave me the idea to convert. I cannot say the Oblates did not suggest it, but I still chose by myself to become a Roman Catholic. I was seven years old. It was the first choice I made in my life that did not follow the tradition of the Weetaltuk family but, as you will soon read, it was not going to be the only one.

When I told the fathers that I wanted to change my faith, they said I needed to be re-baptized but that they would not do it unless I had permission from my father. I asked and Dad did not object. I still remember his answer:

—If you know what you are doing and if it is your own decision, I will not stop you. You can become a Catholic if this is your wish.

When I was re-baptized, I was given saintly names and I became: Jean Marie Edward Ambroise Weetaltuk. This was my first change of name, but I was going to have, a dozen years later, another change of name.

The Mission at Old Factory had also an outdoor kindergarten for young students, both Eskimos and Cree. The Oblates used to give a piece of cake, made by Father Lavoie, to every student attending school. It did not take long before all children went to school. With a bit of experience from East Main, I progressed faster than other kids. Father Labreche was really impressed by my learning skills, and he suggested that I should be sent to St. Theresa School at Fort George to get a real academic education. He asked my dad about the proposal. Dad agreed. He thought it was a good idea to get an education, but it was also a good thing for the family to have one less mouth to feed. That's how it was decided I would be enrolled in school. To kill two birds with one stone it was also agreed that my brother David would come with me.

CHAPTER 2

At the

BOARDING
SCHOOL

By early September, two mission boats came from Fort George[1] to Old Factory. Father Éthier and Brother Martin, two missionaries, were on board. They were travelling around the James Bay to pick up students for school. I remember that one of the boats was a little bigger than the other. I do not know why I still remember that detail, but it is as if the image of those two boats was engraved in my mind. I can only assume it is because those were the boats sent to take my brother David and me to a new world. All the details of that day are still fresh in my memory. One of the boats was named *Notre Dame de l'Espérance* and the other *St. Joseph*.

Like a bad augur, the very day before our departure, a strong windstorm wrecked one of the mission boats, *Notre Dame de l'Espérance*, while it was still anchored. Damages were so serious that the boat could not leave the shore the next day. Since they had only one boat left, the missionaries were not able take as many children as they wanted. That is why that year they only took two students from our settlement, me and my brother. When we left Old Factory in the surviving

1. Fort George was located, at that time, on an island in the middle of the mouth of the La Grande River. The village was relocated on the mainland when the James Bay hydroelectric project was built in the late 1970s. The dam changed the flow of the river and made life on the island dangerous, especially when water was released from the huge reservoir. Actually, experts had anticipated that the island would disappear after being eroded by the currents created by the release of water from the dam. The new village, built on the mainland, is called Chisasibi and is home to one of Quebec's largest Cree communities. It is a bright new town with nice houses and a big mall, though not everything is new; Fort George's old church was moved from the island to the mainland. Some people who still miss their old community travel to the island to remember the life they used to enjoy there.

boat, David and I were pretty scared. The fear of a wreckage added to the fear of the unknown: the boarding school.

Sailing from Old Factory to Fort George was a long adventure. There were 100 miles to go, and we were hardly making fifteen miles a day. Our first stop was at a mountainous island called Wemindji, fifteen miles north of Old Factory. That is exactly where and when David and I first experienced homesickness. Father Éthier and Brother Martin had left us alone and were up on the mountain picking berries for supper. Once alone, David and I looked at the sea in despair as we began to realize that we would not see Mother before next summer. That sad thought made us cry in chorus. After crying so hard from homesickness, we both fell asleep, exhausted from our tears. The two Oblates came back later with two small pails of black and blue berries, not knowing we had been crying. They gave us a cup of berries mixed with milk and sugar. It tasted good. Then they made a fire to heat up some stew. One of them went to get a pail of clear spring water and made tea. Despite our despair, we slept easy that night. The good fathers had their way of comforting us.

The next morning we continued the trip to Fort George with a strong wind. After a few days of travel, we finally arrived. David and I were still wondering who would look after us for the year to come and we were quite unsure of what to expect. I was uneasy and afraid. My brother felt even worse. We were badly missing Mother. A few moments after our arrival we met Father Couture, the head of the school. We were also introduced to the seven Grey Nuns in service at Fort George. Father Couture had a big black beard; in Inuktitut we call it "Umilik." Despite his beard he was smiling. Actually, all the nuns and the fathers were smiling as they greeted us. They were smiling in silence, staring at us with curiosity. All the students staying at St. Theresa School had come to welcome us and they were also smiling. Brother and I were the only ones with a long face.

At that point my brother started to cry in despair. At first I thought it was because of all these happy faces, but I realized he had seen something even scarier. A huge dog, a dog ten times bigger than the biggest dog we had ever seen before. It was so big and so strong that one had to harness it to a cart carrying barrels of water. It was on the move, heading slowly toward us. My brother was soon going to learn that the dog was indeed a bull, a peaceful animal that is as useful in the South as the dog team is in the North. However, David started to cry before anybody could tell him what the animal was. Through his sobs I was able to understand that he was more scared by the bull's way of moving, a bit like an automat, than by its enormous size. That pace was so strange compared to that of our dogs.

Obviously, the students were used to seeing this animal since they already had a Cree name for it: "Mistoss." While I was listening to the children trying to explain to us the habits of the bull, I noticed that all the boys were standing together, while the girls stood apart. Suddenly, one priest gave the signal of departure and the crowd set off in motion. We walked up towards the mission school, the boys in one row and the girls in their own. At one point we all stopped, turned left, and everybody made a sign of the cross. Then, they started to mumble in a language that was neither Cree nor Inuktitut and did not sound like English. What was most surprising was not the language itself but rather the tone; it was almost like a mourning song. It wasn't very scary but it was not pleasant either. I later came to learn it was Latin. After they were finished, they all made another sign of the cross. I crossed myself too. I knew how to do it, as I had learned it from Father Labreche at Old Factory's kindergarten. All the children looked at me with disappointment. Usually neophytes were not able to properly make the sign of the cross, which was a pretext to make fun of them every time. I just had spoiled that joy for them. As for me, I was very grateful to Father Labreche for his good lessons. It was the first time, but not the last, that I was grateful for the education received from the Oblate brothers.

When we arrived at the boarding school, David and I were taken into the boys' dormitory. The nun in charge of boys gave us a piece of cake. She made us sit on the floor against the wall, under a window. I felt like a prisoner. Outside, the other boys were taking a peek at us through the window. My brother didn't like to be stared at by these children he didn't know. He became suddenly very tense and I feared he was going to cry again. But that did not happen. He chose instead to make faces at them with his tongue stuck out. The other kids thought it was very funny and made more faces back at him. After a while we were all laughing. That's exactly when the nun came back. I was expecting to be punished but nothing happened. She wasn't coming to blame us for having fun but rather to take us to the washroom. On our way she told us with a friendly voice:

—Come on, boys! You're going to get a bath. Believe me, you need it after the long trip you have had. Once you are finished, a sister will give you some clothes and you will be dressed like all the other boys.

The bath was pleasant, but we had to quickly leave the good hot water to slip on the uniform. Once we were dressed a nun put a string around our neck with a bunch of medals. They were made of aluminum and pictured all kinds of saints. At that moment, I could not imagine that I was soon going to learn the story of each of them. I remember especially the medals of the Sacred Heart of Jesus and of the Blessed Virgin Mary of the Immaculate Conception. Their pictures were as impressive as their names. At first, I did not realize the reason why we had to wear those strange pendants. I was even scared by the idea of wearing pictures of dead persons around my neck, but the sister explained that saints have the power to help us:

—These are pictures of holy persons who became saints because of their good life. Wearing their image will bring you a lot of good things. They are called Miraculous Medals because they can bring miracles.

That was a strong argument. But, as if that was not convincing enough, Sister added:

—If you pray to them, the good saints will also keep the Devil away from you. The more you pray, the safer you will be.

I was going to realize pretty soon that most of the boys wore at least a dozen medals. The more they had, the more help they would get and the less the Devil would bother them. That was how they understood the teaching of the nuns. The sad result was that boys would go as far as stealing medals from one another. As for me, I never stole a medal. I would have been too concerned about the efficiency of a stolen medal, but many of my friends did not seem to bother. The more they had, the more invincible they would feel. It was that simple.

I was the smallest. Students were numbered from 01 to 19. As I was the smallest, I got the number 01. The nun in charge of the boys spoke three languages, English, French, and Cree. She was from Moosonee, at the bottom of the James Bay. Her name was Sister Louise Martin. My first day in class was a little hard because I could only speak Inuktitut. During the class the teacher drew a picture of a dog on the blackboard. Then, using her stick, she pointed at the dog and said in English:

—This is a dog. Please, repeat after me: DOG.

Then each of the children, one by one, repeated DOG. When my turn came, I said "kimik," which means "dog" in Inuktitut. Everyone in class burst out laughing. I had not realized that it was an English period; I thought the nun was asking each of us to identify the animal. When I understood my mistake, I started to cry. Sister Louise told the class to be quiet as she gave me a big hug. She laughed and said:

—Edward, try again my poor dear. Repeat after me: DOG.

That sister was so good with me. Her kindness made my first day and the following much easier. Actually, she worked very hard for the rest of the year assisting me. I really loved being helped like that. At one point I even pretended to be slow in learning so she would help me more. Because of her persistent help, on top of my Inuktitut, my parents' language, I learned to speak English, French, and Cree. I learnt Cree even before French or English because there were a lot of Cree students at that mission school and I soon got along pretty well with my Cree playmates.

The school routine was pretty strict and tough. The whole year round we would get up at six o'clock in the morning. Our guardian nuns always gave the wake up call in Latin:

—Benedicamus Domino.

Those were the first words I heard for many years, and we would always answer in chorus:

—Deo Gracias.

Then we would get down on our knees with a sign of the cross and start to recite the Lord's Prayer, then the Hail Mary, and Glory Be. We always finished with the sign of the cross. We would only get dressed after all the prayers were done. During the coldest mornings it was as if the prayers would never end. Once we were dressed, all alike, our daily routine began with low mass. Breakfast was only served after the celebration.

Those were the rules of our mission school, but these regulations were not rare in Canadian schools during the 1930s.

The classrooms were located on the third floor of the convent. The infirmary was on the second floor along with the chapel where we attended so many masses. Our dining room, as well as the boys' dormitory that was on the south side, was located on the main floor. To the east side was the girls' room, and at the centre the school's kitchen. The nuns' study and sleeping rooms were on the east side of the second floor. West and east sides had stairs. I must have climbed up and down these stairs a thousand times during the eleven years I spent at the mission. It was always the same sequence every day. Up at six o'clock in the morning, then to low mass, next the dining room, and finally to class on the third floor. For a young Inuk who was used to being free that was quite a routine! No wonder I still remember every single detail of it.

During the day we had two recesses, one at ten o'clock in the morning and the second at three o'clock in the afternoon. Each of us was given a piece of cake for a snack. That is when I learned that size and strength have to be feared. Indeed, survival in the mission school was not only a question of praying to the good saints and the Blessed Virgin but also a matter of avoiding the bullies. I learned from my school years that it is not only in nature that the fittest survive but it is also the rule that governs civilized worlds. My teacher for that life lesson was Isaiah Wiskijan, a Cree from Rupert's House, the biggest and also the strongest student. Once I dared to refuse him a piece of my cake. Before I even realized what I had done, he punched my chest so hard that I almost fell unconscious. I didn't squeal to our nuns. It would have been suicidal: for he would just have punched me harder as soon as he found an opportunity. After that, I always gave him whatever he asked for. The worst was that he was always bragging about his strength and size. We had a soccer ball that this bully would pick up and punch with his fist, right under your nose. He was threatening every one of us, one at a time:

—Look, Weetaltuk, this will be you, if you don't give me your cake.

—Eh! Jimmy, this will be your face, if you squeal on me.

—Eh! James Corston, look at me. That is your nose if you don't mind your own business.

When he was sure he had made his point he would kick the soccer ball. The ball flew over the third storey of the convent, way over the cross. It made me wish to be strong enough to kick him and make him fly like that ball.

Every afternoon we had a lecture on catechism by Father Couture. During these lectures I learned about the seven capital sins. Father taught us that if a man dies before he can repent through confession, he goes to hell. He showed us pictures of Satan, so we would know what he looked like. Most of us had a hard time reading, so Father Couture often used images to teach us. One of them showed the seven gates of hell. That picture impressed me very much, because Lucifer was sitting in the image's centre with a big smile and a fork in his right hand, while other demons were forking the sinners from each gate. It seemed like demons were always ready to feast. Somehow, devils were a bit like the Inuit, always ready to feast. But contrary to what happens in our cold country, demons never had to wait for whales or seals to pop up at the breathing hole. Their meal was always warm and waiting for them, because there are so many remorseless humans queuing in line at the gates of hell.

Father Couture dedicated a lot of time to explaining the difference between mortal sins, also called capital sins, which would send you straight to hell, and the venial sins, which God would forgive, if you asked for His mercy. I pretty soon came to believe that almost every thought, word, or deed, by a man or a woman, were punishable by God. Father Couture had a favourite theme for his lectures: the Ten Commandments. I still remember the first time he promised:

—For those who serve God and obey His Ten Commandments, heaven will be the reward.

I was very upset because I did not know the Ten Commandments and I was eager to learn that secret recipe, which would spare me the eternal suffering. One day I dared to ask:

—Father, it seems almost impossible to be saved. It looks as though you have to be crucified before you can see the gates of heaven. It is so unfair.

The father realized my despair and tried to comfort me. He finally succeeded, as I was not opposed to religion but I was simply overwhelmed by its many rules.

Religion was, to be honest, a true challenge for students like us coming from the tundra with no or little Christian background. We were asking so many questions about all the holy mysteries. Father Couture was always very patient with us and would continually give us answers. Even though the answers were not always clear, we soon became acquainted with the basic concepts of Christianity. Since we were attending a Catholic school, we were being educated as Catholics, and it was very important for us to understand that being Catholic was very different from being Protestant. Indeed, Protestants, although they believed in Jesus Christ, were not going to be saved because they had lost the very track that guides to heaven, Father Couture used to say. He explained to us that once Protestants were Catholic like us but refused at one point to follow the ancestral teachings of the Church and got lost. "Always walk in the tracks of your Elders," my own father had taught me. Listening to Father Couture's explanation, I was thinking that this Inuit lesson could be useful to others beside the Inuit. As years went by, thanks to catechism, students began to take religion very seriously. Some children were obeying the Christian rules pretty strictly, and they were working hard to convince all of us to follow their habits. Every time we took a glass of water to drink, they forced us to make a sign of the cross and the strongest boys would give those who forgot a rough time. One could even be ostracized for not being Catholic enough. The good Father Couture's efforts to turn his little savages into good Catholics had this odd result of giving the bad boys and others an excuse to torment the little ones.

Lent was the hardest time in the year for us kids, forty long days of sacrifice. Always being told to eat less in order to offer your stomach pain to Jesus. It was also forbidden to look at girls, as Father Couture said quite seriously:

—If you look at girls, bad ideas will haunt your dreams and those dreams will make the Holy Mary cry. I warn you. If you take an interest in girls during Lent, you will rot in hell.

It was really hard to control one's thoughts. It even became unbearable the year I met Evelyn Gagnon, a beautiful girl from Moosonee. We used to smile at each other during the year. But during Lent, we could not look at each other for forty days. It was exactly when the Devil would send me the worst horrible thoughts. It is amazing how the Devil works hard to steal our soul. When it was unbearable, I would steal a peek at her, but without a smile. That was strictly forbidden. Sometimes she would look at me in silence too. That was when I learned how to smile inside my heart without a sound. Still I was scared because I knew that fooling the fathers was not enough. Satan, he could not be fooled and he knew what I was dreaming about, and that particular and very desirable thing that I was dreaming about doing with Evelyn was, I can admit it now, a capital sin. I knew it and that knowledge was scary.

As for my brother, he got into real trouble during Lent. I do not recall which year it was but we were still young; it was maybe the first or the second year of our schooling. It was the Holy Week and we were supposed to keep complete silence during the entire week. Actually, we were bound for most of the time to the chapel, where we would pray to the Holy Cross. All statues were covered with purple cloths, the bells were kept silent all week, and the nuns used a wooden rattle to call students. That week was the very week to be quiet. I do not know what happened with David, maybe he could not stand the pressure anymore, but suddenly in the middle of the silence, he curled up his prayer book and used it to made a loud moose call. Unfortunately, Father Couture was right behind him. He told him to come into his office, showing David his twelve-inch ruler. We all saw the ruler and we knew that the punishment was going to be proportionate to the offence. I wasn't able to talk to David before the recess. When we finally met, he told me that Father Couture slapped him so hard that he saw small stars. He swore that after Lent he would not return to the school and would stay forever in Cape Hope Islands. Indeed, he did not make the return trip, because my parents understood that the school and its rules were not made for him.

Nevertheless, Easter Sunday was always a glorious day. The best part of the day was the wake up because silence was broken right after the usual "Benedicamus Domino." That day we would all shout "Deo Gratias." Some kids screamed so loud as if they were trying to let out everything that had been kept inside for so long. Some even burst out crying. As for me, some years I felt so much joy that I thought I was going crazy. When there was a blizzard on Easter Sunday, we would stay inside and play games. If the weather was nice we would go for a picnic at a little shack by a hill called "Monkey Hill." It was named that way because there was an echo and when we shouted at the hill, our voices bounced right back as loud. The oldest kids used to tell the youngest that the voices were made by a monkey, hiding somewhere in a hole, trying to mimic us. That always frightened the poor kids. But when the girls were coming with us, it was even more fun, because they would shout in despair and cuddle up close to the boys, looking for protection. Of course, the girls were just pretending to be scared to be able to get into the boys' arms. Now I realize that the priests also were pretending to believe that the girls were actually scared but let us play this innocent game to get some relief after the long days of Lent. However, back then I was not thinking at all, I was simply enjoying myself because Evelyn Gagnon was cuddling in my arms.

Saint Catherine's Day, 25 November, was a feast always highly celebrated by a picnic. The nuns made toffee with brown sugar molasses mixed with a bit of butter. The mixture was then melted in a pan, and when it was ready, one of the nuns poured it on snow to cool it down. Then, the kids put butter on their hand so the *tire,* or maple taffy, would not stick and before it was totally cold they picked it up, pulled it, and stretched it until it became golden yellow. When it was done, they cut it in small squares to make candies. That was such a treat. I always sucked the candies slowly to make the pleasure last as long as possible. Of course, we were not allowed to eat all of them at once. The nuns would ask us to wrap some of them in wax paper and we would keep them until Christmas. That was indeed the way our school celebrated Saint Catherine, like all Quebeckers do. We also used to sing French Canadian songs on that day. I still remember one of them: "Ah que c'est bon la tire, la tire...."[2]

In the summer of my first year in school, the students from Fort George were able to return to their families, but all other children were unable to get home. Because of the wreckage of the *Notre Dame de l'Espérance*, there was no boat available to sail us back. The mission had only one boat left, a forty-by-eight-feet scow that was already being used to haul hay. The mission really needed that hay to feed its two cows and the bull during the winter. It was the Cree from Fort George who cut the hay for the mission. It was then left to dry in the sun, and later it was gathered and hauled to the mission's barn by boat.

Father Couture gave the students who could not return home permission to go camping for two weeks. He even lent us the mission scow. Father Éthier was our guardian and Brother D'Amour was our captain. With just a 10-horsepower outboard motor pushing the scow loaded up with children and enough materials for two weeks, we didn't sail very fast. Nevertheless, we were all enjoying the adventure and the break from the school routine. As for me, I still remember fondly how Father Éthier was busy trying to keep the boys away from the girls. Away from school and from its punishments and lessons of catechism, we were feeling free and were letting nature drive us. The boys and the girls always tried to pair up with each other, not for real sex, but for games that were the first step towards it. One time we were making so much noise in the bushes that Father Éthier rushed up yelling:

—Hey! Boys, get away from girls. If you don't stop these games immediately, we will return right away to Fort George and you will all be grounded for the rest of the summer.

---

2. "Oh, it's good, the maple-sugar candy, the maple-sugar candy...."

That warning sounded so real that the boys all scattered away and ran in a hurry, pretending to be hunting birds with slingshots.

After two weeks of real fun, we had to finally resign ourselves to returning to the mission. We spent the rest of the summer helping in the gardens. The mission had three large gardens, big enough to feed the mission with all the necessary vegetables for a whole year despite the poor quality of the soil. The fathers were growing carrots, cabbages, beets, potatoes, and turnips. One day, Father Couture came in with a big smile and told us to get dressed. He had something to show us. He took us to the bank of the river where a white tent had been installed recently. Inside were Mother and Father. Mum grabbed ahold of us and started to cry with joy. David and I sobbed, as did our baby sister Ann. In her case she was not crying because she was pleased to see us, but just out of all the excitement. Dad tried to hide his emotion but we could see he had tears in his eyes. Mother gave us news of Grandfather and of other people living on Cape Hope Islands. All were well, which was good to hear. Father Couture gave us permission to stay overnight with our parents. That night we had bannock and tea with extra sugar, just like we loved it. Dad told us that Grandpa was planning to sell his schooner to our mission, since the fathers were looking for a boat to transport the students. Our parents stayed only one week because it was getting late in the summer and they had to leave for their winter camp. They waited for the right wind. The day it turned north, they left, heading back to Old Factory. I'm sure they were thinking of us all day long on their way back.

Later that autumn, Grandpa's schooner appeared at the mouth of the river. The mission had finally bought it. Father Labreche was coming from Old Factory to deliver some merchandise to the mission. Right away Brother Goulet, Brother Cardinal, and Brother Lauzon came to help to pull the boat up the riverbank. It was heavy and they covered the track with slippery oily soap to make its mooring easier. However, that was not enough and they had to call the bull in for extra strength. Apparently Grandpa had accepted $200 for the schooner. Mr. Flaherty had given that boat to Grandpa to thank him for being his guide while Flaherty was mapping the Hudson Bay and James Bay area, as well as the Belcher Islands. Grandfather, George Weetaltuk, indeed drove the famous Flaherty around the region with his dog team while he was preparing the shooting of his famous film *Nanook of the North*. That is something my family and my community are very proud of. To show his gratitude, Mr. Flaherty also gave Grandpa a set of tools. With them, my Grandfather carved canoes that he would sell at the different HBC posts of the region, East Main, Rupert House, and Old Factory.

Each summer, Grandfather set up to make canoes. He always began by steaming cedar wood to bend it into a canoe frame. Grandfather used to say that he learned that technique from Mr. Flaherty himself. He was so skilful that he was pretty soon known all around the James Bay for his well-made canoes. One day, a fisherman from Moosonee heard how handy Grandpa was and asked Grandpa to build him a big fishing boat. Not a regular canoe, but a boat with an iron frame. Grandfather accepted right away, as for him it was just another challenge. Grandpa and his family moved to Moosonee with the fisherman's family and stayed there until the boat was finished. It was named *Joe Groome*. It was strong and well-built. That boat made its owner proud. As for my Grandfather, this was the beginning of a new way of making good money, for after that accomplishment he was asked to build several other big boats. His skills became known all around the region, from the top to the bottom of the James Bay.

A few years later, in East Main, a ski plane had a rough landing and broke one ski on the ice. Jim Bell was the unlucky pilot. He was known to be a very good bush pilot, and he was indeed, but the damage was too serious for him to fix it by himself. He used his Marconi radio to inform the HBC headquarters about his situation. They told him that he had to do whatever it took to be back within one week at South Porcupine. Fearing a lot of trouble if he didn't mind their orders, Jim Bell decided that only my grandfather could save him. He asked the HBC if they could have George Weetaltuk sent from Cape Hope Islands to East Main. Through radio, they reached Grandpa and told him that somebody needed his help. They sent a solid dog team to fetch him with all his tools. Within two days the plane was fixed. Once it landed at South Porcupine, the mechanics checked the plane. They all commended Grandpa's work, saying they could not have done any better. Some years later, the broken plane fixed by Grandfather was put up in a museum. Under the old machine a written note said:

—Miracle Man of the North fixed this broken ski plane.

A few years later, a friend of the family saw the plane in its museum display and passed the information on to Grandfather's Inuit relatives. That is how everyone in the Nunavik learned that George Weetaltuk's skills were famous not only among Inuit, but also among White people.[3]

I met Jim Bell in 1952, when I was on my way to leave for the Korean War. I was already in service and in uniform; I had come to Fort George to pay a last visit to the fathers and the brothers at the mission school. I was going back to Wainwright, Alberta, by plane. To my surprise Jim Bell flew the plane I took at Fort George, a two-engine seaplane. When I realized who he was, I asked him about George Weetaltuk. He recalled immediately the whole story and was very pleased to meet the grandson of his saviour. We spent several hours together and we had a lot of fun. Jim Bell was a real nice fellow. He made a lot of jokes about me being enrolled in the army. I think he thought it was pretty odd for a young Inuk to be on his way to war and could not stop making fun of me. I guess he was only joking because speaking of the true risks was too scary:

—Eddy, listen to me. I have heard that Canadian soldiers are used as training targets for the North Koreans. They practise on our men before attacking the Americans. So be aware.

He said these words with a friendly laugh while wishing me good luck. However, that last joke made me think about my situation. I began to have flashbacks from my childhood, my mother, my brothers and sisters, and my school years. It was like somebody was rewinding my life. I was scared and wondering what had happened and how I had managed to put myself in such a situation.

---

3. George Weetaltuk is indeed well renowned for his many skills. His drawings have helped to make him one of the first recognized Inuit artists in Canada. He was also famous for his carving skills, as he carved the ornate bishop's chair in several northern churches. His boats are amongst his most spectacular achievements. One of them, named *Carwyn*, was over fifty feet long. George Weetaltuk built it in 1944 when he was more than eighty years old. A famous anthropologist, Milton Freeman, wrote a bibliographical note on him (M.M.R. Freeman, "George Weetaltuk (ca. 1862–1956)" in *Arctic* 36, no. 2 (June 1983): 214–15.

But it is not yet time to discuss that; I would rather get back to Grandpa's schooner. Brother Martin worked hard almost all year fixing beds inside the schooner. He even put in a small kitchen stove near the front engine room. He also installed an old Ford engine, water-cooled, to propel the boat. All the kids were excited. We couldn't wait for the spring to come to ride in it. Moreover, a bright new boat meant that all of us would be able to return home next summer.

The brothers named their new boat *Notre Dame de l'Espérance*, like the one that had been wrecked earlier. When it was finally put into the river, after the ice had broken up, we still could not leave for another two weeks because the weather was too bad to travel. Everything was all set up for the trip and we were stuck waiting and waiting. For students it was even more painful than Lent. We were so eager to leave that we built a small grotto to pray to the Virgin Mary to give us nice weather. It was something to see, a bunch of young Cree and Inuit kneeling down and praying for the storm to stop. The Holy Mary must have known that we did not need better weather as badly as we pretended, for our prayer did not help the wind to calm down. Nonetheless, the nuns still encouraged us to pray more and more. They must have seen in our sudden devotion a good way to keep us busy and quiet. Finally, one day our Cree pilot, who knew the James Bay coast well, came in to announce that the weather was just right to leave. I still remember his miraculous words:

—Hey guys! Time to pack up your stuff. Tomorrow is the day. Be ready, we will be leaving as soon as the sun is up.

The next morning we had an early breakfast on the schooner while the boat headed away from the shore. Three brothers accompanied us. We were going back home and all the kids were overexcited. Fortunately, it took only one day to cover the first seventy miles and to reach Paint Hills, thirty miles north of Old Factory, where we stayed overnight. On the high hills there were a lot of ptarmigans looking for berries to eat. Their feathers were turning brown. It was quite a spectacle to see all those birds, some already brown like in full summer, some still white like doves, and others wearing together their winter and summer colours. We asked Father Éthier for permission to go ashore. Two of us,

James Corston of Moosonee and myself, were granted permission to go on to the mainland under the supervision of Brother Goulet, while the others had to stay on the boat and wait for supper to be ready.

When we reached the top of the hill, a rooster ptarmigan saw us and quickly flew up with a loud call for his hens. They all flew for a bit before landing a short distance away. They were staring at us with curiosity. James and I picked up stones, wondering if we could hit one of those birds from a fifty-yard distance. My rock was kind of flat. When I threw it, it sort of curved away, then curved right back, and hit a bird. The ptarmigan's wing was broken and it could not fly anymore. Brother Goulet let out a shout:

—Let's catch that bird. Go for it, boys.

He started to run to chase the ptarmigan. We had a real hard time catching the bird. Although it had a broken wing, it still was very tricky and made us run quite a lot.

Brother Goulet finally caught it and wrung its neck like Inuit and Cree hunters do when they want to put game out of pain. The kids on the boat would not believe Brother Goulet when he told them that I had hit the bird with a rock at that distance. James Corston also tried very hard to convince them of my exploit, but no argument was strong enough. They had a good reason to keep their doubts, since every now and then Brother Goulet would burst out laughing. The good father had had too much fun chasing the ptarmigan that he could not stop laughing while recalling the story. Students were suspicious of his laughter, thinking he was making fun of them. Anyway, by the end of the night everybody ended up laughing. This is a very simple episode of my past but I still recall it with pleasure. Now I am old and I realize that the best times in life, the true happiness, are not when you do extraordinary things but rather when you laugh with friends or family. To be frank, I have to say that the mission school, even if it was tough and I hated it sometimes, it was also like a second family for me.

Next morning we continued the trip to Old Factory. We left at around nine o'clock, which was very late compared to our regular schedule, but nobody was eager to return. We realized that we were near to arriving when we saw a tall cross on top of French Hill. This cross had been planted there by early French fur traders when they established their first trading post in the region. However, they did not stay there for long and moved inland to open a new trading post called Radisson. In the early 1930s a very strong north wind blew the cross down. That was the only vestige of the first European settlement in the region. It was a pity to leave it down; that's why Brother Lavoie hired Dad and Uncle Alaku to put it back up. They worked hard and managed to restore the cross to its former glory. That evening, when the sky turned red, the cross looked like the real Calvary: it was both an amazing and a truly scary sight. Such a spectacle would turn a heathen into a believer.

When we arrived at the mouth of the river, two canoes came to greet us. The first was the mission canoe and the second belonged to the fur trader Jack Palmquist. Mother was waiting for me and was so pleased to see me. I was so happy to be back with her. Unfortunately, Father was away. He had taken employment as a boat pilot. He was working for the summer with Uncle Alaku on a boat of Jack Palmquist, shipping merchandise to the different trading posts all around the James Bay.

I spent the whole holidays with Mother at Old Factory. Summer was the best time of the year: no class, no low mass, no Latin wake-up calls. During that period of the year most of the adults were busy travelling back and forth for jobs or for hunting trips. Only the missionaries stayed at the settlement. That is how I got acquainted with one of them, Brother Lavoie. He was a real outdoorsman. He loved hunting and fishing. I was also very skilful. Actually, he alone had built the Old Factory mission. Almost every summer, when I was back for vacation, I helped him with gardening, clearing bad weeds from his potato garden. As we were working together, he used to tell me stories about the first French people who came to this part of the James Bay. His favourite was Radisson, the first European who visited the region. Brother Lavoie was gardening at the very place where Radisson had built his settlement. One summer, while pulling up bad weeds from the garden, we found old clay smoking pipes. Brother Lavoie told me they were very old and had been brought from

France by Radisson himself or by his men. He saved the ones that were not broken and used them, for several years, to smoke his much loved "tabac canadien" (Canadian tobacco).

At the end of that summer, on its way back to Fort George, *Notre Dame de l'Espérance* stopped at Cape Hope Islands. The Brothers wanted to show Grandfather what they had done with his boat and how well equipped it was now. It was time to get back to school and the mission schooner was busy travelling back and forth, from the bottom of the James Bay (Moosonee) to the top (Fort George), to pick up students in the different settlements and trading posts. The last trip was always to Great Whale River, 100 miles north of Fort George, but the expedition was not always successful, as many Cree from Great Whale disliked the Roman Catholic missionaries. Actually, almost all of them were converted Anglicans. They even had their own Anglican school, where they were taught to beware of Catholics. At that time Anglican and Roman Catholic missionaries would call each other names. As a result, kids were following the lead of their pastors. I remember the Catholics calling the Anglicans "Weepers" and the Catholics in turn were called "Peetuagshoo smokers" (smokers of strong tobacco). Priests and brothers from both religions seldom spoke to one another.

It was very sad to see all those holy men act in such unchristian ways because they wanted to convert as many savages as possible to their own religion. Actually, the Anglicans were doing much better, although the Catholics did their best. I was told a funny story about the competition between pastors trying to harvest souls. It happened much later. If I recall properly, it was during the 1950s or the '60s. The story took place at Eastmain, where almost everyone is Anglican. The Catholic Church tried, nevertheless, to establish a mission there. A priest was sent there and he started immediately to build a small chapel. Once the chapel was finished, the priest began celebrating mass every Sunday, but nobody would come, as everyone was already attending the Anglican service. The priest was desperate until he got a brilliant idea. He ordered a film projector and aired movies at the exact same time the Anglican pastor was celebrating his mass. His trick worked so well that pretty soon almost everybody was attending his shows instead of going to mass. I cannot tell how long that ruse worked. I can only assume the Anglican shepherd must have found a way to bring back the lost flock, as there are still only a few Catholics at Eastmain and no longer a Catholic priest.

Years passed by very fast at the Fort George school. Every summer students went home for vacation. Next autumn they came back, except the few for whom school was over. However, new students always replaced them. Although the school year was punctuated by the religious celebrations, for Cree and Inuit students the rhythm of the seasons was more important. I still recall the excitement we felt when spring was coming or when the first snows whitened the horizon. Those memories are precious; they make me who I am.

My turn to finish school came also. The mission school did not go beyond grade eight. They could not teach grade nine because the mission did not have the funds to maintain lots of teachers at the school. However, the main reason was that the students who had passed all the tests were sent down south to college, where the government took over their studies. Many of my good Cree friends who were sent to attend grade nine in the South came back without graduating. Although they were clever students, they could not adapt to their new life. The mission school was difficult, but still we were together in the North and we still could hear the geese and enjoy the seasons' rhythm. Whereas in the South, alone in these big cities which they knew nothing about, my friends would lose their bearings and become depressed in a few days or else they would be dragged into mean tricks. As for me, I was going to be spared that trauma because when I graduated from grade eight, the Father Director told me that the Inuit were not allowed to study in the South. When I asked why, he answered that the government had decided that Eskimos should be discouraged from moving away from their northern areas. Apparently, experts from the Department of Indian Affairs had decided that it would not be safe to let the Inuit live in the South where they would not be able to adapt to the weather.

I have learned now that the government's plan was not to protect the Inuit from dying of heat, but rather to rationalize the land occupancy. First, Inuit people were encouraged to settle in a few villages instead of being allowed to travel freely on the tundra. Then, during the Cold War, the government displaced several Inuit families far away to Grise Fjord and Resolute Bay in the High Arctic, where no Inuk was living. The idea was to resettle some Inuit families in territories where nobody had ever hunted. It was expected that these families would become rapidly self-sufficient, which would have spared the government money, since it had to take care of the Inuit during bad years. Today, historians say that the Canadian government displaced the Inuit to the High Arctic because it was afraid that the Americans would take over this portion of the territory on the pretense that it was uninhabited. The strategy of the Canadian government was good on paper but this part of the North was not inhabited for a good reason. It was too cold, even for the Inuit, too windy, and nights lasted three months. Moreover, there was almost nothing to hunt. As a result many relocated Inuit suffered from starvation and misery. Several families among the displaced came from northern Quebec, especially from the community north of Umiujaq named Port Harrison.[4]

Because I was not able to continue my studies, I decided to work at the Fort George mission barn. I was sixteen years old and I was getting along pretty well with the Oblates. I had good experiences with farming thanks to my summers with Brother Lavoie at Old Factory, but I wasn't a real farmer and I still needed to study the art of farming. Brother Martin was going to be my boss and my teacher. He only spoke French, which was a problem, since I could hardly speak it. That is why he had decided to split the day in two. During the morning he was my French teacher, and during the afternoon I served as an apprentice at the little mission farm. That's how I learned French as well as how to milk the cows, how to feed, breed, and keep chickens, and how to slaughter pigs. At one point I was given the responsibility of the mission's nine sheep.

---

4. This community is now known as Inukjuak, where several people from Kuujjuarapik and Umiujaq have relatives.

Working as a farmer was a real delight. I enjoyed learning about cattle so much. However, the best part of it was my relationship with Brother Martin. We were getting along so well together that I was really eager to learn French to better enjoy his stories and our conversations. It was also much better to be an employee at the mission school than a student, though some nuns treated me as if I was still one of the students. Sister Alexis, the nun in charge of the kitchen, was one of those few. She would always report my mistakes to Father Couture, hoping that I'd get a tongue-lashing. Luckily for me a young nun replaced her. Oh! What a change. The new cook was so friendly and so nice looking. She was a real beauty, and I was so impressed by her that I hardly dared coming into the kitchen. I had always been uneasy with beautiful girls.

That year, when the time came to slaughter the pigs, I was very nervous because the young nun was there, attending the whole process, as she was going to be preparing the animals to be cooked or salted. I was afraid of not doing it right while I was also secretly hoping to impress her. Fortunately, with the assistance of Brother Martin who realized my embarrassment, I did it like a pro. Working with Brother Martin was always a pleasure, everything was easy and nothing could go wrong. With him I could have tried anything.

I really liked him, and he too appreciated his little Eskimo helper, as he liked to call me. Actually, Brother Martin had a secret plan for me. He wanted me to inherit the family farm he had down south. He was so enthusiastic about the idea that he could not stop telling me stories about his village. From all of his talking, I already knew everything about the region where his family was established. Brother Martin thought it was shameful that I was educated to become a farmer while there were no real farms in the North. That is why he had planned for me to be his heir and to give me the farm of his parents who had just died. It was his dream to help me establish myself in life.

Unfortunately, Brother Martin's dream would not come true. When he shared his project with the other brothers, they called him crazy, because Inuit were not made to live in the South and, more, be farmers. Moreover, he was told that according to Canadian laws,

Inuit were not allowed to settle outside of northern territories. When Brother Martin gave me that news, there were tears in his eyes. He was devastated! Why were the missionaries working so hard to educate the young Inuit to the Canadian way of life if it was forbidden for them to enjoy such a life? He was very angry and he told me that he would no longer stay in the James Bay region, because what the missionaries were doing made no sense.

Nevertheless, Brother Martin did not leave Fort George right away because he was not allowed to quit the mission, but after this disappointment he could no longer think straight. At least that is what the other Oblates from Fort George told me. The only thing I know for sure is that one day he was taken away against his will and sent down south to be confined in a mental hospital. When I inquired what happened to him and where he was staying, I was told:

—Brother Martin is not feeling well. He was sent to a place where someone will be able to cure him. You know, Eddy, Oblates have their own place where missionaries who are exhausted can get rest. Don't worry! He will be well taken care of.

When I asked the name of that place, nobody wanted to tell me. That day I realized the Oblates did not want the rest of the world to know that they were human beings like everyone else. They had to be saints and flawless. They could not have feelings. They could not even be ill or mad. They could not be close with the Inuit living with them. All their true emotions had to be hidden.

When I saw Brother Martin for the last time he was embarking on a mission ship named *Nouveau-Québec* on his way to an unknown destiny. He was broken-hearted! He told me, as if it were his last words, his last wish:

—Edward, my dear son, do not stay in the North. Do whatever it takes but go south. Your real place is there. I promise, you will be able to succeed there. I wish I could have been the instrument of that success but I will pray for you. Do not worry, you have learned good trades. You can be a farmer, or anything else. You are ready for a bright new life. Our laws are too foolish; we should not be preventing Eskimos from going anywhere.

When I told him goodbye, I could not imagine that I was not going to see him anymore. But I was determined to follow his advice.

Shortly after Brother Martin's exile, I left the mission. I was not yet headed for the real South but for the good Old Factory. Nevertheless, I was on the move and I was going to make a living from my new skills. I worked there for a fur trader. I remained his employee for a couple of years and I became chums with Frank, Dennis, Bobby, and Billy, who were living there. These new friendships were going to be instrumental in my quest to become a free Inuk, able to travel all across my very own country.

CHAPTER 3

How Eddy Weetaltuk (E9-422) Became

EDDY VITAL, CANADIAN PRIVATE (SC-17515)

During the few years I worked at Old Factory, my friends Frank, Bobby, Billy, Dennis, and I were making all sorts of plans for our future. In each of our dreams we all had a better life in the South. Not that we did not like the North, but the best opportunities were all down south. Frank already had a good experience of life outside the northern towns, since he had served in the Air Force for a while. That is why he was always trying to convince me to leave. However, I was an Inuk and that was a big obstacle, since Inuit were not allowed at that time to leave the North. That was a serious issue. Frank's friends were always reminding him that taking me along could cause him a lot of trouble. But one day, Frank made it clear:

—He is like my brother. If I go south, Eddy comes with me.

That was clear enough for everybody, and for me it was quite a statement. Frank was like a brother. We were family. I was really proud of that friendship.

From that day on, Frank began to look seriously for a solution for me to leave Old Factory. After many debates, we came to the conclusion that I could not leave in plain sight, for I would be chased by the RCMP. They would most certainly catch me and send me to rot in jail like they did my dad for having plucked that raven, which made him famous all around the James Bay. We already had had a few experiences with a constable named Vanovick, who regularly visited Old Factory. He was very nosy and had a powerful dog team of fourteen huskies and, believe me, he knew how to mush it. I was sure that if he had known our plans, he would have arrested me. Some nights I used to picture myself trying to leave Old Factory and being chased by Constable Vanovick. Of course it was only a nightmare, but still I knew leaving the North would be very difficult for an Inuk like me, especially when the doors to the South were kept by a constable such as Vanovick.

One day, Frank got an idea and suggested that I should change my name. He convinced me that was the only solution. He himself had changed his identity when he deserted the Air Force. Yes, Frank had had a life of adventures before we met him and we all admired him because of that. He had served in the army during the Second World War. But when they were ready to send him overseas to the battlefield, he was so scared for his life that he chose to desert. His name was put on the list of deserters and that is why he changed its identity and had come to the James Bay hoping that in time everyone would forget him. This is the kind of story Frank told us to convince me to change my Inuit name to a European one. Actually, we never knew for sure if Frank was a true deserter or if he had made up this story to polish off his image as a true adventurer. But that was enough to convince me, and my friends agreed that a name change was a pretty convenient solution for me to start a new life down south.

Anyhow, Frank did not need to work hard to convince me to try to get away from the James Bay. I was quite sure that the trades I had learned from Brother Martin were not useful in the North but they could make me a freeman down South. The trip to Moosonee, the very gateway to the South, cost forty-five dollars. It was too much money for me but Frank had decided to pay my travel. That problem being solved, we could then look for a way out. At that time during the summers there were two planes flying back and forth picking up loads of lead from a mine near Richmond Gulf (north of the Great Whale HBC trading post) to bring them to Moosonee. I learned later that this lead was used to make bullets for the 303 rifles that I would later use. When the load was small, they took passengers. There was also a private company, Austin Airways, that was flying out passengers from northern towns to Timmins, Ontario. There, one could connect to trains heading for the real South. We were looking at the different options to get the best price. While waiting for the cheapest ride, we used to spend time looking at the planes flying in and out, and that sight was already making me feel alive and free.

Finally, the day came to start packing up to move on. It was the hardest to tell my parents. Mum objected with tears in her eyes, but Dad said:

—Let him have his life and go with his friends. He'll be well looked after by his friends. They know the White man's society. He will be better off there with them than here, where there is no real job for him.

I too had tears in my eyes thinking of how Father had to work hard to keep the whole family fed. I was so sorry for my parents' poor living conditions and I was so ashamed to run away to look elsewhere for a better life that I emptied my pocket and gave to my mother my last seven dollars, telling her:

—Take it, Mother. It is nothing; there will be plenty more if I manage to find a job in the South. You know, I will be working there and will make a lot of money. Take it, it is nothing, but I want you to have it.

Afterward, I felt a bit guilty for giving that money to Mother. It seemed like I had tried to bribe her to get her blessing even if she didn't approve of my plan. I knew Mother did not like the idea of me leaving our family, and she would have rather eaten less and shared with me the little she had to make me stay.

When I kissed her goodbye, Mother swallowed a big lump in her throat and finally said:

—Okay, my dear Eddy. Go if you think this is the best for you.

She continued crying and I did not know what to do to comfort her. Mother knew I would be gone for a long, long time and maybe forever. That moment was the hardest time in her life. She hugged me for fifteen minutes crying in sobs all the while. She told me a thousand times to take care and left to hide her sorrow.

After that I went with my friends to say goodbye to Father Grenon and Father Vaillancourt. They walked us down to the river. A canoe was waiting to take us to the seaplane. Father Vaillancourt was curious to know when I would return. Within fifteen days or so, I told him. I was lying to his face but I had two good reasons for not telling him the truth. I was leaving the North in secret and wasn't going to divulge to the Oblates my real plan. But I had also another reason. I still remembered how Brother Martin had been betrayed by his friends because of his dream to help me. By moving down south, I was somehow going to be the instrument of his revenge and was already picturing their disappointment when they would learn that I had made my friend's dream come true. In the middle of my thoughts the pilot came to get us, telling us to hurry up. The time to leave for the big adventure had finally come.

That's how Frank, Winnie (Frank's wife), Bobby, Dennis (Bobby's brother), Billy, and I left the North. Once we landed in Moosonee, we were going to get on a train to Cochrane, Ontario. Our only worry was for me to avoid being arrested by the RCMP. At that time passengers from the North were controlled by a police officer and sometimes he would verify their identity, especially when they looked drunk or out of place. That day, the constable who was doing the checking on Northerners did not ask for my ID because I was travelling in good company of young White guys. He could not imagine we were on the move for the big adventure. He probably thought that we were travelling for a quick visit to Timmins, and when he saw me looking so young and so uneasy he even cautioned me:

—Hello, young man. Enjoy your trip and be careful once in the city, it is full of thugs. Don't take any wooden nickels and do not go into any bar. Be careful and you will soon be back to your family. Stay with your friends and everything will go well.

I whispered:

—Yes, sir. Thank you for your advice.

Once we arrived at Cochrane, we went straightaway to the train station. Frank bought the tickets and gave mine to Dennis, so I wouldn't lose it. We were on the train heading south. Everything was so far easy. I was seated in my spot when an inspector came to punch our tickets. Dennis and Frank had gone on a little tour of the train. The inspector asked me:

—Votre billet, Monsieur?

I told him in French that my friend Dennis had it. He told me that he was going to verify if it was true and continued punching tickets of other passengers. I was relieved.

When Dennis came back, he gave me my ticket with a small hole in it. I told Dennis that the ticket inspector had talked to me in French. Dennis laughed and said:

—Maybe he thought you were a lumberjack going to hospital for an accident. You know what? With your new shirt you don't look like an Eskimo anymore, one can easily get confused about your identity. This is very good for you. Continue like that and work on your French. Perhaps it will be useful again. Actually, with your good French and a bit of practice you could easily pretend you're a real French Canadian.

That thought made us all laugh, but the idea was going to stay on my mind.

We arrived late at Cochrane and went directly to book a hotel for the night. Then we went out and had supper at a Chinese restaurant. That was the first time in my life I had Chinese food. I really liked it. The waitresses were all Chinese, and I immediately noticed they did not look like European women but rather like Inuks. I was very surprised because the waitress who placed the utensils on our table brought a knife, a fork, and a spoon for everyone but me. Instead she gave me chopsticks and she smiled at me. Like the train inspector, she too was taking me for someone else. We all laughed when we realized her mistake, and we pretended for the rest of the evening that I was indeed Chinese and my friends made me eat my meal with the sticks. Of course, I had no clue how to use them properly and I made quite a mess. But with the help of my friends, I managed to play my role like a pro and the waitress did not seem to realize her mistake. At least that is what we concluded, since she never brought an extra set of utensils.

After the meal, we went to a movie. As we entered the lobby I had a cigarette dangling from my mouth. The usherette who stood by the entrance door told me:

—Your cigarette, please.

I handed it to her thinking she wanted to take a puff. I didn't know smoking was forbidden in theatres. The usherette seemed to be insulted and told me with anger:

—I don't want it. I asked you to butt out your cigarette.

Frank burst out laughing and Dennis told me that if I continued to behave like that my true Inuit identity would be revealed. After the movie, we all returned to the hotel for a good rest. The next day Frank, who had money, bought a car, a 1952 hardtop Meteor. I wanted to travel to La Passe where Frank intended to settle. La Passe is located in Ontario, just across from Fort Coulonge, which is on the Quebec side of the border.

Before departing we got a surprise. Frank had decided to bring an extra passenger, a postmistress from Moosonee. Frank had invited her to take a ride with us! On our way down the postmistress asked to stop at a liquor store. When she stepped out of the car, Frank told me:

—Eddy, if you want a bottle of whisky or something else, you can have one. Just give her some money; she'll buy it for you.

In those days Crees and Eskimos were on a blacklist for liquor and could not buy alcohol. That was for me a good opportunity to have a new experience. I gave her ten dollars; she bought me a forty-ounce bottle of liquor. I hardly tasted it, as Frank quickly ran out of alcohol and asked if he could have mine. I gave him the bottle:

—Help yourself. I don't like it. It is too strong. Moreover, I am not used to drinking and I fear if I drink too much I will be confused and won't be able to hide my real identity.

We had decided that during that trip I was going to practise my new identity; that's why I had to stay sober.

Edward Weetaltuk, E9-422, wasn't anymore. I was now Eddy VITAL.

That was our plan: my father was a French Canadian from Winnipeg who married my mother, an Inuk from Strutton Island. I had grown up in Northern Canada and learned French from my dad. That was going to be my story. Pretending to be a new person was quite easy and even fun. Each time we met people, my friends would always introduce me as Eddy Vital and I only had to continue speaking French as if I really had French background. English Canadians were totally conned, sometimes someone would simply ask:

—Vital, that's a French name, isn't it?

As for the French Canadians, they did not realize that I wasn't French, since I was speaking French quite fluently, thanks to Brother Martin's lessons. I even spoke it better than some of them.

It is easy to pretend in day-to-day life to be someone you are not, but I knew that I could get into trouble with my change of name. What would I do if some police officer asked me to prove that I was really Eddy Vital? At that very moment my friends' tricks would become useless. Sometimes, I was so stressed out by that idea that some nights I could hardly sleep. After few months I realized that it would be impossible to spend my entire life without having to show an ID. At some point I was going to hit a wall. I came to the conclusion that I had to really become Eddy Vital. To pretend was not good enough. I had to turn Eddy Weetaltuk into Eddy Vital, and for that I needed proper identification. Unfortunately, I had no idea how to get it. That thought scared me and I began to think that my dream of establishing myself in the South might end sooner or later. I was living on borrowed time. Since my days in the South were numbered, I decided to enjoy them as much as possible.

Enjoying life was quite easy, especially with my friends, who always had a plan to go out. Not that they were party guys but they were young and looking for adventure and for women. There was always one of them to convince the others to go out. In those days there was a dancing night for everyone on Saturday and we used to go there. Some weekends we would also go out to play bingo. One night the jackpot was a bright new car. An old lady won the prize, it was a Chevy. I got very upset when I learned that she already had two cars, and I told my friends:

—Why didn't she stay home to give others a chance? I could have used that car. It's a waste: she can't drive three cars at the same time.

They all laughed and told me:

—Welcome to the White man's world, Eddy! People here don't share. You'd better understand that! If you want to survive here, you have to learn to be selfish. Forget the Inuit way.

However, I wasn't going to forget this old lady who had bought a big pad of cards to increase her luck. Another night the floor was packed; few people at La Passe had a car in those days and everybody who dreamed to get one was there. But that night again the luck was on the side of the rich. Going to bingo was for me a real learning experience and I found out a lot about human nature. I still remember seeing people spending their last dime trying to win. The poorest always seemed to be the least reasonable while the richest were always the luckiest. Bingo was so surprising for an Inuk like me used to seeing people sharing and being very cautious with their spending. Unfortunately, nowadays some Inuit have learned the White man's bad habit and waste their money on gambling.

After bingo we used to walk around to get to know the area better. During one of those walks we met soldiers from the Royal Canadian Regiment, posted in Petawawa. They told us that they were training for the Korean War. The next day we went to see them while they were practising. They were already wearing their battle uniform. They looked pretty sharp walking two by two, keeping in step. Seeing them made me wish I were a soldier. However, while talking about it with my friends, the thought of being killed made me change my mind and I decided to look for work instead of becoming a war hero.

Shortly after, I managed to get a position at a lumber camp at James Lake, close to Fort Coulonge across the Ottawa River. The foreman, Mr. Laroche, was very strict with discipline. I still remember that complete silence was enforced on all employees during meal hours. When I complained to my coworkers, they told me that most of the lumber camps had the same kind of rules. This almost comforted me but still I wished the atmosphere had been friendlier. It reminded me too much of the boarding school. I was employed as a chore boy. My main duty was to keep the kitchen and the lumberjacks' quarters full of firewood and water. Most of the time I was hauling dry timbers from the woods with a mare. One day I hooked her to two large dry timbers without knowing she was in heat. The mare suddenly got uncontrollable, jumping and kicking in all directions so much that she broke the harness chain. I could not do anything to stop her from running away in search of a mate. I had to walk all the way back to get a new workhorse at the camp's stable. When I arrived, a young girl came out laughing:

—Eddy, where's your horse?

—She ran away from me. I could not stop it.

The girl and the two cooks laughed, making fun of me because they knew the mare was in heat. The girl said:

—Eddy, I guess you're not a stud, since you did not satisfy her.

I laughed at the joke, although I was feeling a bit ashamed. Some guys brought the mare back later that day and Mr. Laroche released one of the studs to mate with the mare. After she was satisfied, she totally changed her behaviour and became very quiet. When I took her back to the logging area, I could see the difference! She was now moving to my every command.

I was getting paid sixty dollars a week. I used to visit Frank and Winnie every weekend and I would give them thirty dollars, half of my pay, to thank them for looking after me. Billy worked also with me for a while, but he quit pretty soon after because the work was too hard and not well-paid. As for me, I left also when I read in a newspaper that the Abitibi Pulp and Paper company was looking for workers. Abitibi's headquarters were in Timmins. I went with Bobby to their employment office. We took the train, since the ad said that they would reimburse transportation fees. We filled out the employment form and I signed it Eddy Vital. Bobby had all his school and identification papers. Things were easy for him and his application got completed in no time. But when I was asked to show my papers, I was unable to offer anything. I told the recruiter that all my papers were back in James Bay, where I was born. He replied:

—Maybe, but how can I trust you? My job is to verify your identity and I need proof of it.

I was astounded and I was going to give up, when he added:

—However, if you don't have any evidence you can bring a witness who will attest that you are really who you say you are. It's not really allowed but I could make do.

It was my lucky day. I had a witness. I was so happy I could hardly speak, so I pointed to Bobby:

—Here is my witness. He knows everything about me.

Bobby confirmed that he knew me and answered the recruiter's questions with great precision, telling him what we had been practising for a while. Then came the verdict:

—Okay. That's fine, but since you have no ID with you I will make an employment insurance card for you. Do not lose it. This is a very important piece of identification; you could even join the army with it.

I thanked him very much for the card. Once alone, Bobby and I looked at the card. It had my new name on it: Vital, Edward. I told Bobby:

—Thanks for your white lies. We made it, Bobby. We made it! I have a new name. A White man's name!

That social insurance card became my official ID, the one I would show when pressed to prove that I was not an Inuk. Thanks to that card I would finally be able to live in the South. My dream was becoming true, thanks to my friends' help.

After being hired, we were sent to a camp at Smooth Rock Falls, Ontario. Our foreman showed us the routine and we began to work right away. Life at the lumber camp was hard. We woke up early in the morning and right after breakfast we would leave with our lunch box for our strip where we would spend all day. It was a very tiring job. Bobby and I were not used to axing and sawing and we were only cutting one cord a day. We were paid thirty dollars a cord; it was not much money for such hard work. We also anticipated with fear what it would be like during the mosquito season. That is why we started looking for an opportunity to quit. It came under the guise of an army recruiter named Ross. He was on his way back from leave and had stopped by our camp to rest for a couple of hours and greet some old friends. We had tea with him and chatted for a while. When we explained to him how pitiful was our condition, he advised us to leave that nightmare and try our luck with the army. According to him, the Canadian Forces were a wonderful place to work, offering good wages and good food too. It was decided. Next day we were going to hitchhike back to La Passe, not that we planned to enlist but because he had convinced us that our life was worth much more than the lumber camp.

When we told our strip boss that we were quitting, he did not blame us. On the contrary, he told us he understood very well that we were wasting our time cutting wood for pulp. He even gave us a ride to the highway. Not very long after, a very small car stopped on its way south. It was barely big enough for Bobby and me to squeeze in. We had to tie up our luggage on the top of the car. The driver was heading for Pembroke. We were lucky. We told him we were headed for La Passe, only six miles from Pembroke. The driver was a very nice guy and we talked a lot during the travel. He told us that he also worked for Abitibi Pulp and Paper. Like us he found the job awful but had worked there for six long months. Later that afternoon we arrived at La Passe. Bobby phoned Frank and asked him to pick us up with his Meteor. Once again we were out of a job and began to hang around doing nothing.

After enjoying Christmas and New Year's celebrations, my friends Bobby, Bill, Brian, and Bailey, another of our friends, decided again to look for jobs, as we were running out of money and getting fed up with doing nothing. I applied to a lumber company near Petawawa, Ontario, not far from Pembroke's lumber camp. Because of my previous experience, they gave me a job. I was very happy to have a new job but my joy did not last long when I realized that the company was run like a boot camp. The foreman could hardly speak English, but he did not really need to, as he was only shouting insults. The food was meagre and tasteless; the blankets were light, too short, and dirty. It was so depressing that I only lasted one week and so did Brian. Bailey, Bobby, and Bill decided to stay a little longer.

A few days later, once again without a job, Brian and I were making small talk and probably because we had exhausted all topics of interest, he asked just for the sake of chatting:

—Eddy, up to what grade did you go in school?

When I told him I completed grade eight, he was totally amazed:

—Grade eight. So, you can write!

Brian did not really know my story and was not aware of the good education I had received from the Oblates at Fort George. He was suddenly very curious:

—And how many languages do you speak?

I said four, and Brian continued:

—You know, Eddy, with that education of yours, you could get into the army any time you want.

—That's ridiculous. They would not take me because they don't accept Eskimos. You know that.

—You don't have to tell them you're an Eskimo. Just tell them you are mixed-blood. With your new name everybody believes you. There is no reason it won't work with them.

—Are you kidding me?

—No, just try it. You have nothing to lose. They can only reject your application. That's no big deal. I tried myself to enlist three times and I failed the three times because of their stupid tests. They even told me to go back to school. But you, you speak French and English and with a grade eight you will pass all the tests. I swear. Try it. You will thank me later. You'll see. The pay is very good in the army and they feed you. That would be the end of your troubles.

When I got home that afternoon, Winnie was alone. Frank was gone; he too was looking for a job. I began to think seriously of the advantages of having a steady job. I was recalling images from my childhood and I was picturing Mother and little sister crying from hunger. But even more than that, Brother Martin's advice haunted me. I needed a real position. You cannot be really happy going from one odd job to another. That is why Brother Martin had taught me skills. I could not let him down. I had to look for something real. Being a soldier was a career which no doubt would have made Brother Martin proud of me. Later Brian came in for a visit and told me that the parish priest was going to Ottawa. Brian had already asked him if he would give us a ride and he had accepted. I was booked for the trip to Ottawa. During the travel, we told the father our plan. He strongly encouraged us:

—It is wise for young men like you to join the Forces. After I was ordained priest, I served in the army for three years as a chaplain. That was a good experience. You'll see, you will learn much about life in the army. It might even help you to be better Christians.

However, despite everything my friends told me, I was still not convinced of my chances of being accepted. Actually, I was so sure I would be back home the next day that I didn't bring any personal belongings. Meals were free while being tested, that's the main reason why I had agreed to come along. For me, it was still another fun adventure. I could not see it as the beginning of a real career. No argument could convince me that I would fit in the army. After all, I was an Inuk and I had heard that no Inuk had ever been in the Canadian Forces. I was not expecting to be the first one. I couldn't picture myself making history.

However, once in Ottawa at the recruiting office I started getting nervous thinking how stupid it would be to pass the test just to get killed in Korea. In front of the main door I almost chickened out, but Brian managed to convince me:

—Oh, come on! Don't be so scared. After all, they might not even accept you. And if you pass the test, they won't enroll you if you don't want to. We are just going to take a test. It's not a death sentence.

These words reassured me, and instead of thinking that overcoming this ordeal amounted to a life sentence in uniform, I decided to view it as an intellectual challenge. After all, it was only an exam and I was not going to fail it. I had to prove to Brian that I was as good as he thought I was. When we entered Wallis House, where the candidates were taking the tests, there were a sergeant and a corporal. The sergeant asked with a big smile:

—You came to join up?

Brian answered:

—Yes, sergeant.

There was no doubt, it wasn't the first time he was trying his luck. He already knew how to respond to a superior. The sergeant told us to sign our names on a form.

I signed mine as Edward Vital and I gave my address at La Passe. When we were asked for identification papers, I showed the card I was given when I was hired by the Abitibi Pulp and Paper and I told the sergeant that was the only ID I had ever had. He replied:

—That's good enough, young man.

Brian told the officer that we both lived in La Passe and that we dreamed of joining the Canadian Forces. The officer seemed to believe him and asked us to wait in the hallway. While waiting we had the opportunity to watch the many soldiers walking around in the hall. They belonged to different regiments. Brian told me:

—If you want to be sent to the West, join the Princess Patricia Regiment. Do you see, the soldier with red flashes? He is from the Princess Pats; they are stationed at Wainwright.

—I've always wanted to see the West. I will remember your advice if ever I am asked for a favourite regiment. Thanks for the tip.

While waiting, I kept repeating in my mind "Princess Pats" so I would not forget.

We waited a long time but eventually we were called. I was finally going to take the test. Brian was directed to one room and I was sent to another. The test was difficult, since we had to answer all kinds of questions on different subjects. However, I found it fair, since most of the questions related to what I had learned at Fort George. Seeing the other candidates sweating, I thanked mentally the good fathers for their education. When we were done, we were sent to wait in the entrance hall. Later, a soldier in uniform came and posted on the wall the names of those who had passed the test. My name was on the list. Before I could rejoice, I was told it wasn't over. Those who had passed the test had to have an interview with a recruiter.

Once more I was waiting, but eventually my turn came and I got called to meet with a recruiting officer. When he ask me if I spoke French or English, I replied to impress him that I could speak the two. He was surprised and asked me where I had learned French.

—I owe that to the Oblates. I attended a residential school in Fort George. Actually, I speak and write in four languages, including Cree and Eskimo.

That final comment almost failed me. The officer suddenly became suspicious:

—How come do you speak Eskimo? Are you Eskimo?

I replied quickly that Mother was an Eskimo but that Father was White, which made me not Eskimo but Canadian. Then I added:

—My dad's name is Vital; he came from Winnipeg, where the Hudson's Bay Company has its headquarters. He met my mother during one of his trips for the company. When he passed away, my mother raised me up in the North—that's why I speak Eskimo.

I was very lucky that my story convinced the recruiter. He was born in Manitoba and he knew Saint-Vital, a village near Winnipeg, which helped him to trust my name as genuine. He was even quite pleased to recruit a countryman. He picked up his pen and signed, passed. He laughed and said:

—If you want, you can join the Royal 22nd Regiment, the Van Doos, since you speak very good French.

—Thank you for your offer but, if it is possible, I would rather go west to see the place where my Dad grew up. I know that Princess Patricia Regiment is stationed there and I would not mind joining that regiment.

He nodded and wrote PPCLI (Princess Patricia's Canadian Light Infantry) on his paper. That was it, I was in. Then he told me:

—Tomorrow you will be sworn in. You will also receive an ID card. You are now a SOLDIER. Congratulations Private Vital, you're in. Now get ready to leave for Ipperwash, where you will get your initial training.

Once the interview was over, I was given a meal card to eat at Wallis House. I met Brian around five o'clock and told him I was accepted and was going to Ipperwash to be trained at the recruiting camp. Brian congratulated me but was sad. He had been rejected once more. They had paid his fare back to La Passe and he was going to leave. I asked him to take a message to my friends over there:

—Tell them I will be sworn in tomorrow and that I will try to drop by before being shipped to Korea.

Then, I told him that he could have my winter gear; it was still at La Passe with all my belongings. We hugged goodbye and I went back to Wallis House.

That night I could not sleep and began to recall school memories about the war. In 1945, when the Second World War ended, I was thirteen years old and still attending the mission school at Fort George. Although during the first years of war we were pretty unaware of what was happening in Europe, we became at one point quite concerned by it. Our teachers were so emotionally involved that we ended up embracing their fears through the stories of horror they would tell us. We were also told to pray for the war to come to an end and for the Germans' defeat. I was surprised because it was the first time I had seen the brothers and fathers having strong bad feeling against someone. They were always preaching love and forgiveness but this time they did not seem to be ready to forgive the Germans. This is when I realized that war changes the true nature of people.

One afternoon in 1945, while the war in Europe was nearing the end, an American war bomber flew over our school with a great roaring noise, circling around Fort George several times. It was flying so low that we could see the pilot and the tail gunner on top. We all watched it, except Jimmy. He was hiding inside the outdoor toilet the whole time. When he came out, he was white as a ghost from fear. James Corston pointed at him saying:

—You were scared, eh!

Jimmy protested:

—No, I really had to pee.

Bill Gagnon also laughed and said:

—Oh, yes! You were so scared that you almost peed your pants.

We all laughed, and Jimmy's face turned red. After that day everyone began to call him yellow-belly.

When the war ended, all the Oblates from the mission came to the boys' room shouting:

—Hitler is dead. Mussolini is finished.

They made us dance on the floor to celebrate Hitler's death. I was confused because I thought we were supposed to mourn dead people. After that day, we talked a lot about war. It even became one of our favourite games. All the boys wanted to be American GIs. Our conversations were also fuelled by the war that was still going on between Japan and the United States. We were rooting for the Americans and we prayed to God to help them to destroy our enemy. Our wishes came true when the Americans threw a twenty-kiloton atomic bomb on Hiroshima and another on Nagasaki. Again, we celebrated, though it was a real slaughter, hundreds of thousands of innocents were killed and we were all excited and so proud. I was still a kid but I was amazed to see that one country could exhibit so much hatred towards another, as if people from the other country were not real human beings. That concern grew bigger in my spirit when I saw pictures of the Japanese Emperor with his army. I realized that the Japanese looked so much like the Inuit. I was amazed to think that there were people so far away from us but who looked so much like us. It was a true revelation. I was wondering if they thought like us, if they prayed to the same God, if they spoke our language, and if they had heard of us.

Now I wasn't a child anymore and it was my turn to go to war. I was wondering how I would feel once at the front. What does one feel when one kills people? What does one feel knowing one might die at any moment? I was soon going to have the opportunity to answer all those questions and the answers were frightening. Moreover, I was now alone. Brian was gone, back to our friends, and I was all by myself. My dream of freedom and my desire to see the big world had become reality but it was probably not going to be like in my dreams. What would that new reality be like? No one could have told me in advance. It was my fate to discover it all by myself.

I was suddenly interrupted in the middle of my thoughts. It was already the morning and a sergeant shouted:

—Get up! Go down for breakfast. Rise and shine.

That was my first taste of army discipline. It was January 1952, and my first day as a Canadian private had begun. That day I was given a service book and a pay book. Someone took my picture for my ID card and gave me a temporary one with my name, Edward Vital, and my service number SC-175155 printed on it. I had to remember it at all times. So I began to repeat it in my mind.

We spent three more days in Ottawa before leaving for Ipperwash's boot camp. When we came in, there were soldiers all over. They were taking their initial training, learning how to march on a square. Many had trouble following the pace. The sergeant trainer was shouting insults, or he would shove his rifle butt in their ribs to make them understand quicker. In a different corner, other recruits were doing push-ups under the mean look of another sergeant who called them sissies and fags. We were immediately fitted into our uniforms and they gave each of us a sewing kit that the sergeant called a "house wife" for us to sew our red flashes marked PPCLI on our uniform. We were also issued a red square flash indicating that we were going to Korea. However, we were soon going to be so busy training that we would not have much time, said the sergeant, to worry about Korea.

CHAPTER 4

Training to
BECOME
A SOLDIER

Training to become a soldier was divided into different periods, each period being dedicated to the teaching of one single thing. During the first week we had to learn how to get our gear in shape. We actually spent a whole week learning how to handle our equipment, and how to always keep it shiny and tidy. The second week we were taught how to make our bed and how to keep our quarters clean. It sounds funny but it's true, we spent an entire week learning the basic rules of our new soldier's condition. Then the next week, we were taught how to pack: large packs, small packs, medium packs, and basic pouches. We learned everything about the art of packing. Then the fourth week, we were taught how to keep the boots shiny and the uniforms well pressed. They even told us how to wear our beret, but first we had to shrink it to our own size by putting it in warm water until it fit our head perfectly. They also made us understand quite quickly that the brass had to shine at all times. If not, you were given extra duty, and you could even be confined to the barracks for the weekend. That is what I learned during the month of January 1952, my first month of service in the Canadian Forces.

February 1952 was mostly dedicated to drilling us on marching and teaching us how to recognize service ranks. We were taught how to salute and address officers according to their ranks. It was expressly forbidden to call them by their name. Calling them by their nickname would have been the equivalent of a mortal sin. By the end of February we were each issued a 303-calibre rifle. Every morning Sergeant Wall would inspect all rifles, and Corporal Handley was right behind him taking down the names of those whose equipment wasn't perfectly polished. If you passed all the inspections you would get a weekend furlough, but if you failed you were given extra duties that would keep you busy until the following Monday. All weekend furlough passes had to be signed by the company commander, which meant that you had to behave yourself if you wanted your weekend off.

In March we were taught how to march on a square and parade with our 303-calibre rifles. We first learned how to slope our weapons in style at the command: "Present arms." Then we learnt the other ways to carry our weapons. The hardest for me was to "Stand at ease" and relax. To "Stand at ease" one must push one's rifle forward. One time I pushed it too hard and I dropped it. I didn't know yet that I had to fall on my rifle, because your weapon is part of you as a soldier. If it slips from your hands you fall down on your gun. Because of that mistake, I received a punishment and was ordered to run around the parade square with my rifle over my head, in "high port." I had to count out loud each step and run around the parade square until they finished the exercise. I was so exhausted that I was beginning to see stars and I almost blacked out. The world had never seen an Eskimo more tired than me that day. After three times around I did not hear the Corporal Handley shouting to stop!

—Stop! Vital. Stop! Are you deaf? I told you it's enough.

Finally I heard him and I stopped, standing on one foot. The Corporal made me stand at the edge of the parade square as an example to others. I spent fifteen minutes like that. Finally the exercise ended and we were given permission to talk. Corporal Handley asked me:

—How do you feel now, Vital?

—Beat up, corporal.

—Was your rifle heavy?

—Yes, very much, corporal.

Then he warned me:

—If you think your weapon was heavy, that's nothing. It will be much heavier in Korea. Always remember, if you drop your rifle during parade, you fall on it and stay there and you do not move until stretcher-bearers pick you up. That's the rule. There is no exception, even if it is the Queen or the King that inspect the parade. If your gun slips from your hands, you fall on your weapon.

During those three months of hard training, I learnt everything necessary to become a soldier and pretty soon I was like any other soldier. I even had adopted their bad habits, especially the drinking one. When we had nothing to do, we would gather in the wet canteen and we would get sloshed. I was only nineteen years old and I could drink a lot and still be able to wake up the next morning. In those days, beer was only sold in bottles; my favourite was O'Keefe Old Stock Ale sold in green bottles. At the training camp, beside the mess, there were two canteens: the wet canteen to drink and the dry canteen where we used to go to smoke cigarettes while polishing our shoes and shining the brass. One night when I was quite drunk from beer, an old soldier asked me if he could borrow ten dollars:

—I'll pay you back next payday.

I lent him the money not knowing he was soon getting transferred to Wainwright, Alberta. Of course I never got my money back, and when I told the story to my buddies they laughed at me, calling me naive. I was learning that the new recruits like me were easy targets. My friends also advised me not to fall for war stories that old soldiers would tell, because it was a trick to make you feel sorry for them before asking you for money or for a beer.

We were paid every two weeks. Payday was always a joy and pay distribution always followed the same strict protocol. We were called to line up alphabetically. With my name I was always at the tail end and by the time I got paid, I was nearly frozen and my hands were very stiff. Sometimes they were so rigid that I could hardly sign the receipt. We were not allowed to put our hands in our pockets, or even blow on them. They were to be clenched on the side of our battledress trousers. Whatever, I was always very pleased to get my seventy-nine dollars, which was the salary for the recruits. When we were lucky we would get a furlough. One weekend we were given a four-day leave. I took the opportunity to travel to La Passe to visit Frank and Winnie, but they were gone to Port Colborne, Ontario. They were planning to move there once their house in La Passe was sold. Since I had to wait several hours before the next train to Port Colborne, I decided to pay a visit to my old foreman, Mr. Laroche, from the lumber camp at James Lake near Fort Colounge. I found him on the street while he was heading for his favourite place: the local bar. He invited me to have a beer with him. He knew the barman very well and told him:

—Look who's going to get himself killed in Korea!

The barman gave us two free beers and wished me good luck. Mr. Laroche was kind of sad to see me on the eve of that terrible adventure. He said he missed me and that I was a good worker:

—You know, Eddy, at one point, I thought about building a house for you somewhere in Fort Colounge so you would not leave but instead continue to work for me. But now my idea is dead, since it looks like your home is going to be six feet underground.

We both laughed and he added:

—Whatever. You made your choice, but if ever you make it back from war, come and visit us again!

Much later that day, I took the train at Pembroke station to Port Colborne. When I arrived, it was already night and I took a taxi to go to Frank's and Winnie's place. When I arrived, Frank yelled in Cree "pitchuwitchi," that was my nickname, back in the old days. It means, "gum chewer." It was good to hear Frank calling me that. As for him, he was so surprised to see me there:

—How did you find us?

—I got your address from Helen, your young sister. I found her at La Passe.

—That's right. I left our address with her, in case something happened. Eh! It wasn't something but someone.

We laughed and were so happy to be together again. We had a lot of fun, but eventually I had to leave. I gave them my army address and headed back to Camp Ipperwash.

Once back at the camp, I still had two days of leave left. I spent the first day in the camp, waiting for the wet canteen to open. To kill the time, I sat on a bunk and waited for one of my buddies to show up. The first to come was Howard. He was curious about my whereabouts and asked where I went during my two days leave. I told him:

—Just to La Passe to visit my old pals from James Bay.

—Did you meet a nice girl there?

I was not surprised by his question. Howard was known to be a womanizer. He was nicknamed "Bones Howard." When the canteen opened, he invited me for a beer. We drank for two hours. When we were buzzed, he asked me:

—Have you ever been to Sarnia's cathouse?

—Not a chance. I don't even know what it is.

He laughed and said:

—It's a whorehouse. You're a lying bastard. I bet you know pretty well what it is. You probably own all the bordellos up in the North.

After a few beers, we were drunk enough to plan a trip to Sarnia's cathouse.

We left the canteen and walked out the camp's gates, showing our passes to the guard. We took a taxi to the bus depot. Once in Sarnia, we took another cab and asked the driver to take us to the cathouse. He drove for a little while. Then he stopped in front of a house with three small windows on the door. He rang the doorbell. A busty middle-aged woman answered the door. The cab driver said:

—Two customers for you.

She thanked him and let us in. We sat down, Howard in an armchair and me on a chesterfield.

A girl was already sitting on the chesterfield; I sat down beside her. She put away her knitting kit and without any warning she took my hand and put it between her legs. She smiled and checked my erection with her other hand. I was ready:

—What are you waiting for, young man? Go in the bedroom. I'll join you right away.

While I was looking for my way to the bedroom, she went to the kitchen to get a basin of warm water and a bar of soap. Once in the room, she washed herself and afterwards washed my penis in erection. Then she lay on the bed, her legs wide open. She whispered:

—Come, come, I'm waiting for you.

I didn't waste any time and got on top of her. Her vagina was wet and slippery and she was groaning to my every move. It did not take much before I climaxed. She gave me a couple of minutes to savour the moment, and then she went to the kitchen to refill her basin. She washed me again and tickled my penis while making jokes. It was like we had known each other since forever and as if what we had done was without consequence. Once she had finished, she squatted over the basin on the floor, her legs wide open, washing herself. I couldn't turn my gaze from this extraordinary and new spectacle for me.

That's exactly when I realized where I was and what I had done. I was in a brothel and I had just committed a mortal sin. However, even that thought could not make me regret what I had done. The sensation had been so vivid. I was feeling so good, so relaxed, and at peace with myself. I could hardly believe that such happiness was the result of a sinful deed but I was getting anxious recalling the good brothers' advice.

Bones Howard stayed longer than me with his lady and I was getting nervous while waiting for him. I could not bear being alone with my sin. Finally he came out of the bedroom laughing and satisfied. We left right away, and once out Bones said:

—That was seven dollars very well spent, wasn't it? Did she give you a blow job too?

—What do you mean?

—Eddy, how come! You're not a virgin!

He explained what it was all about. I was quite surprised because I had never heard that women could do that to men. I told him:

—You know, Howard, where I was raised, things such as blow jobs and hookers don't exist.

—Maybe, Eddy, but you are not living with the Eskimos anymore. Next time, you ask her for a blow job. You'll like it. You'll see.

Back at Ipperwash's training camp we still had one day left of our four-day furlough. Bones and I decided to work on our gear so we could pass the next inspection easily and without being in a hurry to prepare ourselves. During that day I spent a lot of time recalling all the details of my visit to Sarnia's cathouse. Bones was planning to go back there as soon as we had another opportunity. Of course, I was tempted, but I knew it was wrong for a Christian to go in places like that.

The next morning we had a roll call during our parade square. The Regimental Sergeant Major (RSM) mustered the whole battalion. Once we were all outside, the RSM Lee shouted everyone's names. Each of us had to shout back his service number. RSM Lee was six feet tall and close to 200 pounds. Every one feared him. He was so large at the hips that he had a hard time keeping his heels together at parade. He probably had a special tailor to fix his trousers. After the parade, we had a lecture on demolition. The training continued for several days. Over the next weeks, we were dedicated to learning everything we had to know about camouflage and route marching. We learned how to walk and keep a distance from one another. During that period my superiors discovered the skills I had inherited from my Inuit background and from my father's education. One of them, Captain Crook, was especially impressed by my ability to detect hidden objects even at a long distance. During one march, Captain Crook stopped and asked if anyone had seen something in the open field. I was the only one to say something:

—I did, sir.

—Well, Vital. Tell me what you saw?

—While marching I saw leaves moving over there. I found it suspicious because there is no wind today.

I pointed at the bushes and said:

—Look! It is here. I bet there is something hiding in the bushes.

Captain Crook blew his whistle and a soldier got up and came out. I was right:

—Very good, Vital!

Then he showed us a long line of bushes up on the hill and said:

—Look up, guys. Over there is a tank and a jeep. Tell me where is the tank?

Again, I was the only one to say something:

—It is at the right end, sir.

—How do you know that?

—It's dug in.

—What makes you sure of that, Vital?

—If you look carefully, you can see a pile of sand by the bushes.

—Good, Vital. Now, can someone tell me where the jeep is?

Once more, nobody but me dared to say a word:

—Around the middle of the grove.

—How do you know that, Vital?

—The leaves of the bushes are upside down.

—Who agrees with Private Vital?

Racette, a Metis from Saskatchewan, said he believed me. Captain Crook blew his whistle again, and the tank came out from its dug-in and the jeep from the bushes. Captain Crook congratulated me. I felt like a hero and was feeling good because I knew the Captain would report this performance in my service book. The exercise being over, we marched back to our barracks. Corporal Handley was yelling: "left, right, left, right" to keep us in step together.

The time to leave for Wainwright was getting close. We were given a one-week leave to say goodbye to our friends and family. I went to Pembroke and La Passe to visit my friends. I wanted especially to see Helen, Frank's sister, since she had sent me a letter saying she had problems that she wanted to discuss with me. Once I arrived at La Passe, I met a friend of hers who broke the news to me. Helen was pregnant and was looking to get married fast. She was hoping to marry me because she was alone and far away from her village. I was not the father of her baby but she liked me anyway and she knew I liked her. She needed a husband to give her baby a father and she was convinced I would be a good one. When I finally found Helen, I told her that I could not commit to taking care of her and the baby, because I was not sure when and even if I would ever come back from Korea. I was really sorry for her. I had known her for a long time and she was a very good friend but I did not know what I could do for her. She was very sad. I was her last hope. I knew I disappointed her. I should have married her but I let her down. Today I regret I didn't do something for her but at that time I was young and selfish.

After that sad meeting with Helen, I decided to leave La Passe and I headed for Toronto. I was in uniform and a military police patrol stopped me and asked for my furlough pass. I started to look for it in my pockets but I could not find it. One of the patrollers ordered:

—You're coming with us.

I was not the only one arrested that night. There were six privates with me who had lost their pass. They brought us to some detention barracks and asked us to empty our pockets and to get naked. We were all standing against the wall. There was one big guy weighing at least 200 pounds. He was hiding his penis with both of his hands. The sergeant in charge asked him loudly:

—What are you trying to hide, big guy? Come on! Show it to everybody.

That was enough to make the big guy turn red and his thing shrink to nothing for a man of his size. We couldn't help laughing inside. He barely had anything to show! Some couldn't help a burst of laughter but we were suddenly told to shut up:

—Keep quiet and remember, you are nobody to me and you have no more privileges, no more rank.

We spent the night at the detention barracks. They forced us to carry pouches of sand until dusk. It felt like I was stuck with a bunch of sadists.

The next day I was sent to do the dishes in the kitchen fatigues while waiting for a decision to be made. A provost stood beside me the entire day watching my back and making sure I had the worst possible day. At one point, while I was washing a big pot, he made me put my head in it to scrub it with my tooth, as he said. If ever I was looking at him, or was not scouring hard enough, he would plunge my head in the stinking dishwater saying that was the very place where my head belonged. After a couple of days of such treatment, I was exhausted and almost vomited a couple of times from being so tired. Fortunately, I managed to hold it in. They would probably have made me eat it, otherwise. If mistreating and humiliating prisoners was part of the duty of the military police, they certainly did a good job with me. Finally the time came when I was called to the front office to be released. I was given back all my belongings and especially my cigarettes, which I missed the

most. The sergeant said they had phoned my regiment and found out I
was on an authorized leave. He added:

—I guess you will remember the lesson. From now on, hang on to
your pass, private, because next time you might not be as lucky and get
yourself put into a really tough prison. If you want to know, here it's a
piece of cake.

I could not picture a tougher detention than this one unless, of
course, they made you dig your own grave.

They put me on a patrol jeep bearing a big sign marked PROVOST
and drove me back to Camp Ipperwash. It was good to see the boys
again. They all gathered to hear what detention was like. Racette noticed I had lost weight. I joked about that:

—It's because they brainwashed me and that's where all my fat is.

Then I added seriously:

—But frankly, I feel lucky because I only lost weight. I could've lost
my life in that place.

Petit, a Cree Metis, could not believe me:

—Come on, Vital! It couldn't be that bad. Anyway, if they had
done to me half of what you say, I'd have resisted. I'd have fought back.
I can't believe you let yourself be humiliated like that.

—You don't understand; fighting back was useless. It would have
even worsened the situation. Let me tell you, if you'd resist, they'd hang
you by the nuts and if that were too good they'd find another way to
make your life unbearable.

To change the mood, Howard Bones asked me if I had the opportunity in prison to think of the girl at Sarnia's cathouse. He made me
laugh and we had to tell the others what we had done during our previous furlough. They all laughed and we made plans to return to the bordello in a gang. But our plan fell flat because the next morning we left
for Wainwright. I was very happy; I was finally going to see the West.

Our battalion moved out around midnight. We loaded up in
the sleeper cars of a special train. We were allotted each a bunk, and
thanks to the rocking movement of the train I fell asleep easily. When
I woke up, we were entering Manitoba. The trees were getting more
and more scattered until there were no more trees, only flat land. It was

wonderful to see the prairies. One of my dreams was coming true. I was
on the brink of discovering the big world. I had never seen so much
land so far off in the distance. I kept looking through the window to
fill up my brain with the view. I was dreaming of cowboys and Indians,
thinking they could attack the train at any moment like in the movies.
Racette, who was travelling in the same car as me, asked if I liked the
prairies. He was from Saskatchewan; we were entering his country:

—Very much, Racette. It's so beautiful. The clouds seem to be flying
real high. I have never seen something like that before. It is different
from the James Bay.

Racette was very pleased that I liked his country.

A few hours later we stopped for half-hour at Winnipeg. I was curious to see the big city where my Vital ancestors were supposed to
come from. Unfortunately, we were not allowed to get off the train.
Since I could not step out, I contented myself with looking through
the windows. I was able to see the passengers from another train and
the Regimental Police guarding our own. Sergeant Wall and Corporal
Handley made a quick roll call at each sleeper car to verify that nobody
had jumped off the train during the night. So far no one was absent.
Later we all received a greasy and bad-looking sandwich for breakfast.
We were hungry enough to eat it. At one point someone blew a whistle
and off we went again. Next stop was going to be Wainwright, Alberta.
I was anxious to see my new home. I was wondering what it would
look like. Would it be like Camp Ipperwash? How would the food be?
Would the meals be better or even worse than at the training camp?
When we arrived, we realized that Wainwright was a very small town,
so small that our barracks were much bigger and larger than the town
itself. Once inside, we had a good surprise. Everything was new and
modern, neat, and beautiful. There were even bright new showers with
tile floors. The washrooms were so clean that we were almost scared
to dirty them. Beds were nicely made. We even had rifle racks. What
more could we have asked for?

When noon arrived, they called out for a meal parade. We were
going to take with us our mess tins and utensils when we were told to
put them away and to march towards the mess hall. When we arrived,

they were serving meals on plates as in restaurants. Each of us had a clean cup, knife, fork, and spoon. We were sitting around tables with chairs—not bunks—and only four people around a table. We even had napkins; salt and pepper shakers were also placed on the tables. Several waiters served our meals on trays. I held my breath for a while, hoping they would not take all that luxury away from us for some unknown reason. But they did not, everything stayed like that. It was not another of their sadistic tricks. On the contrary, they were doing everything to please us. There was even an officer walking around while we were eating, asking us if we had any complaints. Complaints? How could I complain in such a place? I was sure that even the Queen and the King were not treated with so much respect! What a difference from Camp Ipperwash! We had everything a human soul could dream of during his journey on earth. It was too good to be true.

Of course, that nice treatment had a price and we paid it by being trained very hard. So hard that it almost made us forget how kindly we were taken care of at the dining room. We would train mostly at night, not too far from the barracks, but sometimes we would leave Wainwright for a one-week exercise. During these long training exercises, of which the goal was to prepare us for the front, we had to spend five to eight days in a trench, eating and sleeping in the mud. A truck came once a day to bring each of us two slices of bread with a bit of ketchup and some fresh water. During the day, we had to be silent and couldn't make a move to prevent the enemy from seeing us. We even had to urinate and crap in our steel helmets while in our six-foot trench. At night we cleaned everything up and re-camouflaged around our trench. The next morning a plane would fly over to take pictures of our position to spot any changes. We were trained to live without leaving any trace. Only flies, drawn by the smell of urine, flying over the trenches could have betrayed us.

During one of these one-week exercises, we practised the assault technique, and for that they had us pass through a swamp full of frogs up to our necks. The water's odour was disgusting and the decomposition was producing bubbles. Each step you took with your rifle above your head was a pain for all your body. There was not one single bone or muscle that did not hurt. When finally we got to solid ground, we had eyes so full of mud that we could hardly believe we were out of the water. Actually, some held their rifles above their heads long after they had put feet on the ground, still thinking they were in water. Our nicely shone gear was wet, full of mud, stained, and looked rusty. Racette, my old buddy, sat beside me and said while lighting a cigarette:

—Eddy, I am so dirty that I feel and smell like I pissed myself.

By late spring our support company asked for volunteers to be trained as mortar operators. When the captain made the request, I thought he said "motor." I always wanted to learn to be a mechanic. Thus when Captain Crook asked who wanted to become a "Mortar man," I put up my hand very quickly. Captain Crook asked:

—Are you really interested?

—Yes, sir.

—Fair enough, Vital. I think you can make a good mortar operator. So, Vital, and you, Neilson, you will transfer today to "Support Coy." Someone will show you where to get your gear.

We both answered "Yes, sir" and marched out to reach the headquarters, where Sergeant Mall was waiting to introduce us to our new company. That's how I became a mortar operator.

At that time, three men were required to operate a mortar. We were trained in groups of three and were told that we would stick together until one of us got killed. Actually, we were soon going to realize that our survival at the front would depend on our capacity to work together and to coordinate our efforts. From now on my life depended upon strangers, who also relied on me to get through a war taking place on the other side of an ocean whose name we hardly knew. Some days, when it was too blazing hot to do mortar drills, we had lectures, under shady trees, about 81-mm and 60-mm mortars, the two calibres the Canadian army was using at that time. In between two lectures, we would ride around in what we called "universal carriers." They looked like small tanks and had an engine right in the middle. This kind of engine was so hot that on summer days it was like sitting on an oven; by the time you got off you were half cooked and in deep sweat.

During training, we had to wear helmets. Those helmets dated from the Second World War. They were Canadian-made but were awfully uncomfortable. Wearing them gave us headaches. However, training was going well, the routine was fine with me, and the pay was good. I had no reason to regret my decision to join the Canadian Forces. Every Friday there was an inspection by Colonel Cameron. One Friday he told us that we were to train in the mountains at Jasper National Park. Korea is a mountainous country and it was important, as he told us, to practise in the same type of environment. We were sent to the Rocky Mountains for a six-week training in high lands. The landscape was so beautiful. I had never seen such tall trees; I could never have imagined that trees could grow that high. The snow capped the mountains and the sky was deep blue. I had never seen such scenery. Our camping area was by a river and the water was cool and clear. Every evening we would go and take a dip. A couple of deer were wandering nearby. It was like being in the Garden of Eden. There were also black bears around that used to come begging for food while we were having lunch. One day I was sitting on a rock eating my sandwich when a bear came up from behind me. On all fours, it was three feet tall, and I was pretty scared when it stood on its hind legs. But instead of attacking, the bear reached out its left paw towards me, like a beggar. I put a piece of bread on its paw. The bear took it and put it on its right paw and ate it. After that, it put out its left paw for some more. Private Yves, who was nearby, threw a piece of bread out, far enough for the bear to go after it and leave us. It was funny to see a big animal like that asking for food peacefully. I was thinking to myself that training in that place must have been going on for a long time for the bears to be so friendly with human beings.

A veteran who had spent several years in Burma during the Second World War supervised us for the night patrols. He was always telling stories about his time there. His name was hard to remember, so we used to call him Captain Burma. Under Burma's leadership we learned a lot about night camouflage. The final week of our training at Jasper we were sent to an expedition in the mountains. We had to climb up a summit with all our gear plus the 81-mm mortar. The mortar's base plate weighed forty-five pounds, the barrel forty-eight pounds, and the pod forty-seven pounds. We were just three men, Desjarlais, Yves, and I, to carry all that weight. Halfway up we were so exhausted that we were granted a half-hour break. Yves fell beside me, closed his eyes, and slept the whole thirty-minute break without even realizing it. We never reached the top because of the lack of oxygen. The higher we got the more our breathing was painful. Before going back, we stayed overnight in the middle of the mountain, close enough to the top to experience the solitude, but still too far away to make it to the top. Despite our disappointment, we had, the next morning, the most amazing spectacle: the rising sun was lighting the mountains surrounding us. It was so unbelievable, as if Mother Nature was offering us all her beauty in one sight. The silence was so intense that it reminded me of the ice floe when there is no wind and one can hear one's own heart. I was feeling good, almost at home.

We thought the descent would be easy, but it was even harder and much more perilous than the ascension. The weight was difficult to balance and we had to be cautious not to start a small avalanche of rocks by stepping in the wrong place. We finally reached a safe and flat area where we had a break. Nearby there was a shallow river where we filled our bottles with crystal-clear water.

Once back from Jasper, we were granted a thirty-day furlough to go back home and to say goodbye to our loved ones before our departure to Korea, which was imminent. My leave travel form was made for Fort George. I could use it to take as many trains or planes necessary to take me to my destination. Once arrived, I had to ask a police officer or a missionary to sign my warrant to prove I really went to the right place. But before getting my leave pass, I was ordered to report to our Regimental Sergeant Major Lee. I was wondering what wrong I had done, because it is usually bad news when you are ordered to report to the Regimental Sergeant Major. I was rewinding in my mind the past several days and I could not see what I could have done. That's when I thought that they had maybe found out my true identity— that they were going to tell me they could not allow an Inuit onto the battlefield and were going to send me back to the James Bay. I was so disappointed. I could not believe that all my efforts were now down the drain. I was so proud to have succeeded in becoming a soldier and now I was going to be expelled from the army. That would have been the ultimate humiliation. I was desperate; I wanted badly to go with the boys to Korea. I had spent so much time with them; I had sweated so many hours with them. I could not believe it was over.

When I entered the office of Regimental Sergeant Major Lee, I was expecting the worst. I could not believe it when I realized that he had only called me in because he was going the same way as me for his own leave. He wanted to make plans for the two of us to travel together. I was so relieved. He told me to make sure to be ready because we were departing early the next morning. That night, I had a last drink with my friends. I was feeling wonderful with my thirty-day leave and $300 in my pocket. When I woke up the next day, I folded quickly all my blankets and sheets and laid them at the foot of my bunk. I did not go for breakfast; I was too impatient and did not want to miss my appointment with Sergeant Major Lee.

That's how I ended up travelling with a sergeant major. All way long he was making jokes, saying he was my guardian and that I had to follow his orders. In fact, he was hardly joking, for he really thought that a young man like me, coming from the Far North, needed help to make his way in the big cities. We took a train up to Edmonton. There, we went to the commercial airport and flew on Trans-Canada Airlines off to Calgary. Then we flew to Winnipeg, where Sergeant Major Lee took a plane for Toronto. Before leaving me, he took care to remind me of what I had to do to get to Fort George. He cautioned me to be careful and not to miss my connections. I thanked him and he wished me a happy landing.

I took a coffee while waiting for departure. My flight number was then announced for Porkus Junction. I felt very much alone and very lost when we landed. The airport was a desert and there were only a few taxis. A cab driver came to me pretending he wanted to help me and convinced me to take his taxi to Cochrane, but once there, he charged me a lot more than the real price. When he left me by the quay where a little seaplane was docked, I recognized immediately George Charity, a bush pilot who used to fly the James Bay region. He was very mad at the taxi driver and to compensate arranged to put me on a small seaplane that was heading to Moose Factory, at the bottom of the James Bay. That was a good deal for me since it was getting me much closer to home. From there I was expecting to be able to take another seaplane to Fort George. At that time there was no regular air link between Moose Factory and Fort George. I expected to wait a while before being able to reach home.

Once I arrived at Moose Factory I had a little surprise waiting for me. Two of my sisters were now living there. Ann, eighteen years old, was taking a nursing course and Minnie was attending the Anglican mission school. Ann was staying in a small shack with Mrs. Hugo Watt. I stayed there for about a week waiting for a plane to Fort George. In Moose Factory there was a bar restaurant owned by a man called England. He gave me a couple of free lunches, knowing I wasn't rich. One day while I was eating there an RCMP officer came in. He hinted to me:

—You must be Eddy Weetaltuk?

—You're right. What can I do for you, sir?

I was trying not to show it but I was terrified. I was in uniform and a policeman who recognized my name and knew, therefore, that I was Inuit, called upon me. I was sure he was coming to arrest me. But I was surprised when I learned that this was not his intention. The policeman apparently did not know about the law restricting Inuit from enrolling. What he had to tell me was no grounds for being scared:

—I know your father well and I have a message to give you on his behalf. He was told that you had enrolled in the army. This saddened your mother, and that's why he asked me to tell you, if ever I came across you, that you should go home.

I was surprised by this request, and answered in one breath, without really knowing what to think of this demand:

—Can you tell him that it's too late since I've been enrolled for three years and that even if I wanted to leave, I wouldn't be able to. But tell him also that I like being in the army and that I have nothing to complain about.

—I'll bring back your message but I'm afraid he will not want to understand. In any case, I was told that you were on your way to visit home, and so you'll be able to explain it to him yourself.

Stepping out, he said to me:

—Hang on! Canada needs soldiers like you. In the meantime, good luck and don't get yourself killed in Korea.

I thanked him. I was pleased and proud because he had recognized the red square flash indicating that I was going to Korea. It made me realize that what I was doing mattered and deserved consideration.

That day the waitress was Mrs. Gagnon, Evelyn Gagnon's mother. When I wanted to tip her, she refused, asking me:

—You are from Fort George, isn't?

—Yes, I attended school there.

—So, then you know my daughter Evelyn.

I blushed. Of course I knew Evelyn. She had been my first girl-friend and I still remembered her. Her mother knew everything about our little romance but did not seem upset. On the contrary, she sympathized with me a lot. We chatted for a while and she told me:

—Evelyn is a big girl now. You would hardly recognize her.

This short conversation made me feel a bit sorry about all the nice people I had abandoned to live a life of adventure out there, in the great world. But it was too late now for regrets; I had to accept my choices.

One morning Mrs. Watt woke me up in a hurry, telling me to get dressed and to pack my stuff within half an hour. Austin Airways was ready to leave for Fort George. I rushed to the plane with my sister right at my back, bringing me a couple of toasts and a coffee. I drank my coffee in no time. The pilot was waiting for me. Ann told me to say hello to Mum and Dad. She was almost in tears to see me leave. A few minutes later I was in the air. I had left my little sister once more. Life was full of departures and goodbyes. I made a quick prayer, asking God to watch over her and help her succeed in her studies. I was thinking that if she could become a nurse, she would be out of trouble. I was so proud of my sister. She was like me, an adventurer eager to take advantage of all the modern world's opportunities. We were so close and I trusted her so much that I told her everything about my change of name. I had told her to contact me using my Vital name if something happened to our parents. Thanks to this confession, I knew I would no longer be without news from my family. I had somehow the feeling that by telling my secret to Ann I reconnected with my family, and I was feeling a bit less guilty for having abandoned my relatives.

When we landed at Fort George, Mother and Father were not there like I was hoping. I stayed at the Roman Catholic mission for a week. My disembarkation leave was running short and I was sad not to see my parents. But still it was nice to be back with the fathers, brothers, and nuns who had helped me so much in the past years. Some evenings we would talk for hours recalling past memories. Father Couture enjoyed telling all sorts of old stories. I remember that we laughed a lot when he told us that some mornings I was sleeping so soundly that he had to wake me up with a jug of water on my face. I was a heavy sleeper and was always late to go to milk the cows in the mornings. Recalling these memories made me realize how fast time was flying by, and how my decision to go into the army had changed the course of my life. After a week of rest, the time came to catch a plane back. The travel back to Wainwright was as long as the way out, but much more depressing. I was leaving my people not knowing if I would be lucky enough to make it back from the battlefield.

When I finally arrived at Wainwright, almost everyone was already back from leave. I was one of the last, but I was the one who had travelled the farthest to visit his family. Soon after my arrival we had a roll call by Sergeant Major Lee. It seemed no one was absent without a legitimate motive. The following week we were briefed by our commanding officer about what was going to happen. We were on the brink of departing for the Korean front. A troop train was going to take us to Seattle. Then we would be transferred onto a ship, the *Marine Adder,* which was going to sail to Yokohama in Japan.

Finally, the day came to move. Everyone was quiet except the corporals and sergeants who were screaming out orders all day long. I suspected that my comrades were like me, too anxious to be able to talk. Like most of them, I never wanted to be a hero, I only enrolled because I needed a job. I was only nineteen years old and I still had a lot to live for. But instead I was heading to the front. I seriously thought of deserting, but I knew the punishment. I had already experienced the army detention and I wasn't going to taste it again. Thinking about what I had endured for misplacing my papers, I was sure the treatment for a deserter, especially a deserter enrolled under a fake identity, would have been unbearable. I was also thinking of my Inuit countrymen and I did not want to bring shame on my people. If I had deserted, everybody would have said that Inuit are not courageous enough for war. At that point I thought that I would rather be dead than bring shame on my family. I was probably the first Inuk to go to war. I had to be strong; I had to prove that Inuit are just as courageous as any other people. I was sad, thinking I could die without seeing my family, but if my fate was to be killed, I was going to die with dignity. I was determined. I was going to show the world how an Inuk fights and dies.

CHAPTER 5

From the Island of Pleasure
TO THE INFERNO

When we arrived at the port of Seattle, the Salvation Army was waiting to greet us with coffee and doughnuts and wished us good luck, like they used to do every time a boat was leaving for Korea. We embarked on the ship *Marine Adder*, which was already half full with American troops, marines and GIs. We would soon get acquainted with them. They had heard quite a bit about us, the 2nd Battalion of Princess Patricia's Canadian Light Infantry. The PPCLI had already won presidential citation in Korea because it had captured the hill of Kapyong. The journey on the Pacific Ocean was long and rough. My comrades were killing time by playing cards and dice or by telling war stories. One day I sat beside an American marine looking at his girlfriend's picture. When I asked if she was his sister, he looked at me with surprise and replied:

—No, man, that's my sweet love.

He was speaking with a southern drawl. I had never heard such an accent before. Later he told me a very tragic story. A marine who was returning from Korea had written to his folks and fiancée announcing he was finally back. But, when he arrived, his sweetheart was not there. She had quit waiting for him. The young man did not say a word and went back into the ship and jumped from the other side of the boat and drowned himself in the sea. I was feeling sorry for that poor marine, and could picture myself in the same situation. But I came later to realize that was a pure fabrication. The veterans enjoyed telling that kind of story to scare the young recruits.

However, I could not wait to arrive at Yokohama. Curiosity was stronger than fear. When we finally docked, everyone took his gear and we all climbed up on the main deck to look at the Japanese who were waving at us from below. I was thinking to myself how these were the same people who fought against us during the Second World War and that we punished with an atomic bomb. They should hate us, like we had despised them. But instead they seemed so friendly. I was recalling the horrors we were told about the Japanese when I was in school and I began to wonder what is true in what we say about other people. I stopped questioning myself when I came to realize how nice looking the Japanese girls were. They were so petite and so elegant, walking with very short steps.

We got off the ship and took a train to Tokyo. Then, we took another train across the country to a city called Kure where we would be stationed while waiting to cross the sea to Korea, heading to the battlefront. On the train I could hear the dispatcher through the loud speakers giving orders in Japanese. It was strange. Japanese sounds very much like Inuktitut, though I could not make out the words. Looking out of the train I could see some of our boys throwing cigarettes and chocolate bars at the girls. They screamed in laughter trying to catch whatever the soldiers would pitch. It was the same game at every station. That was a strange spectacle, but that was indeed nothing compared to what I was going to witness. At one stop, a private in the coach in front of us gave one dollar to a young Japanese boy and pointed to one of the girls. The boy talked to the girl. She then pulled down her panties and lay on her back. At that point the soldier came to her and lay on top of her. When the two started to move up and down, making love in front of everyone, the occupants of all the coaches started cheering. I sort of shied away for a short while. But I could not resist and I looked again. I saw a Japanese police officer passing by the couple. He just walked by without a word, as if he had seen nothing. When they were done, all the train passengers applauded. The girl got up and pointing to us she said in broken English:

—You are all the same!

As the train moved on I could still hear the boys cheering. I was thinking that doing such a thing in Canada would have sent the guy straight to prison. I was very uneasy to realize that we were here to protect and serve but that some of us were doing things because they were in a foreign country and could get away with what they would not even think of doing in their own country. That's when I remembered my dad who had been sent to prison for plucking a raven and I thought there was no justice in this world.

It was sunny when we arrived at Kure. The sun was red because of the city's smog. In school, at Fort George, our teacher had told us that when the sun turns red in late evening it is rising in Japan. It was funny, I was in the country of the rising sun and the sun was actually red when rising. We arrived at the barracks just before supper. We were warned before the meal parade not to laugh at any of the girls who would serve our meals because it was very easy to hurt their feelings and to make them cry. During the meal I realized that one of the beautiful girls was giggling at me and whispering to the other girls. I could sense that she was making comments because I looked Japanese. To please her, I giggled too. She made a gentle bow with her head and looked at me with seductive eyes. Some guys in the room saw the whole thing and one of them commented:

—Vital, she likes you, lucky bastard.

I felt real proud and smiled at her once more. I could guess what she had in mind and it was pretty close to what I had in my own mind. It was definitely a capital sin.

After supper, at the mess, we were allowed to go to the wet canteen. To my surprise, we were served by young girls, while in all the canteens where I had been before the waiters were always soldiers. To see so many nice-looking Japanese women made us all happy and we were making all sorts of plans to party that night. Unfortunately, Sergeant Major brought us back to reality when he told us that we were confined to the camp. No one was authorized to leave the premises. We could drink in the wet canteen but that was it, no permission to leave the camp would be granted for now. Fences surrounded the camp and sentinels were walking back and forth guarding the entrance, carrying bayonets on their 303-calibre rifles. It was quite impressive. At some places the fences had holes and guards were posted to prevent anyone from getting out. I thought to myself that it would have been crazy to even think you could skip out.

Since we were forced to stay in the camp, I spent the evening drinking beer with some friends. The next day, on my way to take my shift at one of the fence holes, I saw something strange. I was half drunk from too much Japanese beer, Asahi, but still I saw this sentry ahead of me laughing. He was standing by the chicken wire fence; on the other side a Japanese girl was kneeling, munching at something with her head in motion back and forth. It was easy to realize what the two were doing. The girl was giving a blow job to the sentinel, who was still wearing his rifle strapped to his shoulder. There was a Japanese policeman walking around, just outside the camp. He saw everything but did nothing to stop them. He acted exactly like the policeman at the train station. I was very surprised to see the police being so lenient. Once they were finished I walked over the sentry and asked him:

—Boy! Did you see what she did?

He laughed and commented:

—No, Vital. I did not see, but I felt it and it was good. You can trust me. She knew her job!

—Did you pay her?

—No, I gave her a pack of Lucky Strikes that an American gave me on the ship.

—Did you see the policeman walking by?

—No. I was too busy coming. What did he do?

—He just walked by. He saw the two of you but he didn't do anything.

We continued our little chat while walking towards my station. Suddenly we heard noises outside of the fence.

—Oh! Oh! Someone is trying to get in. We're gonna catch him, whispered my comrade.

We hid and waited by a bush. Then we saw two pale faces crawling in, from under the fence. We pointed our guns at them. To our great surprise it was our beloved and respected Sergeant Major Lee and one of his body officers.

When Lee saw us he said:

—Privates, don't tell what you saw to anyone. If you leak a word, I swear you will regret it. Though, if you want, you can take the same way, I won't tell anybody. Put your rifles away and if you go straight ahead you will see a cab waiting across the rice paddies. But remember, not a word. And if you get caught I never talked to you.

He gave us a whistle to call the taxi. We ran like crazy to our quarters to store our rifles. There we met Bauer, Yves, and McCambridge. They asked what the big hurry was. We explained that Sergeant Major Lee had agreed to let us sneak out. The three of them got up in a flash and told us to wait for them. They were laughing as they put on their tunics and berets, so excited by the adventure to come.

We walked back to the fence. Once we arrived at the right hole, I said:

—I hope the taxi will take us.

—What taxi?

—Look across the paddies. There is a taxi.

When he saw us, the taxi driver started blinking his flashlight to guide us. Bauer couldn't believe it. When we got in the cab, the driver asked:

—You for Girlsans?

Obviously this was not the first time he was picking up soldiers who snuck out of the camp. When we arrived downtown, the street lights were on. The driver told us to keep our heads low because of the military police. Then he looked in his mirror and told me:

—Not you! No need to hide. You like Japanese.

But later, when he turned around and saw my hair, he changed his mind:

—Sorry, no good. Hair too short, you like army. You too bend your head.

Everybody laughed at that comment.

Yves was the one having the most fun and he could not stop laughing. Every time he looked at me, he laughed. After a while, it became annoying. Bauer tried to shut him up but he could not succeed. Suddenly, the taxi driver yelled to put our heads down and to be quieter, we were being followed by a military jeep. Our driver started to speed up, but so did the jeep. We were being chased. I felt like an idiot to have let myself be dragged into such an ordeal. All of a sudden the taxi made a left turn into a garage that was wide open. The driver rushed outside the car and shut the door behind us. Then he opened another door on the other side. It was a false garage used by the taxi drivers to fool the military police. I started to realize how the Japanese had learned to adapt to the foreign occupancy. The girls made a few dimes from the soldiers while the police pretended to ignore it, and now that taxi driver fooled the military police to drive us to a bordello. I came to the conclusion that the whole society seemed to work together to bypass the foreign rules.

Yves was not laughing anymore. I asked him, referring to the military police:

—How you like that?

Yves was not happy with my joke. He was in a bad mood and no longer knew whether he wanted to continue. However, our driver assured us that we were safe, adding, to make us laugh even more:

—I am judo expert. I throw them away if police catch taxi.

We all thought he was very funny. He was short and skinny; it was so obvious that he would not fight a military squad. Then he added:

—I know safe place for you. No military police. You want to go?

He drove to a very small house. He knocked at the door, said something in Japanese, and a fifty-year-old woman opened the door. Yves burst out:

—Oh no. She is too old.

—No, don't worry. Not her for you. She Mamasan. She gives you very young girls. Girlsans like Americans love. Don't worry. Best girls for you.

Mamasan said something to the driver and she invited us inside. It was just one big room. She made a bow and said something that, we assumed, meant: "Do you want to drink?" We looked at each other and said with one voice:

—Beer, Asahi.

With these words a man got up and left the room. He came back almost immediately with a big wooden box marked Asahi Beer and some ice. Bauer said, smiling away:

—At least if we don't get girls, we can get sloshed.

Ten minutes later our driver walked in with five young girls and said:

—Girlsans, the best!

The girls poured our drinks, lit our cigarettes and when we were ready, they made a bed for each of us. The beds were, in fact, simple mats that they unrolled directly on the floor. Each bed was separated from the other beds by a sliding wall. The girl I was with pulled me over to her bed. She undressed me completely and got naked too. She washed me all over with a face cloth. It felt so nice. We made love half of the night. She was all over me, one minute under, next on top of me. I just could not seem to get enough. She really had mastered the art of making love and I felt like a young boy going at it for the first time.

When I finally had enough, it was nearly five in the morning. She dressed me and walked me all the way back to the camp and showed me a hole in the fence where I could enter safely. She kissed me and said in good English:

—Come again. It's easy. You take the same taxi.

For sure I was going to come back. I walked slowly towards the barracks, looking around to make sure that nobody saw me. I hardly made 1,000 feet when I saw someone else trying to get into the camp. He had stood a ladder against the fence and a young Japanese woman held it while he was climbing. These barracks, where we were supposed to be confined, were a true sieve. Once in my quarters I quietly took my boots off and lay on my bunk waiting for the nine o'clock pay parade.

When nine o'clock came, everybody was there and the place was roaring with sex stories and laughs. Apparently almost everybody had snuck out that night. That payday and the following we were paid in Japanese currency. Most of the guys spent all their money on beer and women. The favourite activity was to go by the river where girls would give you oral sex for $2.50. Although we were soon going to be shipped to the battlefront, no one was complaining, nor was anyone reported absent without leave. Most of us were very young and inexperienced and we were discovering the pleasure of love in the very place where love had been elevated to the level of an art. We were having too much fun to think clearly. Exploring the universe of sexuality was our only concern. Our pay was so good, it made our sex journey almost boundless. The army was good to us. Although I spent all my money, like most of my friends, and did not keep a bill as a souvenir, I still remember very well how the Japanese yen was funny to handle—the bigger the amount the bigger the bill was. At that time 360 yen equalled one dollar and everything was inexpensive. With ten dollars, you could live like a king.

Near the barracks there were two small bars, one called the Ottawa Bar and the other one the Canada Bar. At every table there was a young girl to pour your drinks and light your cigarettes, and you could make her sit on your lap and smoke with you. They always got you "hot to go" but you could not bed down with them, not until they finished their work. Sometimes they had me so excited that I couldn't wait. That's when I would go to another bar in Kure where the waitresses were allowed to fix you up. This bad habit got me in real trouble. One morning that I had visited one of these bars, I did not make it in time for the parade. I was so late that I rushed to the parade in my muddy boots. Unfortunately, there was an inspection that morning and I got caught. Our company had been warned that if someone did anything wrong he would be fined or even transferred to another company. That morning, after the inspection, I was ordered to appear before my company's commander. I was found guilty of disobeying an order. I was fined twenty-five dollars and the commander ordered my transfer to Baker's company. The transfer would be in effect immediately after we arrived to the front line in Korea. Until then I had to behave!

That fateful day came pretty soon. A couple of weeks after my big mistake, we were told that a British ship called *Empire Pride* had arrived to transport us to Korea. When we embarked on the boat for Korea, all of us were sad to leave behind us the island of pleasures. We were at war and some of us would not make it back. Reality had caught up to us. The British boat was in bad shape; there were no beds, just hammocks made of small twine. It was very uncomfortable. They served beer in their canteen, but that beer gave us headaches. The meals were mostly corn-beef, or "bully beef," as Canadians called it to upset the cook. We docked at Pusan in Korea. A band welcomed us playing a marching song. Then, our own company band played "Vive la Canadienne." It almost made me cry for it was reminding me so much of my school days when our missionaries used to make us sing in French. The Salvation Army was there, too, with their usual coffee and doughnuts and asked if we wished to send a telegram to our folks. Some of us did. As for me I did not dare to send anything because I would have to sign with my new name Vital and I did not want my parents, especially Mother, to know that I had changed my name. She had already suffered enough seeing me leaving our James Bay; I was not going to let her know that I had abandoned my Inuit identity for a White man's name.

We got into a couple of two-ton trucks heading for Seoul and from there onto a troop train for Youngdeungpo, ten miles from the front line. We had to get ready to jump into action as soon as a regiment was pulled from the front. We were supplied with bandoliers and grenades to be ready to jump into the mêlée at any moment. We were ready; it was only a question of days. That night, we went to the canteen to drink and to take our minds off things and watch the lightning tear through the skyline. There were so many explosions that it was like someone had turned on the light in the sky. We were all getting nervous. The next night, while watching a movie, we heard gunfire from one of the tents and heard a howl of pain. We all rushed to see what had happened and we found a young soldier who had shot his toe off to be sent back home.

The following night, all companies were ordered to gather. I was, as sentenced, transferred to the Baker's company that was going directly to the front line. The noise from the battlefield sounded like thunder and the flashes looked like lightning. We were all pretty drunk. Some were singing loudly so they would not hear the explosions. Around ten o'clock the bombardments got worse and the whole front line was under fire. Suddenly everything got quiet. The bombing stopped. The air was filled with silence; we could almost hear each other's heartbeats. Nothing happened that night, but I was learning that silence can be even scarier than the noise of the explosions. You get used to the bombs, they become part of your life, but silence is unbearable.

When I joined my new unit, I met Corporal Lefebvre and the two guys I was to work with, Doyle and Brown. The three of us were going to operate a 60-mm mortar. I was acting as number 1, as I was the one with the most training. I reported to Sergeant Major Green, a Second World War veteran. Seeing him with all his medals and ribbons comforted me. I was sure he knew what to do and I was pleased to be under his command. He was always very serene and had a smile of kindness. I still remember what he used to tell us:

—Whatever happens, stay always calm. Don't panic and everything will be all right. Work together; don't lose sight of each other. You are a team and teams win together.

Finally, our turn to jump into the inferno had come. Sergeant Major Green called us and gave us a little pick-up speech:

—Okay, boys, we are going to relieve the Black Watch from England. Enemy has almost wiped them out and they can't hold their position anymore. Make sure you have your ammo and grenades ready. Now pick up your ammo and report to your truck. And don't forget your rifles!

Two American trucks were waiting for us. We moved in convoys at a speed of ten miles per hour. We had no light. Travelling in the dark was pretty scary, even if we had practised that many times. Now it was for real. We arrived around midnight. Our crew set up the mortars and started to fire. It was done so fast that we did not have any time to worry. We were firing three rounds every minute. We could hear our bombs exploding; the range was not too long. When we stopped, the artillery began firing from behind us.

It was so loud that Doyle and I hit the dirt. The anti-tank shells were whistling above us. It shook the ground every time they fired. While the artillery gave its round of fire, we were ordered to dig a six-foot trench and to stay there until everything quieted down. That night we had to wait until 4:30 in the morning. Once the night finally gave way to the day, everything got calm on both sides. We were ordered to go to our company's kitchen tent to grab a hot meal and to come back into our trenches right away. Once back, Doyle and I stayed close to each other. I needed to be comforted and he was the right person, since he had already spent six months at the front line. Later, we saw some young guys from the Black Watch regiment carrying out their dead and wounded on stretchers. I will never forget one of them. He was still alive but badly wounded. He was trying to smoke a cigarette; he looked at us half dazed. He laughed and said:

—Look at them crazy bastards who are going to get themselves killed.

He had been hit in the abdomen. We could see that he had the intestines all ripped out. It looked like he was not going to make it. Doyle told me:

—Eddy, forget about it. Don't pay attention to wounded guys or you will lose your appetite. I am not kidding you. You must learn to become insensitive if you want to survive. You must keep all your energy for yourself. Think of your folks, do you think they want to receive the news of your death?

Once he had finished lecturing me, Doyle continued to eat his ration, as if he had seen nothing. I tried to do the same but suddenly a big roar came over our heads and scared me. It was two American fighter jets flying over us, heading towards the other side of the hill where the enemy was dug in. When the jets got exactly above the enemy line, they opened up their tanks of napalm. When the napalm hit the ground, the sky ripped apart as if it was Judgment Day. Then we heard a terrific blast and we even felt the heat of it. No doubt I was in Hell. Surprisingly, I would get used to that routine. Every day it was the same thing. At night we would fight the enemy with our guns and our artillery, then they would fight back, but when the morning came the American jets would pour tons of napalm over the heads of the North Koreans. It was like we were having two wars at the same time, a conventional one at night and another one, during daytime, that I can't qualify.

Some nights the enemy would not attack and everything was quiet, frighteningly quiet. We were always scared in our trenches of being taken by surprise by the enemy. Some comrades pretended that some nights the Koreans crawled towards our trenches and could get so close that one could smell their breath. The rumour was that the Koreans ate a lot of garlic to keep the Devil away. Of course, I never noticed that smell but the very idea of being that close to an enemy without knowing it was giving me the creeps. One night, I got so desperate that I prayed on my rosary. I was begging God and the Holy Mary to spare me. That is when I realized that I was not wearing the holy medals given to me at the boarding school by the good fathers. I wore only my soldier tag. If I was to get killed, someone would snap off one part of the tag and send it to Ottawa while the other part would stay on me. The war office would then try to locate my family to notify them that I had been killed in action. But my parents might never get the news because I had entered Mary Vital as next of kin and I had given a false address to make sure nobody would track me down. The very idea that my mother might never know if I was killed was driving me to despair. I was feeling like a dog that would be shot and left to die alone.

Our company had incorporated some Korean people as combat support and combat service support. They belonged to the Korean Service Corps, known as the KSC. They would bring ammunitions, food, and water for our boys up on the hill. They worked slowly, trying to avoid mines and bombs. Some of our boys would give them a hard time and called them Kooks. They would even go as far as kicking them, yelling "Haba Haba," which means to hurry up.

One day a team of Koreans from the KSC who had just finished a delivery of water took a smoke break for ten minutes. They squatted in a circle talking quietly while puffing on their cigarette. We were watching them and some of us, I bet, were ready to call them names like usual, when a mortar bomb hit the centre of their circle, blowing apart five of them. We rushed to the scene and picked up the five dead Koreans. Once sheltered, we tagged the corpses, put them on stretchers, and left them outside our bunker to be picked up by the Regiment Inspection Post who would record their death. We all believed that no one could have survived a blast that close. But we were wrong; one of them had only been knocked out by the blast. When the medics came to pick up the dead, one stretcher was empty and the dead man was running down the valley screaming. A medic ran after him. He was heading towards a minefield. He had already used up his luck and it would have been very unlikely for him to make it through the minefield. As for the others, they were really dead and it took three days to get replacements. In the meantime, we had to take their places temporarily and we carried the water. Admittedly, even the least sensitive of my mates regretted the treatment they had put these poor Koreans through.

A few days later, I noticed a beautiful mattress. It belonged to a Black Watch soldier who got killed just before we moved in. Since nobody was using it, I asked the corporal if I could have it to put in my bunker. He refused, saying:

—Sorry. I'll take it but you'll get it if I get killed. What's your name?

—Vital, Corporal.

He wrote my name underneath the mattress and said:

—OK, Vital. If I get killed, you can tell your sergeant major that this is your mattress. But I don't plan to give you that favour quite soon.

I thanked him and was sure the mattress was lost for me. The following night the corporal went out to check the barbwires. The poor guy tripped on an anti-tank mine. His head got blown off. He never knew what happened to him. As for me, I did not ask for the mattress. I was sure it was cursed and I wasn't going to risk getting hit by a mortar bomb trying to collect it.

The corporal was one of our first casualties and losing one of your own always makes you think that you could be next. I could not believe I was there, waiting on death row, while my folks were enjoying a poor life, but still a life, in our James Bay.

We spent Christmas of 1952 at Pheasant Hill on the front line. On Christmas Eve, just about midnight, there was a loud whistle above us. We felt as if we had a major shock, like an earthquake. Then everything became dusty and we could not see each other. We all hit the ground well scattered, as we had been told to do in case of bombing. We waited in that position for fifteen minutes, ready for the next bomb, but nothing came and we finally went back into the bunker. None of us was hit. We had been lucky. No doubt that was our Christmas gift.

The rest of the night was quiet. Still, we took turns standing guard on our mortar. When my turn came, it was already morning. It was strangely quiet for half an hour. Then, I saw a dark face coming up the road that led down the valley. The night was so calm that I could hear the heavy sounds of the man walking slowly. I cocked my gun waiting for him to get closer. When he got close enough, I had my aim on his chest and shouted "Halt." He dropped his container to the ground. I ordered:

—Password.

No answer. I repeated, asking for the password again. This time he recognized my voice and said:

—Eddy, this is me: Golden the Limey. Please don't shoot.

I put down my gun, then asked with relief:

—What the heck are you doing here in no man's land?

—My platoon is running short of water and my captain sent me to get some.

He was indeed carrying a five-gallon jerry can filled with water. I asked him for a bit of water to mix with my rum and I shared it with him. With his British accent he said:

—Real jolly. As good as good champagne! After all, it is Christmas, isn't it?

I wanted to know why he did not answer the password when I called for it. I asked him if it was because he was so scared when I aimed at him that he had frozen. But that was not it; he had simply forgotten the password. We had a new one every night and he could not recall which one was the right one. I was angry and I was still in shock for having almost killed someone at point-blank range, on Christmas day:

—What were you thinking? You should have checked before leaving. You're lucky I didn't shoot you.

—I know, Eddy, that was close. Thanks for the rum. And thanks for not shooting me.

He left to return to his company. I woke up Brown; it was his turn to stand guard and I went to sleep. When I woke up, it was almost noon. It was Christmas and the front line was quiet. There was a small tree near our bunker, and Doyle and I decided to decorate it. We picked up all kinds of junk, anything that looked red or white, and made the most pitiful Christmas tree one could imagine. When we were done, we sat and laughed at the poor little tree. It looked so dramatic. When Captain Lefebvre and Brown finished their guard, they joined us. We opened a case of beer cheering at our Christmas tree and invited anyone who passed by to join us. At the end of the day we were a big bunch of guys encircling our tree. When dinnertime came, we all walked over to the kitchen tent. Inside, everybody was shaking each other's hands. We were given two bottles of beer and two ounces of rum, plus a pack of Canadian cigarettes. Our company commander came down to wish us a Merry Christmas. He read a message from the government of Canada addressed to the armed forces in Korea. It was a dull letter wishing us luck and to come back home soon. While listening to the speech, I recalled my school days when we really had fun celebrating the birth of Jesus Christ, who came to earth to bring peace to everyone. I was nineteen years old. It was Christmas. I had almost killed one of my comrades. I looked around and realized that I was not the only one with macabre thoughts.

After our little gathering, we went back to our bunkers. We waited there a couple of more days and finally were relieved from the front by a battalion of U.S. marines. Twice a month, the whole front was replaced by new troops and was granted a two-week break. When the Americans came in, we noticed they were much better equipped than we were. They were six guys to operate one mortar, while we Canadians were only three. However, since they were more numerous, they made better targets, and if they received a bomb, it would kill more men. That was the kind of joke we would make to comfort ourselves, seeing the Americans better equipped than us. Anyway, we were glad to be out of there. We left in convoys; twenty yards apart from one another, hoping the enemy wouldn't start bombarding as we moved. Luckily, we made it safe to the rest area, ten miles behind the front line.

We were still fifteen miles north of the 38th parallel, but we were out of the enemy range of fire. In our rest area we had a wet canteen where we would spend a lot of time drinking beer. There was so much beer and it was sold for ten cents a bottle. It seemed like it was part of the war effort to make us drink our fear out. During our break, we finally had the time to do our laundry. When the river froze over, we made a hockey rink on the ice. However, sport was not enough to forget the front. Thus most of us would go to one of the nearby Korean villages looking for women. We would pay $3.50 in American scrip for twenty minutes with a beautiful girl. In those villages we could also buy Canadian whisky and gin. How they managed to get those Canadian products there we did not know, but they knew Canadian soldiers were in for Canadian whisky. I guess they also had British and American brands for British and American soldiers. None of us knew the names of these villages because they were identified by number. In times of war a village was not anymore a place where people lived, worked, and loved each other, but only a point on a map. A dot that belongs to us one day but might fall under enemy control the next day. Numbering those villages was a way to make their destruction easier.

I went with a friend of mine to visit two of these villages, numbers 191 and 192. When we approached the first village, there was a group of young girls doing their washing. They were giggling. When they saw us, they all stopped talking and continued their work in silence, but would still give us glances with smiles. One of them looked a bit European with her reddish hair and her large breasts, which was very rare amongst Asian women. She glanced up and gave us a teasing smile. That was enough for my buddy to walk up to the group. I followed him and when the girls saw me, one of them pulled me aside laughing:

—You Korean!

—Yes.

I was not going to tell her that I was Eskimo. She certainly didn't have enough English to understand my story and my Korean was also too limited to get into a long explanation. However, the girls soon discovered my lie because I could not speak Korean. Nevertheless, that did not stop them from inviting us to visit their village. They were living in small huts heated with charcoal. It was nice and warm. We spent enough time there for each of us to spend $3.50 in American scrip. But more than the sexual pleasure, what I enjoyed most was seeing how Korean people were living. They were living with few things but still seemed to be happy. It reminded me a bit of the Inuit way.

We left after a couple of hours and walked further to the next village, number 192. While walking, we were sipping on gin every now and then. When we arrived, we realized that 192 was a small hamlet with only four huts and not too many girls. The few were already busy

with other sex-starved soldiers. There was only one available at the last
hut. My buddy seemed to find her cute and I let him go. I was waiting
outside when the Mamasan told me:

—Wait. I'll get you a nice girl.

She came back with a little girl wearing a school uniform. I was
horrified:

—No, no. I don't want her. She is too young.

Because the Mamasan was insisting, I asked her:

—How old is she?

She put up her two hands with two thumbs down. I said:

—Eight years old! Too young Mamasan. Way too young, she is still
a baby.

—No, not a baby. She is very good. The favourite of the American
soldiers. She already has fifteen American boyfriends.

I was so shocked. I ran away. Now that I recall that episode, I feel so
sorry for her. War is a disgrace, a shame. God must be so sad to see his
poor little children abused like that.

For the following two weeks we cleaned up the camp area and dug
trenches, savouring each and every day before returning to the front
line. Every night we could hear the roaring of the bombs falling on our
comrades. We were hoping that our American friends would hold on.
If not, we would be sent in before the end of our rest to relieve them.
Luckily it did not happen; Americans resisted the many assaults of the
Koreans. Some days later, just before leaving for the front, we were issued more grenades. They were covered with packing grease. We were
ordered to clean them up and to check each detonator. One of the boys
forgot to take the detonator out when he tried the striker cap. The grenade gave off blue smoke; he knew it was going to explode. He yelled:

—Hit the ground! Everyone down!

When Sergeant Major Green heard the shout, he came out of his
tent to inquire about what was going on. The grenade went off exactly
when he stepped out. A piece of shrapnel hit his chest. He was badly

injured and was rushed to the hospital in Seoul. Sergeant Major Cole replaced him and we went back to the front.

We were sent to Hill 187 to replace a battalion from Thailand. Their bunker stunk of garlic. Like the Koreans, Thais believe garlic keeps the Devil away. They had also warmed the bunker by burning gasoline in a barrel and a thick coat of black soot covered the walls. The odour and the dust made the place totally unsuitable. At our request, Pioneers blew it up and built another bunker on the side.

Hill 187 was mostly quiet in the following weeks except for a few rounds of explosions, blasting out now and then, especially during noon hours. The enemy knew our routine and was trying to get us when we were on the move to pick up our rations at our kitchen tent down the hill. One day while we were waiting to receive our ration, Doyle, who seemed to sense that something was going to happen, told us to get back as quick as possible to our bunker once served. We were usually quite fast but that day Doyle wanted us to hurry even more. Brown, another pal, was moaning, as he didn't see the need for such hurry. Doyle was very upset and yelled at him:

—You know damn well why. They always send their greetings around noon. It's noon now and we're going to taste it. Seriously, come on, don't make me nervous, hurry up. We are going to get it today. I can feel it. You too, Eddy. Come on!

Brown just laughed at Doyle, called him "chicken" and told him to go ahead. He was going to finish his lunch before going back. I stayed with him and we ate our meal by the kitchen.

A few minutes later, as we headed back to the bunker, Brown and I heard a loud whistle from behind us. We hit the ground and looked back. Just five yards from us a couple of shells had fallen. It did not take us much time to realize it was two napalm bombs. The grass and the bushes were on fire and the heat was already burning our flesh. We ran away like crazy, trying to escape the inferno, but the flames had already reached our mortar pits and the bomb increments were on fire making loud blowing noises. Captain Lefebvre ordered us to move out, up the hill. I ran so fast that I did not realize I was exposing myself to the enemy. They must have seen me as they sent five rounds of mortar towards me. I started to rush down the hill. While running, I heard a whisper and then the sound of a bomb falling to the ground. I saw the bunker entrance and dashed in. I had been lucky. It was dark in there. I could hear heavy breathing. There were three Koreans from KSC all piled up in one corner. The devilish whistle came again and the bunker shook so hard that I feared it was going to collapse. One Korean said with a shaky voice:

—Chung kook numa hakin ten.

My Korean was not good enough to understand but I was sure he was not telling me a joke.

I stayed in the bunker for a few minutes, just in case they were to send some more rounds of artillery. But they did not. I heard Brown calling:

—Eddy, where are you?

I came out of the bunker and walked back to our pit. The mortar was all black. We checked the bombs and put aside the ones that were hot, to cool them off. Then we replaced the sandbags that had exploded. Brown said:

—For a minute I really thought we had had it.

When we had the mess all cleaned up, I drank a bottle of Asahi with the boys.

Some time later we were told that we were going to be relieved from the front line and given a two-week leave in Japan. That's what one calls good news. A truck came to take us out. The truck was in a safe area out of the range of the enemy's fire, but to reach the truck we had to cross no man's land. The operation was dangerous and we had to follow a strict procedure. We were ordered to line up and to cross five by five. We were going out by alphabetical order. With my name I was going to be the last to be called and I was scared to be hit while waiting. During daytime the North Koreans seldom fired in that direction, knowing no one would dare cross in plain daylight, but at night they would systematically fire at that spot. That day they started their night round exactly when the sergeant called the last five of us. When I jumped into the no man's land heading towards the truck, I heard the devil whistle right behind me. I fell down and the shell exploded immediately, so close that I could feel the heat burning my face. I heard my buddies calling me:

—Come on, Eddy! Come on, hurry up. Don't be silly!

I could not move. I was grounded by fear. I was hearing the voices of my friends but they seemed to be coming from afar. I would have liked to reply but no words would come out of my mouth. Suddenly, Brown called out:

—Eddy! Don't be stupid. The next one to fall will blow you up. Get up.

His voice seemed closer, louder, and so urgent that it pulled me out of my lethargy and I finally got all my strength together and got up as fast as I could. I was exhausted when I reached the truck on the other side. I heard the sergeant commenting:

—Good, very good, boys, we all made it. Let's go.

My heart was still pounding hard when I got inside the truck, but I was feeling a lot better. I was happy to still be alive. We were on our way to Japan for a deserved rest. I had survived my baptism of fire!

CHAPTER 6

CULTURE CLASH

Finally our convoy set off. We were all relieved to be still alive and we rejoiced that we were soon going to be able to sleep away from the noise of the explosions. That night we stayed in a military camp near Seoul. We were packed in a dormitory and the sergeant in charge warned us to keep an eye on our money, because quite a few soldiers had been ripped off by their comrades on their way out. I could not believe that people would do something like that to each other, after what they had endured together on the front line. In the middle of my thoughts, I saw my Metis pal Racette. I waved to him. He came rushing to me, shook my hand and said:

—You lucky bugger! You made it. I am so pleased to see you.

—Me too. I was worried for you.

—You don't know how upset I was when they transferred you. You should have been more careful. What a shame they caught you. But now here you are.

—Yes, and I swear we're going to have fun together in Japan.

We stayed together during the rest of the trip; we had so many stories to tell each other.

When we arrived at Pusan, a beautiful and very clean Japanese ship called *E Sang* was waiting to take us over. All the crew was Japanese, they were very polite and did not waste any time before showing us Japanese courtesy. When we, Racette and I, stepped on the main deck, a man wearing a long trench coat came to us and opened it. Inside the

lining he had all kinds of bottles of whisky. I was amazed; it was like a
display in a grocery store. Then, while making a bow, he offered:

—Take your choice.

I was amused and told Racette:

—They really think of everything.

We bought a little bottle of whisky. We asked if he had any ice and
Coca-Cola. He made a sign and we followed him to his own compart-
ment. It was like Ali Baba's cave: there was everything in there that a
soldier on leave could wish for, from pictures of naked women down to
a magnum of champagne. The Japanese people definitely amazed me;
they knew all about our longings for sinful pleasures and were exploit-
ing our weaknesses with so much elegance. I could not avoid thinking
that their very polite faces were certainly hiding a true disregard for
our civilization.

We landed in Kure late in the evening and were loaded into trucks.
When we arrived, we were told that we could stay at the camp for free
unless we preferred to rent a room in one of the hotels downtown. Of
course, staying at the camp was not an option for most of us, at least
as long as we still had enough money to party. We all picked up our
passes; we had fourteen days' permission leave. It sounded like forever.
I could hardly imagine I was ever going back to the front. Racette and
I took a taxi to Kure. We had much fun going from bars to bordellos
but I am not going to waste your time with more stories of that kind.
However, I remember quite a funny episode from that leave. One day
when we were too drunk to look for a hotel by ourselves, we were going
to take a cab and ask the driver to find one for us, like we used to do in
such circumstances. But that night Racette decided to take a rickshaw
instead. I was not sure but he insisted:

—Come on, Eddy. Let's try it, at least once. You cannot go back to
Canada without experiencing such a ride.

I let him convince me and each of us took a rickshaw. We told our
drivers to take us to the nearest hotel. When I sat in the rickshaw, the
man pulling it gave me a whip and told me to use it on him if he didn't
go fast enough. I laughed and found it ridiculous. But as I was in quite
a good mood, I shouted at him in Inuktitut as if I were mushing a dog

team. After a while, I really felt like I was on a sled, mushing my dogs, and I began whipping on his handrail yelling:

—Oweet! Oweet! Arra! Arra! Aowk! Aowk!

I was laughing and having fun like when I was a kid travelling with my dad on the ice floe. It was a unique moment. Of course, the rickshaw driver could not understand that the ride was bringing back feelings from my childhood. Now that I recall the events I am sure he must have been quite scared. After all, I was a soldier, I was drunk, and I was using the whip like a pro. Since he could not understand my language, he ran faster and faster, trying to satisfy his furious customer. The faster he ran, the more fun I had and the more I was using my whip. Behind us, Racette was laughing his head off, wondering what I was saying and why we were moving so fast. His rickshaw driver was doing his best to keep up behind us but could hardly follow our pace. Finally, we stopped in front of a small hotel called Senesin. The drivers were exhausted. I was impressed by the strength and the endurance of my driver. The more I got to know the Japanese people, the more my respect for them grew, though I was not sure about the idea of asking to be whipped by a customer. I was thinking to myself that these people were a bit like my people, ready to work hard to survive. And, somehow, running and pulling a rickshaw was very similar to running behind a dogsled with someone on it. I gave five dollars to my driver to ease my conscience for having treated him the way I did.

Unfortunately, my conscience did not stay awake long enough and that same night I was going to mistreat another member of those proud and highly friendly people. Now that I recall that time I am pretty ashamed, but I can only explain my situation by the fact that everyone in the army was acting with little respect for the people they were supposed to protect. When we got into the hotel, we asked for a girl to spend the night with, as we were used to doing. Racette got lucky and he had a very nice-looking girl; mine was pretty well-built but her face was not interesting. It looked like someone had kicked her face. At first I thought about refusing to take her, but I changed my mind thinking that I was not going to make love to a face but to a body.

After all, I could still ask her to hide her face, like we used to say in the army: "Just pull down the hood and all the girls are alike."

During the night the girl did everything to please me. I was bastard enough to ask her if she was that good because she wanted to be forgiven for her ugliness. Now I realize that we were actually treating Japanese women as if they were meat in a meat market and not human beings with feelings. The war was turning us into predators, trained to kill men and to chase women, always looking for the youngest and the prettiest. That's what war was turning me into.

When I woke up the next morning, it was nearly eleven o'clock. I was completely naked. I looked all over for my clothes and I could not find them. I immediately accused the girl of stealing my clothes:

—You cypsy, cypsy my clothes.

"Cypsy" meant stealing. In Japan, accusing someone of stealing is a very serious accusation. I knew it, but still I was yelling at her. She put on her kimono and rushed out and came back immediately with all my clothes and my wallet. My boots had been nicely polished, my uniform pressed and my money was still all there. I was feeling so cheap. I didn't know which way to turn. I finally chose to kiss her. A real kiss.

At that point Racette came into my room. He, too, was naked like a worm. He had heard my screaming and was coming to rescue me. When he saw me kissing the girl, he was a bit surprised:

—What are you doing, Eddy? I came in a hurry; I thought somebody was beating you up. You screamed like a pig being killed. What happened?

—Sorry, Racette, if I scared you, but don't worry, I am fine. It was a misunderstanding. I thought I had been robbed but in fact it was the contrary. Now I laugh because I am so happy. These girls are so nice to us.

At that moment, his cute girl came in bringing his clothes. He too was amazed by the treatment.

To show my gratitude I decided to stay a few more days. When the time came to go back to the camp, my girl told me it was too risky to walk in plain view because the hotel was located outside of the bounds and that day there were lots of military police patrolling the sector. She offered to help me get back to the camp and gave me a kimono and a pair of sandals to hide my identity. I accepted her offer without resisting. Since I started misleading people about my identity, I no longer really had any misgivings about passing for someone else.

While I was getting dressed, I heard some kind of radio static and looked out. There was a military jeep right in front of the hotel. I was able to hear them radioing to their base, reporting that they were at an out-of-bounds hotel. They were coming in to check if any soldiers were inside. The girl had anticipated their move, so she put a towel over my head to hide my army haircut and we left the house as if we were ordinary customers. While passing by the jeep, she kept talking to me in Japanese and I replied to her in Inuktitut. I remember telling her:

—Emaha! Emaha!

Emaha means, "hoping so far." Apparently, my disguise was very good and my Inuktitut sounded Japanese enough, since we made it out without being stopped.

When I arrived at the barracks, I still had five days left on my leave. I went back downtown a couple of times to buy a few souvenirs but I spent most of the time at the barracks chatting with the boys. We talked of everything, but usually we were making plans for the future, for after the war, after the army—for the real life we were hoping to still have ahead of us. We also talked about the Japanese women. The boys all agreed that Japanese women were so adorable and I was not surprised to hear that several guys were badly in love with local girls. Some others, actually most of them, had spent all their money on girls. I had been more reasonable and I still had fifty dollars left, which was a pretty good amount at that time.

When the day came to head back to Korea, we travelled on a Japanese ship, the *Wo Sang*. As we embarked everybody was quiet, we all stayed on deck to look at the port fading out. The return journey took place in silence. Some of us were in tears. For most of us, the way the Japanese treated us was a revelation. It was hard to believe that they were once our enemies. It made me realize that politicians can make you believe that wonderful people are barbarians. Once you are convinced of it, it is easy to abuse and kill people, because you believe you are the good ones and the others are just evil.

When we landed in Pusan, someone asked me for a cigarette. I looked in my tunic pocket and gave him one. But while looking for the cigarettes I noticed that I did not have my service book anymore. I realized I had forgotten it in the pocket of my other tunic; the one I had given in payment for two nights in one of the hotels in Kure. It was a catastrophe. I immediately told the sergeant in charge that I had lost my service book. Of course I did not tell him it was because I had sold my tunic, otherwise I would have been charged for disrespect to my uniform. He took my name down and sent a message to Japan in the eventuality someone had found it at the camp. I knew it was not there and I was convinced nobody would find it.

The next day another group came back from Japan. This time Racette was with them. As soon as he arrived, he looked for me. When he finally found me, he said with a lot of fun:

—You old bugger. Why did you leave me behind?

—If I recall, it's you who chose to stay at that Senesin Hotel. You were too busy with that girl!

—Maybe. Anyway, I do not have any grudge against you. I even have a gift for you. Look what I have for you directly from your Japanese girlfriend.

To my surprise, he pulled out my service book and said:

—Boy! How come you are ever lucky like that? You won't believe me but I was just walking out yesterday night to see my sweetheart for the last time when I saw that girl you slept with at the Senesin Hotel. She came running to me and showed me a service book. I looked in it and laughed a lot when I saw your face stamped on it. I told her I'd give it to you. She was just about to cry and told me to kiss you for her. You lucky bastard, what are you doing to women? They all fall for you. Do you know how much trouble you would have been in if someone other than me had found your service book? You owe me one, Vital.

I thanked him for the book and asked if he had spent all his time with the same girl:

—Don't mention it, Eddy. I couldn't get rid of her. She followed me all over.

Of course, he was bragging, as he was indeed in love with that girl and the girl was certainly in love with him too.

What happened to Racette, happened to many of our boys. Since then, I have travelled a lot and I have never met any prostitutes or hostesses who fall in love with anybody. I can only assume these poor girls were so much in despair that they easily fell in love with men like us, rich and coming from America. Or perhaps they were just so desperate that they had no other option but to pretend they were in love to get money from us, unless they were dreaming we would take them back home with us. In any case, love was for them the only way out, the only hope.

A few days later, we were asked to report to our platoon and were driven to the front line. When we arrived, it was mostly quiet except, from time to time, for a few flashes of lightning in the night. Corporal Lefebvre, Doyle, Brown, and Schofield were happy to see me again. They asked why I had been away longer than them. I told them I had been given the choice to travel to Japan by plane or by ship:

—I chose to go by ship because I would be away from the front longer since the two weeks leave began only once we had landed in Japan.

Doyle had had another experience:

—You're very clever, Vital, and lucky too. As for me, I was not offered anything. They flew me directly to Tokyo and two weeks later they flew me back.

We all settled in the bunker and told each other about our adventures in Japan. They really laughed when I told them that I managed to escape from the police because a girl dressed me as if I was Japanese. But their favourite story was my ride in the rickshaw. They found it very funny to hear how my Inuit instincts inherited from my mother—everybody still believed my father was White—came back once I was given a whip. For the following days they made jokes about objects that could remind me of my childhood and that would provoke all sort of strange behaviours. Their schoolboy pranks did not bother me at all. On the contrary, I was different from them because of my culture, but I knew they were not thinking I was inferior. We were soldiers, all coming from various backgrounds but we were all putting our life at risk for our common country and as such I was their equal. I was proud of being recognized for what I was doing instead of being treated differently because I was an Inuk. I was one of them. They were having fun with me and not at my expense. I was Canadian. A Canadian soldier. The first Canadian Inuit soldier, but that nobody knew.

Two more months passed. It was always the same thing, every night we would hear the same explosions and waited to be attacked. Once they were on us, we would automatically fire back to repel the enemy. War was becoming a routine for me and killing the enemy in the distance was almost a piece of cake, until one foggy morning. That day the B company from our battalion accidentally shot an enemy stretcher-bearer. The Geneva Convention, signed in 1949, strictly forbids to fire at rescue teams. The Koreans were not too happy about the shooting, so they warned us, using loudspeakers, that they would take revenge and would attack us on 1 May 1953. They had two months to prepare their revenge. As for us, we had two months to stress at the idea that a large-scale attack would be inflicted upon us and that it would certainly cause great damage. Knowing in advance that several of us would be killed was in itself a punishment. For a couple of weeks we all talked of that threat and were scared, not knowing if the enemy was serious or if they only wanted to make a point. In the meantime, every day, around noon, they would fire their usual round of shells, though they were aiming at our B company more than before.

A few days after that incident I crossed paths with Alec Gray, a guy who had joined the army at the same time as me. I knew him pretty well since we had spent plenty of time together during our initial training. He used to be a pretty religious man. I remembered that he attended church every Sunday. Several months of combat had totally changed him. He was not talking of God anymore, but rather was looking for every opportunity to get high. Every time the front was quiet he would come to our bunker to have a beer with us. He was a stretcher-bearer and was only busy when we had been bombarded and had casualties. Knowing his habits, I began to save my ration of beer to have a little to drink when he would come by.

Alec was very depressed by war. One day I asked him if he was scared to die without repenting for his bad deeds. He told me that a man gets killed whether he is good or bad. That was too true, but still, coming from Alec it sounded pretty depressing. I gave him a full mug of rum to ease his despair and we started to drink. Suddenly, the field phone rang. It was an officer asking for Alec Gray. They exchanged few words. He hung up, drank half of his rum quickly, and left the mug under my bunk saying:

—Eddy, I have to go. Keep that for me till I come back. If I don't make it back, finish it for me. I have to pick up a couple wounded guys. I hope they are not too badly injured. Sorry, but I have to rush.

He left, making sure he did not forget his first-aid kit. Fifteen minutes later we heard a loud explosion up the hill. Brown, who was worried, said:

—I hope Alec is okay.

Unfortunately, a shell had struck him when he was just about to enter Major Roberts' bunker.

The shell had blasted him five yards away. His comrades rushed to rescue him. When they reached him, he was still conscious and kept saying:

—Where's my first-aid kit?

His leg was almost severed. They did their best to stop the bleeding using field dressing, but it was hopeless, he had lost too much blood. When Alec realized that he was not going to make it, he told his friends:

—Tell Eddy to finish it. Tell him to finish it for me.

He delivered his last breath while saying these words. The soldier who carried his body down the hill phoned over to our bunker and asked for me. He told me without any warning:

—Alec Gray got it. He was your friend, wasn't he?

—Yes, Alec was my buddy.

—Then, here is a message for you from him: "Finish it," whatever that means. I guess it was his last wish.

—Thank you. I know what it means.

We hung up. His mug was still underneath my bunk, half full. I took it and I downed it in one go, like he had wished I would. We were all very sorry about Alec's death. He was a good guy who in other times and other places would have been an example of virtue. I will always recall our last talk, and unfortunately, he was right about the war. It does not discriminate and kills the good guys as much as the bad ones.

During the following days our position received a lot of mortar fire. Our support company retaliated so much that they lit up the sky with their 81-mm mortars. When the casings land on the ground, they make a strident whistle. One night, that creepy noise scared a young soldier so much that he lost control. We found him stabbing with his spike bayonet a dozen sand bags like a maniac and yelling:

—I'm too young to die. I'm not eighteen. I'm just seventeen. I lied: I'm not eighteen. For God's sake, let me out. I don't want to die. You can't let me die.

The next morning he was taken back behind lines. An officer wired to Canada to ask for his age to be verified. The answer came a week later. He was indeed underage and had lied to be enrolled. He was sent back, under arrest, to Canada. As you can imagine, that episode reminded me of my own lie and I was crossing my fingers that panic attacks would not push me to divulge my true identity by stupidity.

When the first of May came, everyone had by then forgotten the threat made by the enemy two months earlier. It was a nice day and the wind was calm. Some of us might have noticed that more shells were fired at the B company than in the previous days, but it was perfect weather to fire at the enemy so no one really paid attention to that sign. Thus we were nicely relaxed in our mortar bunker telling stories. Then all of a sudden, there was a sound like a strong blizzard followed by a barrage of mortar shells exploding all across B company ranks. I looked out. On our left it was like seeing a city at night all lit up. The noise was frightening. Our field telephone rang. Corporal Lefebvre answered and yelled:

—We are being attacked!

Explosions of shells were so loud that we could barely hear orders. Our first officer ordered thirty rounds of rapid mortar to retaliate. I repeated his command to my number 2, Brown, who started to fire the shells one after another. I kept watching to make sure that the bubble on the mortar's level would stay in the centre at all times. While we were shooting, tons of shells were falling very close to our mortar pit. It was very dangerous. The three of us knew we could be killed at any moment, but we could not hide, we had to keep firing to prevent the enemy from moving forward. After our thirty rounds were gone, we fired another thirty. Our mortar barrel started to smoke from the heat. We were going to run out of ammunition when the order to stop firing came. Corporal Lefebvre yelled at us:

—Get into your guard trenches and watch the valley below our left! The enemy is estimated to be crawling up from that point. Vital, take the first trench, Brown the second, Doyle the third, Schofield the bunker area, and keep your eyes open!

Then the bombing started all over again. This time the barrage fire came from our right side. The enemy threw everything they had. They even fired with machine guns and several bullets hit my sandbags. The sand was flying into my trench. I could hear the mortar bombs falling all around me. I just lay on the ground, scared to death, I was shaking and my forehead was covered with cold sweat. There were so many bombs falling around me that I thought my last hour had come. Suddenly, a voice came from above. I could not recognize who it was, but it must have been either Doyle or Brown yelling:

—Eddy! Eddy! Are you OK?

I had breathed in so much dust that I was hardly able to speak. When I finally managed to ask what was going on, the voice told me to get back to the bunker as soon as it got quieter. The corporal was going to talk to all of us. Once in the bunker, Corporal Lefebvre told us to get ready to move out. We were not able to hold the position any longer and were going to withdraw at any moment. The mortar bombs kept falling while we were in the bunker. Suddenly our field telephone died out, a shell had hit the line. We were left with only a radio to communicate with the command and to get the order to withdraw. The platoon on the next hill to our left was being slaughtered. At one point, shelling on our side slowed down and we heard a call for help on the radio from a couple of guys who were wounded and stuck in no man's land. Sergeant Major Cole asked for a volunteer to go with him to rescue the wounded boys. I said:

—I'll go.

Then Schofield offered also to volunteer. Corporal Lefebvre said:

—I know the way to settle this between you two. I'll flip a coin.

I chose heads. He flipped the coin on his hand and said with a smile:

—Eddy, you lucky bastard. Schofield, it's your call. Good luck to you.

The two men jumped into no man's land and Corporal Lefebvre left and ran to the bunker, hitting dirt now and then to avoid the bombs. While leaving, he yelled to me:

—Vital, you go back to your trench and watch out for Schofield and Sergeant Major Cole. When they return with the wounded men, make sure no one follows them. If you see any face behind them, ask for the password and if you don't get an answer, shoot and don't miss. That's an order.

Once in my trench, I set up a Bren Gun with a full magazine and I stocked a bunch of grenades in case I needed them. The first time Schofield and Sergeant Major Cole came back they brought Boyce with them. He was lying on the stretcher and his leg was completely severed. He was dying and he knew it. They went back to get Crompton the second time. When they found him, he was already dead and they loaded his body on the stretcher when a shell fell close to them. The blast almost got Schofield, and nearly severed the hand he was handling the stretcher with. They waited for the barrage fire to slow down before they made a move. Crompton's body was full of blood and heavy. When they arrived, the two men were distraught and exhausted. Daylight started to pierce the valley and all the shelling stopped. We went back to our bunker. Schofield was still shaking and told me what he had seen in no man's land and he added that the vision was going to be engraved in his memory forever:

—You can't imagine what it is. The worst is when the shells explode. They light the sky and expose the bodies lying all over. There is also the wounded asking for help or begging for mercy killing. It's a real slaughter. A nightmare.

His trousers were red, stained by the blood of Boyce and Crompton. The blood was still warm and its odour was so strong that I was nauseated.

Everything looked devastated after the heavy attack. All the bushes had been burnt around our bunker area. Our mortar pit was caved in on one side. Luckily, our ammo had been spared. The valley was in smoke for hours. Corporal Lefebvre had a pair of binoculars and was looking for wounded and dead soldiers down in the valley. When everything had calmed down, he sent our stretcher-bearers to pick them up. A Pioneer was leading the way with a mine detector, marking the safe area. The enemy was doing the same for their own dead. This time we could see their white armbands. A spotter plane was flying above taking pictures of the battlefield. Later on, officers would be busy counting the casualties on each side. No doubt someone would claim victory in both camps.

Our support company had suffered many casualties and because of that we became short of mortar men. I was qualified to operate an 81-mm mortar and was called up and asked to pack my gear to join the support company. It was nice to be back with my old crew. Lieutenant Barnam was commanding the support company and Sergeant Robertson was the operation commander. I was assigned to Plante's mortar, where I was asked to be number 2 to replace his buddy who had been wounded and sent back home. The support company used loudspeakers to give orders to the mortar operators. One section had a 107-mm artillery mortar; its barrel had rifling inside to make the bomb twirl. Its blast was so strong that it suctioned the shirt to your skin. At every blast you had to put a cotton batting in your ears and open your mouth or your nose, otherwise your ears would bleed. The old crew that I trained with in Wainwright was all there. Misner, Mason, Plante, Spence, Gauthier, they were all there, all my buddies. Desjarlais and Misner started to tease me and to make fun of me because my stupid mistake had sent me to the very front line.

Now that I was with the support company I was to discover a slightly different routine, but the job was still basically the same and the enemy was still firing at us. Some nights we were so busy firing back that even the cooks were helping us to open cases of ammo. Sometimes the barrels of our 81-mm were so red-hot that one night Plante lit his cigarette on a barrel while waiting for it to cool off. After the big attack of May first, our support company spent a lot of bombs to make sure the enemy would not come any closer to our lines. Sometimes I was number 1, sometimes number 2. I was pretty fast in pushing bombs into the barrel. One night that I was acting as number 2, we fired thirty rounds of 81-mms and I sent all the bombs before the first one hit the ground. The officer in charge called the fire controller and asked who was number 2 on that mortar. He had never seen such beautiful grouping of mortar fire. All the bombs had fallen on the same spot. The officer commented:

—If there was anyone there, he must be in pieces. Very good, Vital.

Desjarlais heard and, amused, added:

—Attaboy, Vital! You get compliments from officers now! Watch out, you might be promoted.

We went for divisional rest towards the end of June. We did not move far away from the front but were settled in a quiet place where there was a little stream with cool spring water. It was really nice. We built a small pool where we would dip when the day was hot. Although we were on rest, we still went from time to time to our training area to work with live mortar fire just not to lose our touch. A rumour was circulating. A ceasefire was going to be signed. When the time came to get back into real action, we were all hoping that the ceasefire would spare us another two weeks on the battlefield. We were informed that if the ceasefire was signed, a searchlight was going to be lit up. Every night we were all looking at the skies hoping to see the sign that would deliver us from the inferno. While the chiefs at the headquarters were working on the conditions of a ceasefire, the battlefront got quieter. Nobody wanted to put the truce in jeopardy.

While waiting for more news from the headquarters, we would take rides with the army trucks. One day we went to visit the battlefield where our 2nd Battalion won the United States citation. It was a very long valley where our guys had been boxed in. The enemy's artillery pounded them from all over. They had no other option but to advance and to charge Kapyong's hill, which they managed to take over, to everybody's surprise. For sure, the 2nd Battalion paid a heavy price and experienced a lot of casualties. None of us really knew how many men they lost, but when we visited the site we could imagine the extent of the suffering. Although the trenches had been filled in, we could still see boots, helmets, and bush coats sticking out. A foul smell contaminated the air. It was coming from the decaying corpses left behind in bunkers and buried in the trenches. It is understandable that the stretcher-bearers could not pick up all the dead soldiers because the bodies had disintegrated and their parts were scattered by the violent explosions.

Our rest reached its end, without a ceasefire being signed, and we were sent back to the front by the end of July. During the peace talks, we stayed in our trenches. Our superiors were making sure we were still ready to repel the enemy in case the combat would resume. However, we were told not to fire unless it was a direct order. It was important to give the ceasefire a chance to be worked out by the headquarters staff. We kept our fingers crossed and our cannons silent. Everybody stayed quiet for a while on both sides, but one night we heard a thunder of artillery at the extreme right on hill 355, one of the biggest hills in North Korea. We were all depressed, wondering who were the "war mongers" who were putting an end to our hope. It happened to be the enemy, who was trying to take a last crack at hill 355. They wanted to add that last piece of land to the North Korean territory before the armistice was signed—a last effort, another dozen casualties just for a few hundred square yards of devastated land. Apparently, the North Koreans almost knocked the Allied Forces off the hill but at the end could not take it. The word came that our company was going to take over the defence of hill 355.

A British company was sent to replace us. They brought their own artillery and we were ordered to start pulling out our six mortars. We loaded our weapons into our convoy and moved to hill 355. Once there, we set up our fire behind the crest line. We ranged in to make a line of fire so as to offer good protection. Then we settled down in our bunkers. Later that day we heard a barrage of mortar hitting the position we had just left. All night long the enemy hit the same position. The next morning, when we came to pick up a 107-mm mortar left behind, we realized that the British had been badly hit. Five of their mortar men had been killed during the bombardment. Desjarlais could not believe it:

—Vital, how come we are that lucky? If we had stayed here one more night, it would have been you or me dead.

We loaded our 107-mm mortar and headed back to hill 355. When we arrived, Gauthier asked:

—What did the pit look like after they'd been hit? I hope they weren't all slaughtered.

Desjarlais and I made a joke about the situation. We didn't feel like talking about dead comrades, so I said:

—We did not pay much attention to those English guys. As long as our mortar was OK, we did not ask many questions.

—You selfish bastards, concluded Gauthier, laughing.

During the following week, things calmed down a bit and we were acting as if the truce was near to being signed. Gauthier and I went every day to take a dip and wash our clothes in a little stream further down the valley. We used to go there around noon with a couple of beers. Sometimes shells would fall but they always landed too far away to worry us. However, one day bombs started to fall in a much closer range than usual when I was cooling off nicely in the river. It started to be very creepy and we ran up bare-balls to our bunker for cover. No need to mention that our pals made a lot of fun of us later on.

July went by, August was almost there, and we were still hoping for a ceasefire to be signed between the parties. We knew that difficult talks were going on at Panmunjom and we were trying to avoid making any mistakes. I will remember forever the night of 27 July 1953. We had been warned by our officers not to shoot one single bullet, the ceasefire was almost signed but the enemy was nervous and a mere little mistake, a single death, could put all the headquarters staff's efforts in jeopardy. Believe me, that night I didn't sleep, I was too busy listening for any suspicious noise. I was determined to prevent whomever from provoking an incident which would have rekindled hostilities. That night I prayed a lot. I had not prayed for a while, but that was the right moment to get back to God. I said my bedtime prayers at least fifty times. They were the only ones I could remember. I was looking for something beautiful enough to convince the Holy Spirit to bring His wisdom to hundreds of half-drunk soldiers. But it was hopeless, my brain was empty and I could not remember any of the wonderful prayers I had learned from the Oblates. Finally the morning of 10 August 1953 came and nothing had happened. It was six o'clock and everyone was asleep. The silence was absolute. I sat near the field telephone, sipping on a bottle of Asahi, waiting for something to happen.

CHAPTER 7

LIFE
GOES ON

At exactly ten o'clock the morning of 27 July 1953, the telephone rang, and a voice came through loud and clear:

—War is over. Cease firing immediately.

I ran out and screamed as loud as I could:

—Cease firing. Cease firing. Cease firing. War is over. OVER. It's over, guys.

Everyone ran out of their bunkers except Gauthier, who was in a deep sleep. I ran over to Gauthier's bunker and woke him up. He did not know whether to believe me or not. He picked up the field phone and got this:

—Alto. Yes, private, war is over. A ceasefire has been signed at Panmunjom.

He dashed out swinging his bush jacket in circles. Then he threw it on the ground, stepping on it and yelled at me in French, knowing that only I could understand his swearing:

—Tabernacle de calice, Eddy. Cette calice de marde est finie. Bring me that case of beer. I've been saving it for this moment. Let's party!

I dragged the case of beer from underneath his bed and opened it. We yelled to our other buddies to come and join us. They all came; even our platoon sergeant joined us.

That day we received the order to expend all the boxes of ammunition that were open. We fired them into no man's land. Later we were informed that the next day we were to move back ten miles away from the front line. We were curious to look at the other side before leaving. A few of us went up the hill to get a view of the enemy position. It was like an anthill. Someone burst out:

—Oh my god. Look what we were up against!

The entire valley was swarming with people. Some seemed to be waving at us, and we could hear them chattering down in the valley. We waved back at them. Peace was that: making friends with yesterday's enemies. Some of the boys on the other side were wearing hats with Chinese writing on them. They were all dressed in white. It was a comforting sight.

Both sides expended their ammunitions by firing into no man's land. We were very cautious, for we did not want to hit North Koreans. Now that we were at peace we had to take care of our enemies like we used to do with our own boys. We were sending a flare signal to warn the other side when we were ready to fire. Then we would shoot with no rush, no pressure. Everything seemed so easy now, even operating a cannon was simple. For that operation I was given a very easy job. I sat on top of a hill with a giant red flag. Every time we were ready to blow, I raised the red flag to warn everyone to go under cover. The noise in no man's land was incredibly loud but so pleasant to hear. It was the song of peace. Since that day, every time I hear fireworks it reminds me of that feeling. Firing was now fun. It was even more fun than practice because we didn't have to worry about pleasing our sergeant. We were just shelling to waste all our ammunitions.

After our stock was all gone, we packed our mortars in a 2-ton truck. It was already dark and the crest line was radiant. Hundreds of trucks and jeeps were illuminating the night with their headlights. We could not believe there were so many vehicles on both sides of the front line. It looked like ballet; each step of these war monsters was easing our souls. I took a break with few comrades. We sat quietly, facing the hills, to contemplate that spectacle and to savour slowly the life ahead of us. That was true happiness.

The next morning, we cleaned up the minefields and blew up hundreds of dud shells. That cleaning job kept us busy for three weeks. Then we destroyed our own bunker, the last position we occupied at hill 355. When we were finished, we waited for orders to be shipped back to Canada. We were to sail from Inchon Bay to Seattle. Before leaving, the U.S. marines gave our battalion a brand new bugle engraved with the words "To third battalion P.P.C.L.I from U.S. Marines —1952–1953 Korea." That was their way of showing their appreciation for our support during combat. We were very proud to be congratulated by the U.S. marines. After all, the marines were known to be the best soldiers. To be congratulated by them was a real honour.

The journey back from Korea to Seattle was long but we had done our duty and the feeling was good. When we passed by Japan, the island of pleasure, all the good memories came back to mind. For days, my comrades talked about the women they had met there. Several of them swore they would come back to get their sweetheart. Some had already asked if they could marry their Japanese girlfriend but they were told it was strictly forbidden. Nevertheless, the boys were making all sorts of plans to return. Still, most knew that once in America they would not have the money to realize their dream. Even if they had found the means to come back to Japan, it would have been so difficult to find women they met years ago, especially during wartime. Now that I think back, I feel sorry for those girls who must have waited in vain for their loved ones. Several of them had babies who looked like American or Canadian soldiers. It certainly must have been difficult for them and for their children who grew up wondering why they did not look like their friends. At that time none of us were thinking about these kinds of things. We were too busy feeling sorry for our own losses while rejoicing because war was over.

Now that I have seen my own village being occupied by an army of workers when a large hydroelectric complex was being built,[1] I realize what these girls endured. In the 1980s the Quebec electric power company had sent 100 men, sometimes more, to camp beside our

---

1. This is the Great Whale project that was supposed to be done in Phase II of the hydroelectric megaproject in James Bay, developed from 1975 onwards by the state-owned Hydro-Québec. The project was never realized but preliminary work took place in Kuujjuarapik, formerly Poste-de-la-Baleine, from 1975 to 1981 and from 1989 to 1992.

community. They met with local girls, offering them alcohol, cigarettes, and drugs and sometimes love too, exactly like we did in Japan.
Once they finished working on the project, they were sent back down
to Montreal. None of them returned. Now if you stroll in the village,
you can see several young adults with mixed parentage. If you ever see
them, think about the hardships their mothers endured.

Now that I am an old man I am wondering if there is not a Japanese
person with some Inuit blood in his veins. Maybe his mother missed
a father for her baby. At least, the baby, if I fathered one, didn't have
to face racism or discrimination because he looked like an American.
That was another good point of being an Inuk in Japan.

For an unknown reason, we could not dock when we arrived in
Seattle. Instead, the captain decided to head to Vancouver and let the
Canadians off first. When we arrived, the harbour was celebrating the
end of war. There were paper streamers flying all over and bands playing.
Almost every soldier was welcomed by his family. I was one of the few to
be alone. There was nobody to greet me except, of course, the Salvation
Army with its coffee and its doughnuts, as always. I could see some of the
parents in tears of joy. I was feeling alone and I wished I had someone
to celebrate with. It was a glorious day and I was sad. I sent a telegram to
Winnie and Frank telling them I was coming back home and wishing to
stay at their place while I was on leave. I had nowhere else to go. I could
not dream of going to my parents because I knew that no plane would fly
to James Bay until January when they could land on skis.

The 3rd Battalion PPCLI received a thirty-day disembarkation leave.
I spent the whole time at Welland, Ontario, where Frank and Winnie
had bought a farmhouse. Once back from my leave, I was transferred
to the 1st Battalion PPCLI, which was a parachutist unit stationed in
Calgary, Alberta. But before joining my new assignment, I was sent to
a training camp in Manitoba. Training was interesting but exhausting.
To become a qualified parachutist you had to make five good jumps
from a C119 aircraft and on top of that you had to complete one night
jump. Once you had succeeded, you would receive your wings.

Beginning in the cold month of February 1954 we spent six weeks
in training. Every morning we would get up at five o'clock for our

half-hour road run, come back for showers and breakfast, and then our day would begin. We were issued bunny suits[2] so we would not be too cold. We were also asked to wear a parachute on our back all day long, or almost all day long, to get used to wearing it. After drill hall, we exercised at the mock tower, where we jumped off and practised the art of landing. Little by little we learned how to tame our fear. We learned not to look down as we jumped but always out towards the horizon so that we would not get dizzy and freeze in panic. We had to make eleven good exits from the mock tower before we could move to the next step. The last week of our training, we jumped from a silo tower with a real parachute. We were strapped into a chairlift and lifted to just about the top and there released. When I realized I was falling into the void, I was so scared that it felt as though my heart went right up into my head. I closed my eyes waiting for the crash. I feared my guts would spill open and my head snap off when I hit the bottom. But nothing happened. That was it. I was on the ground. I had managed to survive my first tower jump. The worst was over for me. Four more good jumps from that tower and I would experience a real leap from a plane.

Unfortunately, I got sick around the end of February. I was pretty ill and was admitted into the hospital only to be released around the middle of March. I was then able to make my other landings. Then I made four jumps out of a C119 cargo plane. I was now waiting for my final jump, the night jump. I waited several days, but the wind was too strong and the officers in charge considered it to be too dangerous to jump. After a long wait, they finally decided to make us jump during daytime, when the wind was better. They blindfolded us to reproduce the night conditions. I managed to do a perfect landing and the next day I was presented with my parachute badge. I returned to my unit in Calgary and reported to my company. During the rest of that winter of 1954, we made various jumps in the surroundings. Each of us had to practice at least once a month to earn his thirty-dollar bonus, granted to a parachutist.

During one of those exercises at Lloyd Lake, Mason, one of our buddies, got shrouded in his parachute and fell on the ice in the middle of

---

2. A full-body protective suit.

the lake. He bounced back into the air like a mannequin and shattered all his bones! The morning of the accident, he was on the second lift and I was on the third. The first lift went all right but the wind changed suddenly, right when Mason jumped. The wind blew in his parachute and it got wrapped all around him, so much that he could not pull his reserve cord and crashed on the frozen lake. The jumps were cancelled for the rest of the day. But the next morning we had to resume the exercises. You can imagine that there were not too many happy faces in the aircraft that day. Even though some smiled, I could tell this was fake. Engines were roaring, and the plane was moving slowly towards the dropping zone. Once arrived, we were told to stand up, hook up, and check our equipment. I was the first on starboard, the guy on the other side made the sign of the cross. We were all standing in, ready to shuffle, when the usual shout came from the dispatcher:

—Is everybody happy?

A very faint "Yeah" came from the jumpers. The light turned green. It was my turn to open the dance. I jumped, trying not to think, following mechanically the instructions learned during my training. I was so stressed that when I went out I started to count out loud to calm down: "One thousand, two thousand, three thousand...." I should have counted to myself because I landed with my mouth wide open and I bit my tongue. It bled badly. My clothes and my reserve parachute got covered with blood. When my sergeant saw me like that, he asked if I was injured. I told him what it was all about, which made him laugh. That night at the wet canteen, everyone was talking of the accident and the ones who jumped that day were proud because they did not "chicken out."

Later during the spring of 1954, we were told that volunteers were needed for the 2nd Battalion in Germany. I put my name down with another guy from my company. In no time we got our needles and all our documents ready and were given a forty-eight-hour pass to celebrate. We were invited to a farewell party. That night I drank so much that I got lost on my way back to the garrison. The last thing I remember before passing out was that I paid ten cents for a paper toilet seat at a Greyhound bus depot. The police must have picked me up there, as I woke up in a cell.

The next morning I had to appear before a magistrate and was fined $25 plus $3.50 for the court costs. Captain Honeymoon, a big, stout officer from my unit, came to bail me out. He was very understanding and did not patronize me. He knew, as he said, that such a thing can happen. However, he told me to report at the holding wing to our regimental sergeant major. RSM Gardener was well known for his loud voice, as if he had a built-in speaker. Some called him the Ventriloquist, When he asked me:

—Why are you reporting to me?

I told him it was because I was volunteering to go to Germany. That was obviously not what he was expecting me to say and he shouted to me:

—Private Vital, you are reporting to me because you are a disgrace to your uniform and your regiment. You are not going anywhere except to receive your sentence.

Effectively, I was redirected to an officer who asked:

—Are you Private Vital, SC-17515?

—Yes, sir.

—I have bad news for you. You are accused of disturbing the public order and being drunk in a public place. The offence happened last night at approximately 04:00. You were found sleeping in a pay toilet and when spoken to by a constable, you could not answer because you were under the influence of an excess of alcoholic beverages. Do you plead guilty or not guilty?

—Guilty, sir.

I was fined another ten dollars and given seven days of detention according to Section 118 of the military code.

I finally got out of the holding wing and went back to my own company to continue parachuting exercises. I was very disappointed. Because of my stupidity, I had missed my chance to go to Germany. During the following winter, we went to Yellowknife for winter training comprising many survival expeditions. We would go out on snowshoes and drag our equipment on toboggans. I was in my natural environment but most of my friends found survival in the North difficult. The smallest thing demanded so much of their energy; they even had a lot of trouble tying on their snowshoes. That's why, although my technique was not in the army manual, I showed them, with the instructor's permission, the Inuit way to slip on snowshoes without having to tie them in the cold. This took a little practice but finally they got used to it and appreciated the difference. I was quite proud of my contribution to the team.

Details of this winter spent at Yellowknife are now fading from my memory but some episodes and images come back like flashbacks. For example, I remember that we were served our meals in thick foil containers and Private Hogue and Private Diggs, my Black friends, hated so much the army food that they lost their appetite. For outdoor training we had to wear our parkas and a white lining over them for camouflage. For jump exercises we had to hook our rifles and snowshoes over our rucksacks in addition to our reserve parachute. One day Diggs told me that he felt like a mummy being strapped in with all that stuff:

—That's funny because we are in the Canadian North but we are dressed up like Egyptian mummies.

At night we would sleep in our bell tents that we tried to warm up with our gas stoves. We were three to a tent. It was quite cold sleeping in those tents and a mist of frost formed inside the tent during the night. Luckily, we were quite comfortable in our warm sleeping bags. Before the sun went up, we pulled down our tents and hurried to melt snow to make tea. After a light breakfast, we loaded our toboggans and got going. Once the exercise was over, we would fly back to Calgary. We were literally piled up with a C119's cargo. It was so full of equipment that we had to lie on top of the gear. The captain in charge had a hard time counting us in such a mess.

I will never forget one of these trips. We were quietly flying over the Northwest Territories, and everybody was sleeping when suddenly we heard the voice of the captain on the speakers. One engine was on fire. I looked around and the only thing that looked like an emergency exit was a window on the ceiling's roof. I felt naked not wearing a chute but I would rather jump than ride down in flames. While I was making plans to escape from fire, the captain announced he was going to circle in order to stop it. If that didn't work, we would have to land as soon as possible. Luckily the flames went out on the second circle. The captain decided to continue to home base with only one engine. Most of us would have rather landed and waited for another taxi but nobody asked us for our opinion. I must say that we found the rest of the trip pretty long and stressful.

When the captain announced that we were flying over Edmonton and it would not be long before we reached Calgary, we felt relieved. We opened a couple of cans of corned beef and ate them with some biscuits out of our c-rations. That was the only thing we could find to celebrate this happy ending. When we landed, there were several trucks waiting to drive us back to the barracks. After that episode, routine resumed and the weeks went by slowly. Day after day, night after night, time stood still, frozen like a cold arctic day. During most of the nights, I was busy partying with my pals. Some mornings I would come back with a black eye, wondering how and where that had happened. Archie, a guy from my company, introduced me to a few girls that we would visit during our furloughs. Several of them had run away from home and were in real trouble. I still remember one of them, Sarah. She was very young and very sweet but she was so naive and innocent. It was pitiful to hear about all the misery she was enduring on skid row. She was from an Aboriginal background and had come to the big city seeking freedom and looking for Prince Charming. I regret I didn't do anything for her before she disappeared for an unknown reason. I feared the worst and I looked for her without luck. I quit searching for her after a while, thinking it was useless.

Later, I met another girl, Joanne, and we soon became very friendly. She reminded me of a girl in my old school days at Fort George. She was bringing back memories from my childhood. From that time when I was still innocent, still a Weetaltuk, still an Inuk living with his family on his own land. I was now drinking too much and my life was a waste. Getting close to Joanne was a way to keep faith, to keep hope for a better future.

Every summer around August we would get our thirty-day annual leave, plus an extra eight days for travelling if we went out of the province. That year I decided to go to Edmonton rather than out of the province. I ended up going there with Diggs and Loyd. Once in town

Loyd and I looked for a hotel. I paid for a week and Loyd paid for one night, since he was going to stay at his sister's place the next day. The next day Loyd and I went to her place. She was staying with one of Loyd's friends. We bought a forty-ouncer of rye whiskey, which we drank in no time. I was so drunk that I was worried I would pass out with all my savings in my pocket. I went to the bathroom and Loyd's friend followed me and we began to chat. He told me that my hotel was not safe, as it had been broken into many times. He advised me to hide my money in my paratrooper boots. I followed his advice and went back to the party and drank more. Pretty soon I fell asleep. When I woke up, Loyd's sister was lacing my boots. When I asked her what she was doing, she told me:

—Don't worry, Eddy. Your boots were unlaced and I was lacing them up.

Somehow I didn't believe her and I got up and left right away. Loyd said he would meet me there later. I took a taxi and once in my room, I got into bed right away and fell asleep on the bed. I was so tired and drunk that I must have forgotten to lock my door because the next thing I knew the light was on and Loyd and his pal were in the room. When I woke up again, I had a lump on the side of my neck and a swollen cheek and jaw. I unlaced my boots to check if my money was still there, but it was gone. I looked around; the only money left was thirty dollars in my wallet. I had been robbed and bitten during my sleep.

I started to look for Loyd and the other fellow. They were downstairs. When they heard me, they came running upstairs asking what had happened to me. I told them what happened and that I had a strong suspicion that one of my friends had robbed me. I told Loyd and his friend:

—You were the only two who knew where my money was. It must be one of you who stole my cash. Just give me my money back and I'll forget everything.

They denied taking it but I could not believe them. I ran downstairs and called the police. They came right away. I told them what had happened and that I suspected my comrade and his friend, though I could not prove anything. Loyd put on an act saying he was so sorry for me and to show his good faith he said he could spare me seven dollars. I refused his money but he put it in my shirt pocket saying he wished he could do more. I could not believe it and the police officers were also a bit sceptical. They asked Loyd and his friend what they had done the day before and what were their plans for the next few days. And they were told to keep their noses clean otherwise the smallest complaint against them would have them arrested without hesitation. However, the police did not search them and let them go free.

After the police left, I spent a short time wondering if I should not go back to the barracks, since I had no more money to support myself. I thought about trying to get a job in Edmonton but there was not much employment in the neighbourhood. Finally, I decided to hitch-hike back to Calgary. It was hard to get a ride inside the city limits and several people gave me distasteful glares. Finally a car pulled over and the driver gave me a lift to the outskirts of Calgary. Once more I stood by the highway with my thumb sticking up. I was very hungry and I was feeling cheap. It was an hour before someone stopped. Once downtown, I rented an apartment for two weeks. With the little money I had, I could not afford much more. After I had settled in, I went to the Queen's Hotel for a few beers, hoping to meet some of my pals. I was lucky. Lynch, a Korean veteran who used to be in my regiment, was there with his girlfriend. I asked him if he knew where I could get a job. He referred me to a nearby sawmill. I went there right after a quick stop at the Esquire Café, where I had a good meal. Once at the shop, I had to wait a long time before being introduced to the woman at the personnel office. When I finally got to her, she gave me a form to fill in. When I was done, she looked at the application and told me:

—I really like your handwriting. I am sure you must be well-educated. Take your application and go downstairs to meet with the foreman.

She gave me the application sheet with a note she had written while she was talking to me. The foreman told me I had the position and I was going to get sixty dollars a week. It was less than what had been stolen from me but it was enough to survive. Still, I was broke and it was going to be tough to wait until the first paycheque. Luckily, Joanne, Lynch's girlfriend, knew my situation and a couple of times brought me a bag full of food: chicken, bread, and butter. Such friendship made me feel like I was back home again. I knew I was just a half-breed Eskimo for most people, that is to say someone who did not belong there. But when I was with my fellow soldiers, I was really a part of the big army family. There, I belonged.

I spent the rest of my leave in Calgary. When I went back to my garrison in early September, our commanding officer told us that we were to leave for Germany next October where we would be stationed for two years. I was all excited about going to Europe. I had always wondered what kind of people the Germans were. I was very curious to see if they were as bad as we were told in school. Now I was going to find out. I was thrilled with the idea that I would soon be able to make up my own mind about the German people.

During September two Inuit, Elaisiak and Sakvoyak, from the Northwest Territories joined our regiment. We all knew that when the time to move out to Germany came, they would not follow but would rather be posted somewhere else in Canada. Back then Inuit could not leave the country because the Canadian government had decided to keep them in the North. That's why one of these Inuit soldiers was sent to Churchill in northern Manitoba and the other posted at Yellowknife, Northwest Territories. I spent the month of September with my fingers crossed, hoping I would be able to go with the boys to Germany. October came with no sign of me being suspected to be "Eskimo." Finally, the list of names of those who were to be posted to Germany came out. My name was on it. What a relief! Nobody had realized I was living under a fake identity. Diggs and Main were the only ones who knew my story but they kept it quiet. I was very grateful to them.

While waiting for departure, we visited our friends in Calgary to say goodbye. For most of us it was just another occasion to party, but for some, departure meant leaving a sweetheart. The ones really in love were desperate. I felt sorry for these mates but knew well that deep inside it was much harder for these girls, as many of them had no other support than their boyfriend. Private Crane, who was in love, decided to marry Audrey, an Indian girl, but he was short of two dollars to buy his marriage licence. I gave him the money as a wedding gift and wished him good luck. One of the girls I used to party with wanted to marry me and was even willing to accompany me to Germany. I was not thrilled by the idea because she was six months pregnant and I didn't know who the father was. I knew how difficult her life and her baby's life would be without a father. She was Indian, had no job and no relatives in Calgary. Hell was her only future. I understood so much her despair. I hesitated a lot but I finally decided not to marry her, because I feared everybody in my garrison would make fun of me. I was picturing them laughing at me:

—Hey, Eddy! How are your wife and my kid?

Later, one evening in October, when we were standing on parade square in full marching order, Captain Potts and Sergeant Major Austin were calling the roll. There were a few missing soldiers, those who could not find their gear in their quarters at the very last minute. One of the late guys was standing at the edge of parade square. Sergeant Major Austin called his name and gave him permission to join the parade and asked him:

—Tell me, Private, are you late because you were stuck at the Chicken Inn? I bet you were kissing your girl goodbye. I hope you kissed her well because you might not have another opportunity.

Everyone burst out laughing but we also understood we were going to be on the move soon. It was around 8:00 p.m. when we were ordered to pack our stuff and to get ready. In no time, the rumour of our departure spread and all the Chicken Inn girls came to see us off.

We were packed in sleeper cars and once again we rode across the prairies. We travelled for days and nights until we arrived at the Montreal harbour. The Salvation Army was waiting to bid us goodbye. A first-class tourist vessel belonging to Cunard Lines, named *Ivernia,* was waiting for us. It was a beautiful ship with all the facilities you could dream of. It had a theatre for movies, bars, beautiful dining rooms, well-trained waiters who balanced their trays regardless of how rough the sea was. Bellboys would warn us when it was time for meals. I could hardly believe I was sailing in such luxury. It was like I was part of the upper society. For an Inuk like me coming from the Canadian tundra, it was a real achievement. I could not avoid thinking of my family and all the misery my father had endured to feed his family. I was definitely lucky and grateful to God for having spared me and let me enjoy a bright life, filled with adventures. That night, I could not fall asleep; memories from my childhood were coming back. I could not avoid recalling my first trip on a boat, when the missionaries took my brother and me to the residential school at Fort George. That memory brought tears to my eyes.

In the middle of the Atlantic we were hit by a big storm; the waves looked like endless mountains. One of our buddies was almost swept away by a giant wave. The waves were so powerful that they even broke several thick windows. During the storm, I went to the theatre to watch a movie, thinking it would get my mind off the storm. During the show, because of the violent pitching, the piano came off its six-inch spikes and crashed onto the first rows of seats, smashing them. I was lucky I did not choose to sit close to the screen; it would have been the end of my adventures. What a strange end it would have been for an Eskimo to be crushed by a piano in the middle of the Atlantic! Finally, after a long journey we arrived at Rotterdam in the Netherlands. While waiting to disembark, we had a roll call. When Captain Potts called my name, he asked if I could speak German. I answered:

—No, sir, but I will learn.

—I don't doubt that, Private, since I was told you already speak four languages. We'll count on you to show the Germans that Canadians are good boys and can learn their language well and quick.

I was thinking it would have been a pity to be crushed by a piano before getting that compliment from an officer.

Once we disembarked at Rotterdam, we got onto trains heading to Germany. It was my first time in Europe and I was eager to learn more about this mythic continent. As our train started to move, I looked at the houses, which seemed to me very crowded. Once on the outskirts of the city, I looked at the sky. It was dull grey. At one point the train stopped on a bridge and from where I was seated I was able to look at the street. It was built of cobblestones. There were hardly any cars but I had never seen so many bicycles. They were lining up for blocks waiting for the green light to go. These cyclists were all workmen and workwomen. I felt sorry for them to be stuck in such a grey environ-ment and forced to cycle every day back and forth to their work, sum-mer and winter alike. Before entering Germany, we passed through Holland and I saw a couple of those windmills like the ones in the Eu-ropean masters' paintings. When I was in school at Fort George with my brother David, pictures of these paintings were on our copybooks. I felt lucky to be able to see with my own eyes the inspiration for such well-known masterpieces. I was thinking that I should write to David, who had trouble filling his notebooks with mathematic formulas and irregular verbs, that I had seen the originals.

As we crossed the border into Germany, the train was stopped by customs. The Polizei entered the train to check how many troops there were inside. This was the first time I ever heard German and it sounded a bit like Inuktitut to me because of their special sounds, "aaks" and "arrgs," and of course the famous "Achtung." The German police wore beautiful green uniforms and marched very smartly. They were also very polite. I was thinking to myself how I was in the very country that had terrorized and almost conquered the world and these men were once the most feared soldiers. Soon after reaching the border, the train set into motion and raced across Germany. First we crossed Dort-mund, then Iserlohn, Hemer, Deilinghofen and finally we reached our destination, Camp Fort MacLeod, next to Fort Prince of Wales, an-other military facility of the occupying armies.

The Canadian, U.S., British and other armies that were stationed in Germany were there to protect Germany from the Soviets as well as occupying forces. We were told to be exemplary. We were supposed to behave as well as, or even better than, in our own country. This wasn't Japan or Korea. Here we were ordered to act as civilized persons. For two years we had the same commanding officer, Lieutenant Colonel Defaye, and he never missed an opportunity to remind us of the rules:

—If anyone gets caught disturbing peace or fighting, whatever the reason is, he will be sentenced to thirty days of detention. I will not bother asking any questions. I don't care if you are responsible or if you are the victim. If you are in the middle of a fight you will serve your time in an army prison, take my word. I will not bend the rules for anyone. My best advice is to stay as far as you can from trouble and potential places of trouble. You know what I mean.

When I was on leave, I enjoyed going to Iserlohn and Dortmund to visit German cities. I was also looking for a girlfriend who could speak English so I could learn German from her. At first I had no success until I met a private in Iserlohn who had a lot of experience in the place. I asked him if he knew some girls who could speak English. He told me he had met one at Heinz's Gasthof, a bar where old paratroopers from the Second World War used to hang out. He warned me:

—The girl speaks good English but she is money hungry.

I decided to meet her anyway and he showed me the way to the bar. The bar was located down a narrow street. Inside the bar, the light was dimmed low. We picked the first table on the right. Heinz, the owner who spoke a little English, asked what we wanted to drink. We ordered an Iserlohner Pilsner, a mild beer. There was a Lotto Mat, a small gambling machine in a corner of the bar. Around 2:00 p.m., we put ten pfennigs in it. While we were playing, my friend pointed at a girl who just came in:

—There is your girl!

She was a tall blonde with blue eyes that really sparkled. She looked so swell. My friend pulled out a ten-mark bill and flashed it around telling me this would make her come over to play at the Lotto Mat. Indeed she came over pretty soon after. My friend asked if she wanted a beer or a cognac. She ordered a cognac and we had another beer. He asked her if she wanted to sit down with us. She agreed but she sat far away from me, staring at me with curiosity, which made me feel uneasy. Finally, as I could not stand it anymore, I told her:

—I don't know what makes you look at me like that, but I am not Chinese if that's what you want to know. I am half-Eskimo, half-Canadian and I don't bite people.

She looked surprised, stared at me for a minute or so, and finally asked what my name was. I told her:

—Eddy. Eddy Vital.

Then she said very kindly:

—Nice to meet you Eddy. My name is Clara and I don't bite either, unless you ask for it!

She spoke such good English that one could think she came from England. We chatted for a little while. At the end of the night I asked if I could come back to see her.

—Any time, Eddy. You will always be welcome.

She added that she liked Canadian cigarettes. I gave her my spare pack and told her:

—Next time I'll bring a carton for you, if you teach me German!

—It's a deal, Eddy. A carton and you will speak German!

Finally, I was getting to know real German people. I was so happy and so fond of Clara. She was so beautiful, so clever. She was everything a man, every man, was looking for. Once back at Camp Fort MacLeod, I continued thinking about that beautiful encounter. I could not wait for my next leave to see Clara again. I was so scared that in the meantime another man would steal her heart. The next day I told all my friends about Clara. They made fun of me because I was in love after just one evening with a girl. I did not pay attention to their sarcastic remarks because I was too happy and too busy counting the days before I was going back to Heinz's bar. The next leave was one week from then. It was almost an eternity for a young man in love. What I did not know was that one week was indeed nothing compared to the time I was really going to wait before meeting her again.

CHAPTER 8

In Prison and
IN LOVE

I spent the rest of the week at the wet canteen trying to kill the time before going back to Heinz's bar to meet Clara. However, instead of drinking just enough to have nice dreams, I drank so much one night that I got really high. Once in that state, I couldn't wait any longer before seeing her. I decided I was going to find her at any cost. Because of my drunken condition and because I had no pass, the guard refused to let me out when I tried to walk out the gate of the barracks. He told me to sober up and sent me back to my quarters. I went back to lie down but I could not sleep. I kept thinking about Clara. I figured I should find an excuse to leave the premises. I did not know what excuse would be good enough, so I decided to get up and go to the canteen to have a strong coffee to clear my mind. Unfortunately, that did not work out and the waiter told me to get back to my quarters and sleep it off, but it was in vain. Clara kept coming into my mind and I still couldn't sleep.

In the middle of the night I went out and checked the wire fence surrounding the camp. It was hopeless; I could never jump over it. I was going to abandon the idea when suddenly I remembered I had brought a good pair of wire cutters from Korea and they were still in my kit bag. I hurried back to get them. A few minutes later I had cut a big hole in the fence at a place where nobody could see me. I was so drunk and so angry because the guard did not let me out that I cut a huge hole, big enough to drive a two-ton truck through. Once on the street, I got a taxi to Iserlohn but I did not go directly to Heinz's bar, thinking the military police might be checking the place looking for soldiers without a pass. Instead I went to the train station and had some German white wine to kill the time. I was still thinking about getting to Clara but my plan was to look for her in the morning when the military police were usually less suspicious. The German wine was too much. When I finally thought it was time to get on the move, I was so drunk that I could hardly walk. The military police spotted me right away. They stopped and searched me. They found the wire cutters, used to open a hole in the barracks' fence, with my initials on them. I was driven to the guardhouse and locked up for the rest of the night.

The next morning I was returned to my quarters and ordered to put on my uniform and march to the battalion's orderly room. They had me stand against the wall for what seemed an eternity. Finally Sergeant Major Austin bellowed my name. I stepped forward and I followed him. We turned left and marched until we halted in front of the commandant's office. Then we made a left turn to face it. I stood between my escorts waiting in front of the door. When it opened, he shouted my name and asked if I was "SC-17515 Private Vital." I answered and he charged me under section 118. Then he read the military police report.

—At approximately 04:00 Private Vital was found at the train station in Iserlohn supporting himself against the walls unable to move, obviously under the influence of alcohol. When approached by military police, he tried to resist arrest. When searched by the arresting officers, he was found with a pair of wire cutters bearing his initials. It was later discovered that these wire cutters had been used to open a hole in Camp Fort MacLeod's fence by which Private Vital had escaped.

I was asked if I pleaded guilty. I did so. As a result, I was rightly sentenced to thirty days at Soest's prison, sentence starting immediately. While serving in Korea, I heard a lot about American jails or detention stockades. The boys used to say that you were allowed to smoke and you did not lose your pay. I was soon to discover that it was quite another story in our jail. I tell you, Canadian army prison is not a picnic.

I was driven to the Soest prison in a jeep. It was a long drive. I took advantage of it to smoke as many cigarettes as possible. The driver told me that once inside it would be forbidden. When I arrived, I was turned over to the sergeant. He made me circle around the centre of the detention barracks three times on the run, my rifle at high port over my head. Sweat was pouring down my face. I was breathing heavily and at one point I saw stars and feared I was going to pass out. Finally the sergeant yelled to halt. I remembered not to call him "Sergeant" but "Staff." Indeed, everyone was addressed "Staff" in prison, except for "Sergeant Major," who was addressed as "Sir." He ordered me to come inside and then to place my whole kit on the floor, except for my dog tag. After he checked out everything, he ordered me to put my kit back together and to put on black coveralls with a yellow round target on the back. Then I reported to the store man, a lance corporal with a big yap who yelled at everyone.

I repacked my kit and took everything except my rifle and marched to my cell, a sergeant yelling from behind me "left, right, left, right" the whole time. Once in my cell, he pushed a galvanized rusty bucket towards me and sneered:

—Clean it shiny!

I answered:

—Yes, Staff.

This one was definitely trained to get prisoners to hate him. I started to scrape the bucket with a bath rock. Once I was finished, I was instructed to lay out my kit on the wooden bed. Only then did I take the time to look around and to assess my new situation. The bed had no mattress, no sheets, no pillow, only a blanket. On top of the wooden plank there was a Gideon Bible. Above the bed there was a small trap window with three steel bars letting air and light through. The guard had told me I was not allowed to close it. To the left of the bed was a wooden table. All of this was going to be home for the next month. That was tough but it could have been bearable if the guards had not done their very best to make you feel miserable.

Every morning we had to wash ourselves with cold water, even though there was hot water in the prison. We also washed our clothes in cold water and let them dry on our wooden table. As we were doing the washing, the guard walked back and forth in the corridor staring at us. Every now and then, we could hear the clanks of cell doors releasing prisoners who were done with their washing. Once outside of the cell, we had to stand by our door. When everybody was ready, we were ordered to march with our buckets towards the ditch. But before we could empty them, we had to run around the square twice, sometimes three times. Then we had to stand to attention with our bucket in the right hand waiting for the next command. Once the buckets were emptied, we would march back to our cells to work on our kit, which meant polishing our boots all day long by spitting on them. What nonsense! How could they believe that such meaningless treatment would improve someone's personality? Spitting on my boot was driving me crazy. That life was so remote from my Inuit life in the tundra.

Every morning after breakfast our kit would be laid out on our wooden bunk and the camp commandant would inspect the premises, going from cell to cell. During the inspection one had to stand to attention against the bottom wall, nose almost touching the wall, waiting for the inspection to be over. Part of the routine was the commandant's ritual question, asking if anyone had any complaints. Of course the only possible answer was a humble:

—No complaint, Sir.

One night, I could not stand the cold anymore and I closed my trap window. One of the staff noticed it and decided to teach me a lesson. He put me in front of the window, opened the trap, and forced me to stay in the breeze. The cold nearly knocked me out but simultaneously sparked memories from my childhood in northern Canada. Suddenly, I was not in prison anymore, but back in the tundra, in a small Inuit house with a candle keeping me warm. No more lock, no more hole in the door, and no one peeking at me. I had no electricity or wood stove, but I was not cold in my warm caribou parka. I was feeling good, the breeze was killing my sinuses but I was happy. I was a free man, an Inuk. If the guard had known the good he was doing me, he would have stopped the punishment right away.

Guards would take every opportunity to humiliate the inmates. They would not give you your food but would rather throw your loaf of bread and you had to catch it like a dog. If anyone spilled his food, he would have to take his spoon and eat the food from the floor. Every night before we went to our wooden bed, we lined up for the shower parade. The guard would select a detainee to turn on the showers. One of the guards always chose Antonio, an African-Canadian detainee, because his organ was supposed to be bigger than others'. He would send him naked to turn on all the showers. While he was walking, the guard would make fun of him, speaking of his "tar paper penis," and the poor guy would answer:

—Yes, Staff.

The staff would watch to see if any of us was trying to steal a peek at Antonio. If he caught anyone looking at him, he would take the man's name and cell number and the next day that man would be the one to turn on the showers and the guard would find a way to make fun of him. Once I dared a look to see if Antonio's feelings were hurt by the guard's insults. Seeing Antonio's eyes I realized how desperate he was. It seemed there was no end to him being tormented because of his skin colour. It was well known that Antonio was serving a five-year sentence for stabbing two Germans who called him "Black Bastard" in a restaurant. He was proud and had fought for his honour. The humiliation he was subjected to in that circumstance must have been so painful for him. I was very sympathetic to him but could not say a word because I would have been punished for showing my disapproval of the guard's behaviour.

Unfortunately, the staff read my mind and next day it was my turn to be the laughingstock. The little runt of a lieutenant corporal who was on duty that night hated my guts only because I looked different. He sneered through the lineup and stopped in front of me, got close to my face, stared at me with hate in his eyes, and tried to distract me from looking forward. He yelled:

—Are you Vital? Are you the bastard who looked at Antonio's balls last night?

—Yes, Staff. I am.

Obviously he was waiting for me to say no, so he could call me a liar. Since I had managed to avoid his trap, he redirected his attack:

—Are you that freaking Eskimo who can speak four languages?

—Yes, Staff, I am.

—So, Private Vital, if you got Eskimo blood in your veins, get into the shower and turn on the cold water tap and show everybody how an Eskimo showers.

After that episode, the pitiful days went by but nothing really special happened to me until one night. The sergeant who had caught me closing my trap window and who had been snooping around me ever since, came into my cell. He made me stand to attention against my table, put his left leg over it, and asked:

—How long have you been a detainee?

—Twenty-four days, Staff.

—You must find the time long, Private. Long enough, isn't it?

—Yes, Staff.

—I guess you understand that you're in here because you're a retard.

—Yes, Staff.

—So, to encourage you, I have decided to allow you a cigarette.

He took a puff of his cigarette and slowly blew smoke in my face asking:

—Do you deserve a cigarette, Vital?

—No, Staff. I don't deserve a cigarette because I closed my window when I knew it was forbidden.

—Good, Private. Good, you're learning. Keep learning like that and you will get a cigarette. In the meantime, keep your cell tidy and your table clean.

Then he butted his cigarette out on my clean table and walked out. As soon as he was gone, I scraped out the dark spot and threw the butt in my bucket.

The next morning I got up and made my bed as usual. However, this particular morning everything went wrong for me. I happened to be the last in the meal lineup and when my turn came to yell my number, I only yelled "24," while I should have yelled:

—Detainee 24, on parade, Staff.

Because of that mistake, we all had to start over. Then, the same sergeant who had come to my cell the night before forced me to say that I did not deserve breakfast. The snoopy sergeant came into my cell and checked my table and asked if it was clean. I said:

—Yes, Staff.

—No, it isn't! It's dirty. Look at that!

And he pointed at the burnt spot he had made with his cigarette. He ordered me to report to the commandant. I felt like the world had come down on me.

I expected to spend more time in detention for insubordination. To my surprise, the commandant was lenient and only fined me five dollars. He warned me to keep a low profile for my last days of detention. After that episode, the guards were easy on me and finally the day came for me to be released. It was the happiest day of my entire life. Actually I was the happiest man on earth. I still remember when the sergeant told me to get all my gear packed and to turn in my bucket, my brush, and what was left of my soap. When I went through the door of my cell, I passed by the lieutenant corporal who had made fun of my Inuit background and forced me to take a cold shower. When he saw me gleaming with joy, it was like I had slapped him in the face. He was furious and sneered at me with his crooked smile and stared into my eyes with hate and mumbled:

—Don't worry. You'll be back, Eskimo-boy, and I'll be waiting for you.

Before being released from the prison, I was directed to the sergeant major's office. He gave me my belongings out of the locker where they had been stored while I was away. I had two packs of cigarettes plus two dollars Canadian and forty Deutschmarks (DM) in my wallet. Sergeant Major told me to keep out of trouble. I thanked him and was marched out. The provost who brought me in was happy for me. To celebrate with me he gave me a cigarette. I told him I had two packs but he insisted:

—Take it, it's on me. Anyway, yours are probably dried up.

I was just about to burst into tears. It had been so long since someone was kind to me. I was feeling so good. I was free and I was having a smoke with a real human being. I inhaled so much smoke that I got dizzy and felt drunk, but the feeling was so great.

That night everyone cheered to see me back. Corporal Lewis asked if I wanted a few days off. I almost told him I did not deserve it, when I realized he was really offering me a pass. I put on my civilian clothes. Diggs and Main lent me fifty Deutschmarks. Everyone was so friendly, even old Larrison, our company sergeant major, seemed to understand what I had endured. When I came to him with the pass prepared by Corporal Lewis, he did not hesitate to sign it. Before leaving the barracks, I went to the barbershop to try to make my bald head look like a brush cut. Unfortunately it did not work out because my hair was really too short but that was nothing to ruin my day. When I headed out the gate, the sentry guard did not even check me. Once out of the gate, I took a taxi to Heinz's Gasthof in Iserlohn, hoping Clara would be there. It was early afternoon when I walked in the bar. Clara was there. She gave me a big hug and a kiss. I had brought a carton of cigarettes like I had promised. She had tears in her eyes and ruffled up my hair. Heinz sent over a round of beer and said it was on him. Barney, a friend of mine, had told Clara my story and how I had gotten myself in trouble. Now that I was with Clara I was ready to forget all the humiliation and suffering I had endured for a month. I was back with my pals and I was in love!

My relationship with Clara became steady pretty soon. We were lovebirds and were acting like an old couple. I made the habit of giving her 40 DM every time I was paid so she could buy herself new clothes. She had an odd job in one of the factories in Iserlohn and barely made enough to support herself. I was proud to be able to support a woman. I felt like a real man, at least like a man ought to be in a modern society. Actually I didn't tell her my real background. I didn't want her to know that my parents back home were the poorest of the poor. So poor that they had to live in tents and had barely any food to eat. I wanted her to think that my relatives were wealthy like all the other Canadians. I figured that what she did not know would not hurt her.

I knew pretty well what my fellow Canadians thought of the Aboriginal people at that time. That is why I did not brag about my origins but I did not forget where I came from. I would write, from time to time, to my sister Ann and I sent her some money for my parents. I knew it was not enough, almost nothing compared to their needs, but I could not afford to send them more. I needed my money to be able to stick with my pals. I remember that that year, just before Christmas, I went over to the Westfälische Bank and withdrew 1000 DM. I gave

400 DM to Clara and was counting on spending 100 to buy some Christmas gifts and sending the rest to my parents. But once my shopping was done, I realized I had nothing left. I was feeling so selfish. I had spent all my money on useless purchases while my parents were lacking everything.

That 23 December we had our Christmas dinner at the barracks. Our senior officers served us. This was the only time we could tell the officers what to do. After the feast we returned to our quarters to change into civilian clothes. We were issued a four-day pass. The canteen was opened and with my cigarette cards I was able to buy a couple of cartons. Clara liked Black Diamond chocolates. I got her a box. I had a couple of beers at the canteen with the boys and then got a ride to Iserlohn's Gasthof. I gave Clara her carton of cigarettes and the chocolates. We chatted for a while, and then we went to Willie Herring's, a friend of Clara's. He was a former paratrooper who had been wounded during the Second World War.

When we arrived, the party was already on. Willie had a full closet of strong liquor of all kinds. He invited me to take everything I wanted and to make myself at home. I asked for a cognac; he pulled out a bottle and told me to drink it slowly, as it was very strong. The night was very pleasant. Willie and I had a lot in common, we had both been on the battlefield and we talked a lot about war. I was amazed when I realized that I was getting friendly with someone who had fought my country. That is when I decided I should go back to Korea to see for myself who the people I had fought really are. When I told Willie I wished my family could see how great the party was, he took some pictures for me to bring back home to Canada. Unfortunately, my dad would die before I could show him the pictures.

Willie was married to a woman everyone called Pepe. She was a smart woman, chubby and very natural. She used to talk to me in German and Clara would translate. Pepe's and Willie's place was next to the Cathedral. When bells rang for the midnight mass, we were already very high. Only Pepe was sober enough to go to church. She left us saying she would pray for all of us. Willie opened two more bottles of cognac. We drank them and suddenly Clara stood up, saying that the place was too hot and to our surprise, she began to undress. Willie and I felt embarrassed and turned our heads away, but some guests were laughing looking at Clara singing half-undressed. I turned red with blushing; I went outside for a few minutes to get some fresh air. When I came back, everyone seemed quiet and Willie proposed a toast to Christmas. We put on some good Christmas music and Clara cuddled up close to me. I still remember the record. It was *Little Drummer Boy*. That night Clara and I slept on the kitchen couch that Pepe had prepared for us. This was true happiness.

We slept like angels and woke up around ten o'clock the next morning. Pepe was just returning from low mass. Bells were still going strong. She told us not to hurry and poured us coffee. Once awake, Clara looked at me. She was embarrassed and asked me:

—I hope I didn't hurt your feelings last night when I took off my top. I don't know what happened to me. I guess I lost control. Will you forgive me?

She was so cute, so adorable. I told her with a big smile:

—Of course I forgive you. I love you so much, Clara. I love all of you, even your mistakes.

Clara jumped off the bed to tell Pepe and Willie what I had just said. Then she came back in a hurry and gave me a big hug and kissed me on the cheek. Willie shook my hand and kissed Clara. It sounded like we were engaged.

Later that day we all went to Heinz's Gasthof, where Clara's aunt and Iris were waiting for us. Iris was Clara's little daughter. She was in the aunt's custody. Indeed, when Clara gave birth to her baby, she was too young to take care of her child. Clara's aunt had decided to foster her niece, but every time she came to town she would bring Iris with her so she could visit her mother. When Clara introduced me to her aunt, I told her in English:

—Nice to meet you Madam. It is Christmas and I bought a gift for you.

The aunt looked so surprised and turned to Clara with a question on her face. Clara translated to her aunt what I had just said. Then she explained to me why her aunt looked so surprised. In German the word "gift" means "poison," that's why she looked so surprised!

Iris used to call me Uncle Eddy. The more I got to know her, the more I was getting attached to that little girl. At one point I even considered adopting her. But to adopt Iris I would have to marry Clara. In fact, I really thought about making the big proposal but I decided not to because I knew I could not get married without revealing my true identity and that would have been the end.

Besides, I was not sure how long Clara would have stayed with me after she found out how really poor my family was. She was trying to get out of poverty herself and I don't think she was dreaming of adopting the Inuit way of life. Indeed, after my time in Germany was over the only way for us to stay married would have been for me to come back to Canada with her. Once in Canada it would have been a rude awakening for her. I was picturing her having to sleep on the floor of an overcrowded small matchbox-house, while the cold blizzard blew outside for nights and days. How could my swell Clara have slept among the many children shivering in the cold and crying all night long because of hunger?

My gut feelings were confirmed by a story I had heard and that definitively convinced me I should not marry Clara. Apparently a few years before my stay in Germany, a Native Indian from Canada married a beautiful German woman. Before marrying her, he had told her that he lived on a beautiful farm. But once back in Canada, after he had finished his service in Germany, his wife realized that the beautiful farm was in fact an Indian reserve with no running water, no sewer, and no facilities, and that his folks were living in an old shack. When she realized the living conditions of the Indian people in Canada, she just jumped back onto the train and headed to Germany. Once home, she told her sad story to everybody and cried for months. She was really in love but could never endure such poverty. I sure did not want the same thing to happen to Clara if she married me. I was twice as badly off as this poor Indian fellow. Somehow I was hoping Clara would thank me some day for sparing her going from poor to poorer. However, it was a real torture for me not to be able to envision my entire life with her by my side.

During the time we were in love, Clara and I wanted to be together as much as possible, but there was always something happening that kept us apart. Once I ended up again in the Soest prison for fighting with a German police officer. When the fight began, Clara cried, telling me to stop because she did not want us to be separated. I felt very much the same way but powers from nowhere pushed me to keep kicking the officer. As a result Clara and I were kept apart for another thirty days. Though, this time I only spent fifteen days in prison, as I was released to go on a forced march with my company. It was a sixty-mile march from Deilinghofen to Sennelager. That punishment felt like a picnic compared to detention, though my heels started bleeding on the third day. I was not the only one in that shape. Captain Honeymoon, who walked behind me, was too overweight for this sort of exercise and was in a lot of pain. I can still picture him with sweat running down from his forehead, burning his eyes. Despite the pain, he kept talking to me. At first I could not understand why he was not saving his energy but I came to realize that speaking was his only way not to collapse.

Finally, we reached Sennelager. When we entered our camping area, Colonel Defaye took a salute. As we marched past him some of us were stumbling, exhausted by these three days of forced walk. We could see that Colonel Defaye's arm was not as high, as proud as usual, and it seemed to take him a great deal of effort to salute, though he could still afford a smile. We finally dropped our gear. Diggs and Main came over to cheer me up and to invite me to join them at the wet canteen. We all had a cold beer; the first swallow was pure satisfaction. Later, we sat on a grassy area and relaxed. We could hear the roar and rumble of other fellows, clanking their bottles of ice-cold beer together. The day after, we went over to the rifle range to practise our firing. After the end of the exercise, we headed back to Camp Fort MacLeod.

At last, I was back to my sweet love. A few days later I was granted fourteen days of leave and I tried to convince Clara to come with me on vacation. Many of my friends were taking advantage of their leaves to visit Europe's beautiful cities: Copenhagen, Amsterdam, Hamburg, Strasbourg, München, Köln, and I wanted to do the same. Unfortunately, I could not convince Clara to travel; she preferred to stay in Iserlohn to work. She wanted to send money to her aunt for Iris. Since I could only see Clara during my holidays, I chose to stay close to her.

I was already taken away from her too often due to my mischief and to army requirements that I was not going to go on a tour without her.

Life as a soldier in Germany was nice and easy, as long as you did not get in trouble, and I liked Germany very much. It was a beautiful country and the people were friendly. Our marches in the countryside were not hard because we travelled on paved roads, which meant we did not eat dust all day long, in comparison to Alberta and Manitoba where there are mostly gravel roads. When in exercise, we camped in fields by farms where we could steal fresh potatoes, turnips, carrots, apples, and other fruit. We did not feel guilty, as we knew the farmers could claim reimbursement for the damages made by the troops to their farms. I really enjoyed camping on the farms because it reminded me of the training I received from Brother Martin. Some nights I would picture what my life would have been if he had realized his dream of giving me his parents' farm. I really had a preference for an outdoors life. I think I would have enjoyed being a farmer. I like animals and I like working hard. Farming could have been a nice way for me to make a living. However, I am not complaining. I also enjoyed the army because it allowed me to discover the world and the different people who inhabit it.

I noticed quite rapidly that German people are very religious. When walking in the countryside, I was surprised to see that many crosses and statues at the edges of the fields. They were always in good condition, tidy with flowers growing around. I also noticed that Germans were respectful of their fellow men and I rarely saw a German refusing food or money to a beggar. The more I was learning about Germans the less I was able to understand how they could have committed such atrocities during the Second World War. The only explanation I could come up with was that even the most advanced civilizations are governed by human beings, and when they abandon God, they fall under the Devil's influence.

I was amazed by the way German people were keeping their trees, parks, and gardens always clean. I remember one of the beautiful camp-sites where we stayed for a while. The road going to it was tree-lined on each side. The trees were majestic; they must have been planted over a century ago. They were all lined up as if they were themselves soldiers at parade. I was also impressed by the relationship the Germans had with nature; they had a lot of respect for it, especially for the animals. They also enjoyed hunting. Even though they only did it for pleasure and not for survival like the Inuit, they had developed very sophisticated techniques. They were very well organized and took a lot of precautions to never shoot anyone by mistake. They used to set small cabins high in the trees. Some hunters would hide in them while others would make noises to chase the deer in the direction of the hunting nests. Every time they killed a deer, they would never fail to celebrate the hunt at a local bar. I realized how important the celebration of the hunt was for them, but sharing food was much less important. I realized that this was a big difference between Inuit and Germans.

I was also pretty amazed to see that Germans, like Inuit, have their hunting stories. Some are memories of good or special hunting trips. Others are myths that are passed on from one generation to another that every hunter knows. When my German friends realized that I was fond of hunting stories, they began to tell me a lot of them. There is one story that I will remember forever. The story goes like this. In old ages, hunters from an isolated village saw a very large deer roaming around in the woods. But that deer, a big mare, was not a regular deer, for it was wearing a cross right between its antlers. The rumours of that miraculous deer spread around and people became scared of going out in the forest in case the deer turned out to be a devil or a bad spirit. However, one man, Jägermeister, the mayor of the town, did not believe this story and decided to go hunt this mysterious animal. The next Sunday he went out, promising he would soon hang the trophy on his wall. Once in the forest, he suddenly saw the biggest deer he had ever seen. The deer started to walk towards him, staring at him. The mayor aimed at the deer right between the eyes but at the exact moment when he was going to shoot, a bright cross appeared between the antlers. The mayor was paralyzed with fear. He dropped to his knees and crawled towards the cross while a voice was asking him:

—Jägermeister, why don't you go to church on Sundays? Go back home and tell your people to follow the Ten Commandments instead of destroying God's creation.

Jägermeister was so scared that he could hardly speak. The deer sent by God finally vanished in the bushes and the poor man hurried back home and told everyone what had happened. After that people from his town became very pious and no one ever killed a deer again.

Months went by and I was beginning my second year in Germany. Clara and I were getting closer every day and I was behaving like I was her husband. Hence, I have to say she did not like it when I would tell her what to do. She was a free woman and did not want to fall under the influence of a man. As a result we often argued. One week when our battalion was leaving for a three-day outdoor exercise, I told Clara to stay home and not to go out at night while I was away. I knew it sounded as if I was jealous and I guess it was real jealousy. She told me not to worry and promised she would stay home and wait for me. Somehow I did not believe her. I suspected she was planning something, that's why I warned her, telling her that she would regret it if she did not follow my advice. The next day I left and I could only hope she would keep her promise.

The second night of our trip we camped in a field. I was ready to fall asleep when my tent began to shake. I yelled to my neighbour, Yastry, a Metis from Saskatchewan, to stop shaking my tent. He laughed and told me that his own tent was also trembling and he thought I was trying to scare him. Since it was neither he nor I, we concluded a storm was beginning and got out of our tent to check if the pegs were well fixed, but to our surprise everything was calm, oddly calm. A full moon was shining; there was no breeze and not a soul in sight. Obviously, it was not the wind. Again, I asked Yastry to admit it was him, but he swore that he did not shake my tent. Since it wasn't me either, we decided to call it imagination and went back to sleep.

However, before falling asleep, I recalled stories from my childhood. Everything became clear. My tent did really shake and it was a sign, like the signs sent to the Inuit by the Spirits. Such signs happen when the Spirits want to warn you because your loved ones are in danger, hurt, or need help. However, I tried to get rid of the idea by telling myself that it was only a superstition. After all, I was now living in the modern world where there is no such thing as Spirits, signs, and other irrational thoughts. Comforted by that idea, I fell asleep and woke up the next morning without any bad ideas. But around noon a man approached me and asked if I knew a girl named Clara. Reality had caught up with me. I may be living in the rational world but I was still an Inuk and the Spirits had talked to me. That man was going to tell me that Clara was in danger. I was so shocked that I could hardly ask:

—My girlfriend is named Clara. Something happened to her?

—She was injured in a car accident. There was a man with her. Did you know him? His name was Fraser.

—Was...?

—Yes, he died in the accident.

—I don't know him. How is Clara?

—She broke an arm and a wrist. When the ambulance came, she was screaming your name and asked that you be informed of her situation.

—Thank you, sir.

As soon as we arrived at Camp Fort MacLeod, I rushed to the hospital but instead of being happy to see me, Clara blamed the accident on me, saying I had wished her Bad Luck. I argued, saying that she should have listened to me and stayed quiet at home. After that accident, our relationship changed a lot and we were now always quarrelling. I was young and very stubborn and did not know how to express my true feelings. Finally, during one of our quarrels we broke up. I thought she would come back because she was so much in love. But she was too proud to make the move, and I was too stupid to run after her when there still was time.

We did not see each other for a year but she was always in my thoughts and I was making all sorts of plans to get back with her. Life was ugly and phony without Clara. When the time to get back to Canada came, I started to look desperately for Clara. I did not want to leave Germany without saying goodbye. I was also secretly hoping to reunite with her. I wanted badly to see Clara but I did not know where to find her, thus I looked for her in every bar. One night, I walked into the Texas Bar and I saw Clara. She was with a man. I thought: "She is really finished with me." Still, I wanted to talk to her, but when I walked towards her, she got up and walked out. I don't know if she saw me and chose to ignore me, or if she left without seeing me, and I will never know because I didn't have the guts to stop her. I took a last long look at her, saying to myself, "Goodbye dear love," and she disappeared into the night. I knew it was the end of the love story of my life. I was really beat-up and I felt like crying but instead I got drunk. That was the only reasonable thing to do. I had met the best woman on earth. I should have married her but I didn't because I was too ashamed of my background. Such stupidity had no cure. Today I think if I had been courageous enough to tell her my whole story, that I was indeed a poor Inuk trying to survive under a fake identity, she probably would have understood and loved me all the more.

The day was approaching for our departure and the Canadian customs officers were checking our boxes before we sealed them for shipment. We were to proceed from Deilinghofen to Rotterdam, where a tourist ship from Cunard Lines named *Neptunia* was waiting for us. I was full of regrets about Clara so I tried to change my frame of mind by making plans for the life ahead of me once back home. But despite my efforts, I was always thinking of her and wondering if I would see her again, or if there would be another girl to take her place. I was also anxious to know if she would marry another man, maybe the one I saw her with at that bar. I hoped the guy was wealthy enough to spare her from misery. I knew how she felt about being poor. I was thinking how we were in the same situation, Clara and I, trying to find a way out of misery. I am grateful to the army for helping me to make my life much better. I hope Clara found her way too. Now that I am old and back in my community I try to help others to improve their lives, and I hope that young Inuit boys and girls will read about my humble life and will find in it inspiration to achieve their goals. Nowadays, traditional values are not so popular among the new generation. The elders' advice is not always listened to and many young have lost faith in God and in themselves. I wish to tell them: your life belongs to you. You are the ultimate master of your destiny, so don't let despair, alcohol, or drugs control you. Be yourself, be proud. Be proud of being Inuit and always remember that our ancestors had to fight every single day of their lives to survive. It is now your turn to be strong and courageous.

It was a long trip back from Rotterdam to Montreal. The last day on board we had a pay parade. This time we were paid in Canadian dollars. It was a sign we had to forget Germany. I was the last to be paid, as we were called alphabetically. When my turn came, the paymaster ran out of twenty-dollar bills. I ended up getting my $300 pay in five-dollar bills. He laughed when he saw the tall stack of fives he was giving me. Later that day we were handed our leave forms. I was freed from any military commitment. I had to consider two options: I could either embrace civilian life or apply for another three-year contract. Despite the numerous mistakes that I made while stationed in Germany, I was hoping that the army would accept my request for a reengagement. I was not ready to go back to the hard Inuit way of life and I did not know what kind of job a former soldier could find in the civilian life. I was afraid of ending up on skid row if I did not sign on for another term. All these thoughts scared me and I kept my fingers crossed, hoping my request for reengagement would be accepted. Army was my daily meal and lodging ticket, as well as my second family.

Luckily I signed on for another three years. This time I was stationed in Victoria, British Columbia, where I finally stayed for seven years. At first sight, I loved Victoria. It is a beautiful and peaceful city. Winters are not too cold there and summers are not too hot, and there are no mosquitoes or blackflies. At night you can see the lights of Seattle. Still, what I preferred in Victoria were the totem poles carved by Henry Hunt, the disciple of the well-known Chief Mungo Martin. I spent many hours admiring these totem poles. Being with them was bringing comfort to my soul. Although Victoria was a very nice place, I did not feel completely at home. As the years passed by I was becoming more and more sensitive to my Aboriginal inner nature. Admiring the memorial of Chief Mungo Martin was doing something good to me. It was soothing my spirit. It was also helping me to be proud of being a Native man. I was pleased to see that an Aboriginal like him had gained international fame. I was told he donated a beautiful totem pole to Queen Elizabeth II, who in return gave him the most elaborate burial ceremony ever given to a Native Canadian. Mungo Martin wanted to be buried where he was born and he was given that honour with all the rites the highest officials get when they die. Henry Hunt, who at the time had become a friend, gave me some pictures of the ceremony. I kept them preciously in my guitar case until someone stole it with the pictures in it. I deeply regretted that loss.

Ever since that time, whenever I see a postcard of totem poles it reminds me of Henry Hunt, who explained to me how to carve them. I still remember when he told me stories about the early days when Aboriginal people from the West Coast were travelling in canoes made from cedar trees. They were carved out from one single big log. He would spend hours explaining how his people used to carve. These canoes were very strong and could last a very long time, even in seawater.

During my stay in Victoria, the Queen of England, Elizabeth II, came to inspect our company, the 1st Battalion Princess Patricia's. The Queen came with her husband, Prince Phillip. She stood up on a jeep while we paraded before their Majesties. I guess they put her on that jeep because they didn't want her to get dusty, since there was a breeze blowing sand and dust that day. There were thousands of spectators around us, who had come just to see the Queen. She gave us a speech and thanked us for our good work during the war. She was given a 21-gun artillery salute. When the first gun fired, it was so loud that an old spectator had a heart attack and died.

In 1962, my sister Ann sent me a letter asking me to come home. Dad had had his first heart attack and was not feeling good. I was driven by despair at the thought that my father could die without seeing me. That is when I decided I could not renounce my father at the very moment he was going to leave earth. I went to see Captain Vick, who had known me for a while. I trusted him and told him everything. I explained that my name was not Vital but Weetaltuk and that my father was an Inuk like my mother and that I was not a Metis but a full-blood Eskimo from the James Bay. He was very understanding and promised that he would not expose my lies or reveal the reasons for my leave application. He then gave me a form to fill out and forwarded it to be approved at the headquarters in Ottawa.

When I received Ann's letter, I was stationed in British Columbia, where I was acting as regimental police supervising young recruits. It was October 1962 and by June of next year my request for compassionate leave still had not come through. It was already the time for our annual six-week training and we had to get on the move. I was getting very worried about Dad as the weeks rolled by. One night, I could not stand waiting anymore for my leave. I had to find a way to get my freedom back, since I couldn't get a leave. Deserting was not an option; consequences would have been too serious. The only solution I could figure out was to be expelled from the Forces for a major offence.

The best idea I came up with was to get caught stealing a case of beer from the kitchen's cooler. This type of mistake would not have sent me to court-martial, but they would no doubt have forced me to resign. That night I sneaked into the kitchen and when I heard the guards doing their rounds I dashed out with a case of beer and made enough noise attract their attention. When they heard the noise, they rushed into my direction. When they flashed their lights on me, I lay flat on my stomach with my arms around the pack of beer. I was handcuffed and they turned me in to the company's sergeant major that sent me, as usual, to the detention barracks. Next day I was bailed out and waited to be sentenced. A few days later I appeared before the commanding officer, a lieutenant colonel. As usual, he started by asking:

—Are you Private Vital sc-17515?

—Yes, Sir.

—You are charged with a theft of a case of beer in the company's cooler at 2:00 a.m. Do you plead guilty or not guilty?

—Guilty, Sir, but with an explanation.

Then I explained that my father was sick and that I had been waiting for eight months for an answer to my application for compassionate leave. I had quit hoping for the leave and had figured that my best chance to see my dad a last time was to be thrown out of the army. He replied:

—It's a disgrace and a stupidity to be charged with theft. I am sorry for you but stealing a case of beer will not solve your problem. And you won't be dismissed. Nevertheless, I'll be lenient with you, as I sympathize with your problem.

He fined me sixty dollars and promised he would try to get me home on the annual leave. I reported to my company and told my buddies that I was only fined sixty dollars. They found it hard to believe because such behaviour should have sent me to jail for a while.

We were going to receive our annual leave after our usual training in Alberta. I was expecting to be released right after. But instead I had to head back to Victoria with the rest of the company. Instead of travelling towards home, far away in the North, I was going further away towards the Pacific Ocean. However, shortly after we arrived in Victoria I had a good surprise. I was asked to report to my company commander. He told me that I was granted a thirty-day compassionate leave. He had kept his promise and had organized my trip to Great Whale, at least for the part he could control. I flew from our base to Trenton, Ontario, via Winnipeg. Once in Trenton there was no flight out to Great Whale. I followed the backup plan he had prepared for me, which was to reach St. Hubert's Air Force base near Montreal, where it was possible to find a plane to Great Whale. Since I had my uniform on, I thought it would be easy and cheaper to hitchhike from Trenton to St. Hubert. An Air Force sergeant offered me a ride to the town outskirts. It was already dark when he let me off at the highway. I felt very much alone. Freight trucks one after another were speeding their way to Montreal and none of them was ready to stop to pick up a hitchhiker. I was getting cold and desperate standing there. Finally a big truck pulled over. The driver said he could give me a ride, but not as far as St. Hubert, and asked if that would help. I thanked him; anything would be better than spending the night in the ditch. He drove all through the night and let me off on the highway near Montreal. It was getting into the wee hours and I was exhausted, hardly able to keep my eyes open. Finally, an old couple stopped. I asked them in French if they were going to Montreal. They were not but they were so surprised and so pleased to hear an Eskimo speaking French that they offered to drive me right up to the St. Hubert Air Force base.

When I got to the base, I showed the guard my leave form and destination. He made a couple of phone calls to find out if there was a flight to Great Whale in the coming days. Apparently there was none. Thus someone advised me to go to Ottawa where I could get a flight to

Churchill in Manitoba and there I would possibly find a flight to Great Whale. What confusion! I was sent from one place to another. I was so desperate to see my father. I now had to return to Churchill, 3000 km northwest of Montreal. I was going to have to turn back and cross half of Canada before finding a taxi to go north. In the meantime, the corporal showed me a place to bed down and told me to be ready to get up early the next day, as there was a Douglas DC-3 leaving for Ottawa and I had to take it. I did not have much option but to follow his "advice."

That's how I ended up in Churchill. Once the plane was on the ground, the door opened and let us out. A cold breeze hit my face. I was lightly dressed and it felt like the wind was going through me. I could hear the sea roaring. The cold and the sea together reminded me of Cape Hope where I was born and spent the first years of my life. I was getting close to home after too many years of absence. That was a very good feeling. I was taken to the reception quarters where I was to wait until I could get a flight to Great Whale. A corporal told me I had just missed a ride with the RCMP. I enquired around to see if there were not some private planes that could fly me. I found out that there was a taxi-plane offering tours around Churchill to the tourists. But for $100 one could only get a thirty-mile ride. I figured it was a waste of time to ask how much they would charge to fly me to Great Whale on the other side of the James Bay. I decided to wait at the army base and to kill the time I visited the town of Churchill. I liked Churchill. With its two Native communities, one Cree and one Inuit, it reminded me very much of Great Whale. The Cree settlement was called Camp 10 and the Inuit settlement was called Camp 20. Most of the Inuit families had been moved to Churchill by the government from northern Quebec because at that time Churchill's economy was booming and a workforce was needed. While I stayed in Churchill, I had the opportunity to observe that the whole town was living to the rhythm of the army base and of the harbour. It was a big harbour where huge boats would dock to ship grain to be exported to Europe, I was told. Grain was brought from the Canadian prairies to Churchill via rail. It was amazing and odd to see such animation in a northern community.

Fifteen days later I was still waiting for a plane. My leave was running short and I wired to Victoria to my commanding officer requesting an extension on my leave. Extension was granted for another thirty days. Ann must have heard that I was trying to get home, as she sent a telegram from Great Whale telling me to go to Montreal and to get on Nordair. I had never heard about that airline. I knew that Austin Airways sometimes flew to James Bay from Timmins, but Nordair was new to me. However, I could trust her since she used to be a stewardess and knew of all the airline companies. When she became a stewardess, in 1959, she was the first Inuit to occupy such employment. A Canadian magazine, the *Star Weekly,* published her picture on the front page of the 28 March issue. A friend of mine, Willie Gow, saw her picture and her name on the front page. They had called her Witaltuk, as they had misspelled Weetaltuk. It really sounded like my new name. Willie was very curious. He showed me the magazine saying:

—Look, Eddy, here is your sister. She must be your sister; she has your eyes, Eddy. She is your sister.

—No, Willie, she is not my sister. She might look like my sister but I tell you, she is not. You know all Eskimos and half-breed Eskimos look alike when you're not one of them. It's the same thing with the Chinese, isn't it?

—Yaaa! And her name, what's that name? Witaltuk. I bet Vital is a nickname for Witaltuk. You're a damn liar.

Anyway, he gave me the *Star Weekly* and did not make any more fuss over it. I am sure he had uncovered my secret but had chosen to keep it. That's something I liked in the army: you could trust your comrades.

Ann worked as a stewardess for two years. Then she got pregnant and went back home to live with Mum and Dad at Great Whale, where she met up with an employee of Marconi, Terry Witfield. They fell in love and got married. Actually, that created a big problem, because Terry's work contract specified he could not fraternize with the Natives of the village he was stationed at. Their love story that almost turned sour made the front page all across Canada and the U.S. and later both Ann and Terry appeared on a television program called *Front Page Challenge*.

In her telegraph Ann had advised me to take Nordair, but unfortunately when I received her telegram I was not allowed to buy a plane ticket from a private company, while I was able to travel for free on the government-chartered planes. I was very disappointed until I met an Inuk at Camp 20 who worked as an interior decorator. I knew him from Old Factory where we attended school together. He said he could help me and bragged about the money he had set aside. I jumped with joy and bought a couple of cases of beer to celebrate the good news, not knowing he was lying. He used to make promises to get beers from naive people like me. After that false hope it was already too late to look for another solution. It was time for me to head back to Victoria. I had spent all my leave in Churchill, so close but still so far away from my family.

A few days later the corporal advised me to get my gear packed as he had found a lift for me to Winnipeg. The morning of my departure I got a phone call from Camp 20. It was the same con artist from Old Factory who wanted to see me. He had heard I was leaving and wished to apologize. I had only forty-five minutes before my plane took off. I called a taxi and rushed down to his place. He wanted to take a picture of me in uniform with his wife and their two girls. I found the request odd but I agreed anyway. I was to find out later that it was a trick. Once he had the film developed, he used it to pretend that he was me. He went to Churchill Hotel. When there were people passing through, government employees or tourists that came to see the polar bears, he would tell them that he was stuck here, wasting his leave waiting for a plane to bring him back to see his family. In order to soften the hearts of his victims, he would show the photo of me, in uniform with his wife and daughters. People felt sorry for him and would spare him some change and few beers. Later he went back to Great Whale and he continued pretending to be a parachutist from the Canadian army. He even managed to steal from the post office a letter I had sent to my sister. In the envelope there were photos from the training camp and from Victoria. He used these pictures to support his pretense. He even told the war stories I had told him while in Churchill. It was a strange turn; I had been ripped off of the fake identity I had forged for myself.

When I arrived at the home base in Victoria, everyone was getting ready to head back to Germany. We were going to be stationed there for four years from 1963 to 1967. Once again we stencilled our gear. This time we did not sail but flew to Germany. It was October 1963 when we landed in Düsseldorf. Buses were waiting to drive us to our destination. I ended up again at Camp Fort MacLeod, six miles from Iserlohn. Once at the camp, we were given a three-day pass to get to know the surroundings. Since this was my second time, I already spoke a bit of German and knew where to go to have a pleasant evening. I knew all the taxi drivers who usually waited at the gate and I also knew every bar and all the restaurants at Iserlohn and the nearby towns. I took with me a group of my buddies that were in Germany for the first time; we went to a restaurant and then to Myer's Bar. After a couple of beers I told my friends that I wanted to go to Iserlohn. I wanted to see if Clara was still there. When my friends understood that I already had had a girlfriend in Germany, they were all quite impressed.

We took a taxi to Heinz Wesinger's Gasthof. I was hoping he was still the owner of the place. I paid the taxi. The place had not changed at all. Heinz and his wife and their children were still there. I had left the place six years ago but I still remembered everyone's name and they all remembered me. Heinz's wife almost burst into tears when she saw me. I asked about Clara. She told me:

—Clara drank a lot after you left. She was so sorry she did not see you before your departure. I guess she was hoping to get back with you.

—Where is she now?

—She left for Canada after she married a Canadian soldier. It was five years ago. I heard they are living in Winnipeg.

She gave me a picture of Clara. The picture had been taken when she had her broken arm. She had some sort of unknown feeling in her eyes. But she was my Clara. The only woman I ever loved. I did not ask for her address. After all, why should I bring back the past? I had lost her by my own mistake and I had no right to disturb her new life. I was thinking that maybe she had a happy life, with kids and a loving husband. I was sad thinking that maybe her life with that man was better than the one I could have offered her.

CONCLUSION

My second stay in Germany went by so fast. Too fast. I could not appreciate it as much as I would have liked because I knew that once I would be back in Canada I might have to return to civilian life. I had been an infantry mortar operator for twelve years and that would not help much in real life. I started to wonder what I could do once demobilized. I thought about taking up training as a heavy machine operator. Then I thought about a transfer to the Air Force because they had a base in Great Whale. If I was lucky, I could be posted close to my people. I figured out the best way for me to be transferred to the Air Force, and be posted at Great Whale, was to be a cook. I knew they would be pleased to have a multilingual cook, capable of speaking French and English to the soldiers, and able to speak Cree and Inuktitut to deal with the local population. That is how I asked for a cook's training course. I explained my motivation to my commanding officer. He thought it was a clever idea and promised he would recommend my name to the sergeant in charge of the kitchen. I waited a couple of months and finally on 22 November 1963 he told me to report to the kitchen. The following morning at 5:30 I was all dressed up in white and ready to learn new skills.

I spent the whole day on my feet and was given the dirtiest duties one can imagine. When night came, I was exhausted and went back to the camp to lie down on my bunk and fell asleep right away. I was too tired to join my pals at the wet canteen. Later that evening my friend Brabant woke me up:

—Eddy, turn on your radio and listen to the news. President Kennedy has just been shot!

On every station it was the same news: Kennedy had been murdered. I got dressed and accompanied Brabant to the wet canteen. We had a couple of whisky shots to calm down and talked about Kennedy all evening. In the following days I listened to the news. I heard that in Japan emotions were very high. Germany was also in real sorrow. They remembered him with love because when he came on tour in Berlin he said "Ich bin ein Berliner." Kennedy was respected all over the world for his great contribution to peace. How come someone kills a man who fought so much for peace?

Since there was hardly anything more for me in Germany, Clara being gone, I focused on my cook's training. I almost quit drinking because I did not want to end up one more time in military jail. All I wanted was to learn a trade, which I did within a year. Then I was assigned to our company kitchen. On 14 May 1965 while on duties I received a telegram from my sister Ann saying my father had passed away from cardiac arrest. My lieutenant asked if I wanted to go home. I thought by the time I got there he would have already been buried. Instead I sent a telegram back saying I had received the news. I was allowed to spend the rest of the afternoon in the wet canteen. My captain and a few friends joined me later. I spoke of my family back home, telling them how my dad was a hard-working man. I was near the end of my contract with the army and I decided to tell my friends who I really was, where I came from. I explained how poverty and lack of opportunities had pushed me to leave my family to look elsewhere for a way to have a better life. When I was done, I felt so relieved. Eddy Weetaltuk was finally going to be reborn.

We were sent back to Canada after three years in Germany. Once landed, we were given a furlough. I took a train to Montreal and then the bus to Quebec City. I arrived at around 10:00 p.m. Ann was waiting for me in tears. It had been a long time since we had seen each other. We went to her apartment, a basement she was renting with four other Inuit girls. Two of them were students from Inukjuaq, which was called, at that time, Port Harrison. I still remember their names: Sarasee Smiler and Ann Palliser. The other two, Ann and Marge May, were from Fort Chimo (Kuujjuaq).

One day my sister came home telling me that her boss, Mr. Gourdeau, was going north with a DC-3 belonging to the Government of Quebec. She had asked him if I could come along and he had agreed. We left at 4:30 in the morning and had two stops before Great Whale, Schefferville and Fort Chimo. My sister Ann was part of the trip, working as an interpreter for Eric Gourdeau. When we got off the aircraft at Great Whale, there was a group of Inuit waiting for us. Among them was Mother. She had aged. She now had thin lines all over her face. She was standing, smiling. She looked so happy. Her son was back. I went over to give her a hug!

There were tears of joy in her eyes. Eric Gourdeau got a jeep for me to drive us home. She was now living in a very small square house with an oil stove. She had a chamber pot and a bathtub, but no running water. Mother was living there with her granddaughter Salamiva and my brother David's kids. I am really grateful to Salamiva, for she took good care of her. Mother loved Salamiva very much. I stayed with them for the few days I was in Great Whale. David, his wife, and their youngest son were living in a tent beside the house. At night, we could hear the young boy cry because he was cold. I felt so sorry for him that I sometimes got up to bring him close to the stove and the heat. Lying in that little square overcrowded matchbox, I thought about Korea and all the places I had been. I couldn't help but feel sad for my loved ones. We were in 1967, man had just walked on the moon, and my brother was still living in a tent and his son was suffering from cold in one of the richest countries on earth.

While I was in Great Whale, Mother sewed me a parka with the material she could scrounge. I spent my entire leave visiting family and friends. I also hunted ptarmigans like I used to do when I was young. One day, while following the birds' tracks through the woods, I saw David Masty and his wife, struggling to pull their sleigh loaded with green frozen pinewood that they had cut to make firewood. They both smiled when I waved at them. I wished I had my camera with me to prove to the Southerners, munching cakes while watching TV, how hard people of the North struggle to survive. At that time there were still many Indians and Inuit living in tents, depending on hunting and fishing for survival. The years of good hunting were getting scarce and many had to depend on government relief that was barely enough to keep them alive through the winter, especially the ones with children. Some hoped a miracle would happen and spare them from cold and hunger. But even though they would go to church every day, it was not going to change anything, since God could not melt away all the snow in the North so they could be warm.

The days passed by so fast. I was so pleased to be home, but I was also sad to see so much poverty and also because I realized how poorly the White people treated the Native people here. One night Father Ostan invited me to the Great Whale "Social Club," a place where the local White people would gather to watch movies and have a drink. Indians and Inuit were not accepted. I was allowed to get in only because I accompanied Father Osten; however, when he ordered a beer for me, the bartender refused to serve him, saying that Eskimos were not allowed to drink alcohol. The father tried to object, saying that to refuse a drink to a service man who had put his life at risk for his country was not right, but the barman did not change his mind. Upset, the father gave me his beer and told me to drink it, whatever people would say.

When Nordair finally came, most of the village gathered to see me off. I boarded the DC-4, an old Second World War bomber, and waved to the crowd. They all shouted "Hurrah!" with their hands raised. It was good to know I had friends. Once in the air, a stewardess served us drinks. I had a gin.

When I arrived at Montreal airport, I took a taxi to the train station, downtown, and there I bought a ticket to Edmonton, Alberta. I spent my last hour in Montreal having a couple of beers and relaxing, thinking of my buddies from the army. I knew they would all have their many stories to tell. Surely most would lie about their adventures, but it was nevertheless going to be fun listening to them. Once landed in Edmonton, I went to the barracks. The boys were amazed to see me wearing an Eskimo parka sewn by my mother. Finally, a few days later, my request for transfer to the Air Force came through. I was accepted with three other guys: Jerry, Anderson, and Goulet, an Indian we used to call for fun "Chief." Jerry and I were transferred to Saint-Jean-sur-Richelieu, Quebec, thirty miles south of Montreal, where we would receive a basic training. Once the training was completed, I was told I was going to be posted in a military college in the region of Montreal. I was very disappointed, since I had only asked to transfer to the Air Force in order to be posted at Great Whale. That's when I decided my army career was over. I was fed up with my life far away from my people and my community. I had seen the world: Japan, Korea, British Columbia, Seattle, Germany, Alberta, Manitoba, Montreal, Quebec, and so many other places. It was time for me to get back home.

After fifteen years in the Canadian Forces, I was now on my own. I did not know what my future would be like but it was mine to discover and I was thrilled by the new adventures to come. My first move was to look for a job in Saint-Jean but there was no opening for me, so I headed back to Quebec City to visit my sister Ann and to tell her I was now out of the Services and wanted to move back to Great Whale and look for a job over there. Once again, Eric Gourdeau said he could help me find a position. I flew to Great Whale with him. I was happy; I was again heading home and I was thinking it might be for good. Once we arrived, Eric talked to Roger Beaudoin, the local agent of the Direction General du Nouveau Québec (DGNQ), Quebec's Northern Affairs department. They arranged a job for me at the army base kitchen. I was going to help the cook and his wife. At first I thought my life was going to turn out perfect. I was back at Great Whale and I was going to work as a cook at a military base. It was as if I was back to my former life, the good life I had in the army, except it would be even better since I was home. But it was nothing like that. I was not anymore a member of the Forces but a civilian and treated as such. I was in the real world and in that world the strict but fair rules of the army did not apply.

I also came to realize that the North had changed and the new generation of White people coming to work here were less friendly. School was not a good thing for us anymore but a nightmare for some young. That was for me a huge disappointment. Especially when I realized the cook I was going to work with was racist and hated the Cree and the Inuit who were working with him. He thought nobody but he was a hard worker. According to him all Natives were lazy, liars, and stupid, including me. Although I had been a soldier and fought for our country, I did not deserve his respect. Working in those conditions was a shame and I could hardly stand it. When I was a soldier, I had been treated with respect. Everywhere I had travelled I had been treated fairly and now I was in my own community but I was not anymore good enough to deserve respect.

Moreover, this man was ripping people off. He used to get beautiful Inuit carvings by exchanging them with local sculptors for beer or food when they were broke. He would then sell the carvings for a high price to the government's employees when they came to Great Whale for business. He knew I was aware of his little dirty business and he was anxious to get me out of the kitchen. He finally had me fired on the false pretense of being late too often. That was actually the same reason he gave when he wanted to get rid of his Native employees. But in my case nothing could be more wrong because I was still under the influence of the army drill. Routine and wake-up calls were still the way I functioned. I went over to complain to Mr. Beaudoin, the DGNQ's agent. He offered me work in the office with him and Mr. Landry, the accountant. I worked there as radio telephone operator and as a Cree and Inuk translator. That was a good position and it was nice working with good people.

Some time after being settled at Great Whale, I met Debby, an English teacher from Montreal. We thought we loved each other enough to get married. She really loved the North and asked me to teach her the Inuit way of life. I was proud to be her guide and it reminded me of Clara teaching me German. Now it was my turn to be teaching someone. Though Great Whale had changed since I had left, I knew it was still the right place for me. I spent months teaching Debby how to survive in the tundra. She was very good at walking in snowshoes and she was amazing when walking on slippery rocks. She went as far as carrying firewood on her back like Indian women do. She really mastered the hard life of the North only to be told in disgust, by her family and her friends, that she was wasting her time learning the way of life of the savages.

Our wedding ceremony was at the small Roman Catholic chapel on the base. The wedding was one of the biggest that ever took place in the village of Great Whale. Tommy Hoare was my godfather, since my dad had passed away. Guy Dufour was my best man. Debby's mother and sister Dorothy came to the wedding from Montreal. My former boss was asked to bake a wedding cake but he refused because he hated me so much for having found a good job after he fired me. The agent of the DGNQ told him to pack his belongings and take the next Nordair flight back to Montreal. I was proud to see a Quebec government employee upholding justice for an Inuit man. I was definitively home. This was the end of my adventures in faraway places.

A new life was ahead of me. The life of an Inuk in his village. Like many lives, my life was not perfect and I endured some sorrows. My marriage did not last long and I saw several of my relatives suffering from poverty and disease. But it was my life and I know one can't expect too much from this life on earth. Thanks to my travels, I have learnt that no one can change the world, not even through war. I also realized that we are responsible for our own destinies, and that we have to accept our fate but without giving up. For many years we have been badly treated by our government and many of us have lost faith in ourselves. Those Inuit who blame the government and the White people are not completely wrong, but that should not distract us from working to control our own lives. I hope my story will help the young Inuit to find the inspiration to strive to maintain their heritage, because it is the only way to avoid losing one's soul.

THE EXPERIENCE OF EDDY WEETALTUK IN THE CONTEXT OF ABORIGINAL PARTICIPATION IN CANADIAN WARS

BY *Thibault Martin*
TRANSLATED FROM FRENCH BY JEREMY PATZER

The numerous discussions that I had with Eddy Weetaltuk brought me to realize that his military experience significantly contributed to the way he understood and regarded his Aboriginal status, and it induced him to explore the nature of the relationship between this country's original inhabitants and other Canadians.[1] After Eddy's death, I wanted to know if his experience as a soldier and the effects it had on his personal development were unique, or if they reflected those of other Aboriginal veterans. I thus began my research and quickly realized that work on the subject was rare—up until the Royal Commission on Aboriginal Peoples (RCAP)—aside from a few exceptions which include Gaffen (1985), Kulchyski (1988), Dempsey (1989 and 1983), Davison (1993), and Whiteside (1973). RCAP was put into place during the 1990s and shed light on colonialism's detrimental effects on Aboriginal Canadians. The RCAP was an attempt to forge a new relationship between First Nations members and the rest of the Canadian population. Hundreds of Aboriginal members, including numerous veterans, testified before the commission. Their stories revealed both the importance of Aboriginal peoples' contribution to Canadian war efforts and the vast inequality and abuse suffered by Aboriginal veterans and their families. Since this commission, federal institutions (the Department of Indigenous and Northern Affairs, the Department of Veterans Affairs, Library and Archives Canada, and the Department of National

Defence) have published various texts in an admitted effort to correct this oversight. The experiences of these veterans also drew interest from numerous historians (Brownlie 1998; Dempsey 1999, 2006; Drees 1997; Innes 1997, 2000, 2004; Lackenbauer 2007b, 2004; Lackenbauer and Mantle 2007; Lackenbauer, Sheffield and Mantle 2007; Morton 2008; Sheffield 1996, 2001, 2004, 2005, 2007; Sheffield and Foster 1999; Stevenson 1996; Summerby 2005; Talbot 2011; Winegard 2012). Most of these publications concern enlistment requirements, the heroism of Aboriginal soldiers, and their unfair treatment, with some denouncing their having been "forgotten" and, in the case of Poulin (2007), the lack of information on the contributions of Aboriginal women. Despite these works, many sociological aspects of this issue have still not been examined. Perhaps the most important is the impact veterans had on the organization of Aboriginal political claims.

Of course, several historical pieces exhaustively explored the events, the circumstances, and the socio-economic consequences that Canada's wars had on its Aboriginal peoples. In these publications, however, the role war played in the construction of Aboriginal societies' collective identity is only of minor and incidental interest. My objective here is to mark out the contours of such a process.

I would therefore like to show that war has participated in this process in two ways. First, it is during or after the wars that the Canadian state accelerated economic and legal measures that contributed to the marginalization of Aboriginal Canadians. Second, their participation in Canadian war efforts awakened Aboriginal Canadians to the unequal treatment to which they were subject. This gave birth to a pan-Canadian political rights movement, the origin of the current discourse that sets up the Aboriginal (inclusive of all legal statuses) as a specific social category different from that of "Euro-Canadian." One can thus speak about *Aboriginalization* to reflect the workings of a double process: the state's implementation of specific conditions contributing to the marginalization of Aboriginal peoples and also their self-identification with a shared, *sui generis* condition distinct from that of members of other societies.

Construction and Instrumentalization of the History of War

Over the past twenty years historians from federal institutions have produced nearly exhaustive research underscoring the importance of Aboriginal contributions to Canadian war efforts. This work, the primary objective of which is the construction of a Canadian national identity, seeks to give back to the Metis, First Nations, and Inuit their place in this history. The history that the Canadian state elaborates, thanks in large part to the historians within its departments and agencies, is a celebratory epic, an ode to Canada's unique contribution to the Western project of a more just world. In this narrative, Canada is presented as a diverse nation, yet one that moves collectively and with conviction towards a brilliant future where equality, democracy, justice, peace, fraternity, and freedom of commerce shine like so many military medals and decorations earned in the field.

Yet, a nation's idealized self-image requires reconciliation with its past, and the writing of history, a simultaneous confession and cleansing of past transgressions from collective memory, becomes the instrument of this reconciliation. From this perspective, Canada must wipe from its "historical slate" the inequitable treatment of Aboriginal Canadians: dispossession, displacement, sterilization of women, forced adoption of thousands of children, and the creation of residential schools to acculturate them (Steckley and Cummins 2010). Over the past two decades the state has begun to recognize past errors and has set about reintroducing Aboriginal Canadians into national history such that it can become the history of all Canadians. Recognizing First Nations' contributions to Canada's war efforts and paying homage to the sacrifices made on their part is integral to this process. Certainly, one must not be naive, for while this reconciliation serves as a sort of recompense for errors committed against Aboriginal Canadians, it also unburdens the collective conscience of Canadians and, in the end, allows them to define themselves as a generous and progressive nation—the ultimate goal of the official history of Canada.

One must remember that history is not an objective fact, but a narrative. As a historical phenomenon, war is socially constructed, so much so that the different societies that compose Canada do not have the same interpretation of it. In this vein, it has been recognized that French Canadians and Quebecers have had, and continue to have, a view of war that diverges from that of the rest of Canada. Likewise, the interpretation Aboriginal Canadians have of war and its consequences is different from that of Quebecers. Indeed, such interpretation is rooted primarily in values native to their cultures. Thus, there is more than one Aboriginal construction of war. In addition, this construction of reality is the result of a circumstantial involvement of First Nations members in war. War as a social construct is therefore formed from within the society in question. This is why the narratives of war history depend at once on the intrinsic culture of each society and the extrinsic events that contribute to their participation in war.

An example taken from the Canadian experience can serve to illustrate this proposition. It concerns the resistance movement of the Metis of the Prairies. While this event has been qualified as a "resistance" movement by French Canada and especially by the Metis themselves, it was known for a long time from the English-Canadian point of view as a "rebellion." Similarly, when one spoke from the Metis perspective of Louis Riel's assassination at the hand of the government, from the other side of the cultural divide one spoke of the "execution" of the Metis leader for "high treason." One easily understands that this difference in the verbal expression of facts is simultaneously the cause and effect of the narration of several parallel histories, each one belonging to a particular society. For some time, however, English Canadians have more or less adopted the vocabulary of the Metis to describe the events surrounding Louis Riel's resistance. This change in understanding of past events indicates the reconstruction of history at work in Canada today. It can be interpreted as the result of the will of the Anglophone majority to construct a common history including Canadians of all origins.[2]

From this perspective, writing the history of Canada requires that one accept the postulate that Canada has more than one past. It then requires that one listen to its different histories. Of course, taking an interest in history written by Aboriginal authors can be unnerving for non-Aboriginal readers. Thus Georges Sioui's *For an Amerindian Autohistory*, which presents the arrival of Europeans in the New World

from an Aboriginal perspective, was not published without engen-
dering controversy. Aboriginal historian John Moses, author of a substantial report *A Sketch Account of Aboriginal Peoples in the Canadian
Military*, also elucidates a different perspective on this question. It is
remarkable in this respect that Moses dedicates two-thirds of his book
to events that precede the First World War, while the historian Gaffen
(1985) and the Royal Commission on Aboriginal Peoples' report
(RCAP 1996), both of which look at the same subject, spend the majority of their analysis on wars of the twentieth century. Moreover, when
Moses describes conflicts, he does so by examining the standpoints and
strategies of Aboriginal nations in relation to their own context and
their own ambitions, rather than from the point of view of rivalries
between European nations. Such a reading leads to interpretations
that minimize the role we generally attribute to certain events while
emphasizing others. For example, when Moses deals with the Patriote
movement, which is, from the point of view of Quebecers, an integral
moment for Quebec nationalism, he is content to simply mention that
it took place and blends it in with the unrest that took place across
Canada and the United States at the end of the nineteenth century.
His interests lie less in the causes of the revolt than in the details of
how it was crushed, which he attributes in part to the intervention of
an Aboriginal contingent. Such an analysis thus minimizes the importance of the confrontation between French and English Canadians—a
particularly preponderant one in Quebec historiography.

　　Aboriginal Canadians thus construct their own war histories, and
in order to understand history in its entirety we must also take into
consideration the histories told by members of Canada's First Peoples.
However, listening to these alternative narratives requires taking interest in the Other and their world view. In order to do this, we must not
perceive the Other solely through the restrictive lens of our relation
to them, but rather we must try to understand[3] how they perceive this
relationship. This reversal of questioning is not easy, but it is the condition of possibility of any process of *understanding* as envisaged by
non-positivist sociology.

War of Equals

From the first contact between First Nations and Europeans, war was at the heart of their relations. Contrary to popular belief, Aboriginal peoples were not subjugated by Europeans (Delâge 1985) during the conflicts that took place in the era of conquest. Of course, First Nations were sometimes drawn involuntarily into conflicts that did not concern them, and Europeans sometimes used First Nations to fight in their place. But First Nations also engaged in and initiated conflicts related to their own political and commercial interests (Moses, Graves, and Sinclair 2004), as Delâge (1985) demonstrated in his well-known *Bitter Feast*. Thus the Six Nations (Haudenosaunee) proved to be a particularly fearsome power interested in both military and political terms. They almost succeeded in having the French at their mercy thanks to a strategy that saw periods of combat, truce, alliance, and negotiations in which the goal for the Iroquois was to gain control of routes for the fur trade (Moses, Graves, and Sinclair 2004). Moreover, from the Great Peace of Montreal (1701) until the Seven Years' War, the expansion of New France rested largely "on the participation of the Native peoples residing within the French sphere of influence" (Moses, Graves, and Sinclair 2004, 9). In essence, far from being passive actors, Aboriginal leaders maintained, notably during the seventeenth century, important diplomatic relations with different European nations with the aim of getting the most from their alliances (Basile 2001).

From this perspective, and as Moses, Graves, and Sinclair (2004) suggest, one must not see the treaties and alliances prior to Confederation as acts of submission. In several cases, such alliances were considered opportunities by First Nations. And when they engaged in alliances for military or strategic reasons, they did so as between equals on a nation-to-nation basis. The Aboriginal chiefs who signed these agreements did not feel themselves—and, for that matter, were not—positioned as subordinates or dependants, but as allies. Thus, in order to encourage the alliances they needed, representatives of the European monarchs adopted certain rituals and practices[4] of the First Nations during the ceremonies ratifying the accords, thereby confirming for their leaders equal footing within the relationship. One can also find numerous examples of situations where representatives of the Crown (be it British or French) admitted their vital need to obtain help from First Nations. During the attempted American invasion, Major General Isaac Brock, commander of the armed forces of Upper Canada, announced to Shawnee warriors and their chiefs that the King of England himself requested their aid because his soldiers needed to learn their techniques to make war in the forest and defeat the Americans (Moses, Graves, and Sinclair 2004, 19).

Of course, these alliances were not without risk. Military loss and victory were both possible outcomes, so much so that even in times of adversity, the First Nations felt their commitment to their European ally was important. This was the case for Aboriginal warriors fighting on the French side until the very end: their defeat on the Plains of Abraham on 13 September 1759 (Gaffen 1985, 11). Despite this defeat, Obwandiyag, also known as Pontiac, Odowa Chief, organized an attack against the British in the Great Lakes region in 1763, hoping to open a new front that would favour the return of his French allies (*Canadian Encyclopaedia* 2006). In a more general sense, defeat was generally not interpreted by First Nations as the consequence of a relation of subordination but rather as a military setback, as indicated by an Aboriginal chief allied with the French: "although you have conquered the French, you have not yet conquered us! We are not your slaves" (cited in Moses, Graves, and Sinclair 2004, 10).

Thus, when First Nations engaged in combat or in alliances with European forces—for the sake of strategy, loyalty, or necessity—they did so as equals and not as dominated peoples. They anticipated and accepted the consequences of their choices in advance.

After the Treaty of Paris in 1763, which saw to the end of France's political presence in Canada, the British Crown possessed the only "signature" that could forge an alliance with First Nations. The word "signature" merits quotation marks here because it properly evokes the European contractual conception of alliance, while many Aboriginal groups were of the mind that they were engaging in a relationship based on reciprocity. This means that the First Nations, in allying themselves with the King or Queen of England (since all alliances were from then on made in the name of the British Crown) thought they were entering into a relationship of mutual obligation (in the Maussian sense of the term), according to which allies should offer each other mutual assistance. This is why, in 1775, several First Nations came to the aid of England during the first battle with the Americans (Moses, Graves, and Sinclair 2004). In July 1812, when American troops penetrated the Canadian border, it was thanks to the decisive support of Chief Tecumseh of the Shawnee Nation that the English army succeeded in stopping the enemy invasion (Stanley 1985). First Nations' contribution to the defence of the territory was considered indispensable, and several generals did not hesitate to acknowledge this. General Brock, for example, described his Shawnee ally by writing that "a more sagacious or a more gallant Warrior does not I believe exist" (cited in Moses, Graves, and Sinclair 2004, 19). There were other American attacks in 1814 and these too were pushed back thanks to the loyalty of certain First Nations. This faithfulness was recognized by the British Crown, who awarded ninety-six medals to Aboriginal combatants in recognition of the military aid they provided from 1793 until 1814 (Summerby 2005, 9).

Military engagement on the part of Aboriginal Canadians has not been limited to the defence of Canadian soil, however. Some volunteered to fight in foreign countries alongside their English allies. Nearly 400 men, mostly Metis, earned a reputation for their ability to manoeuvre their vessels during the Nile Expedition of the Battle of Khartoum (Summerby 2005, 9). Superior officers shared the opinion of Lieutenant Colonel Coleridge Grove: "The employment of the voyageurs was a most pronounced success. Without them it is to be doubted whether the boats would have got up at all, and it may be taken as certain that if they had, they would have been far longer in doing so, and the loss of life would have been much greater than has been the case" (cited in Moses, Graves, and Sinclair 2004, 55). Numerous First Nations and Metis individuals volunteered during the Boer War as well. Private Walter White, a Huron of the Anderdon band of Wyandot, near Sarnia, was the first soldier killed in combat on 18

February 1900, "much in advance of any other British dead" (Moses, Graves, and Sinclair 2004, 61).

Nevertheless, participation in England's defence did not convince Canada, once it gained its independence (1867), to respect its obligations to its Aboriginal allies. Yet, according to the conditions stipulated by the British Crown, once Canada became a nation it was meant to respect the agreements that had been struck by the Crown. Unfortunately, Ottawa respected neither the letter nor the spirit of these agreements and, far from protecting Aboriginal peoples, the Canadian government left European settlers to seize their lands. This attitude set off a first wave of indignation from Aboriginal Canadians, who wanted Canada to recognize that they deserved, for their efforts, rights to land in the country that they had risked their lives to defend. This is in essence what John Brant Sero, a Mohawk and veteran of the Boer War, expressed: "We believe we have an interest in the empire, bought by the blood of our ancestors" (cited in RCAP 1996, 7).

The First World War and the Increasing Marginalization of Aboriginal Canadians

When the First World War erupted, many Aboriginal chiefs encouraged members of their communities to come to the aid of their ally, the British Crown (Gaffen 1985), with whom they felt to be engaged in a reciprocal relationship following the signing of pre-confederate "peace and friendship" treaties (Dickason 2002). Some of them had already died on the battlefield when the authorization to accept them in the Canadian Armed Forces had finally been given—more than a year after the beginning of hostilities (RCAP 1996, 8). Until that point, recruiters did not know how to respond to Aboriginal Canadians who wished to enlist, since there were fears that they would be unsuitable for fighting in modern wars or that "the Germans might refuse to extend to them the privileges of civilized warfare" (Militia and Defence 1915, cited in Talbot 2011, 100). Others feared Aboriginal soldiers would be unable to withstand the European climate or tuberculosis but, in addition, many recruits refused to fight alongside visible minorities (ibid.). They would not always accept them, for fear that they would be tortured by the enemy if captured. Despite this reticence, the momentum of Aboriginal volunteers was not slowed and they continued to enrol in large numbers. More than 4,000 status Indians (according to Moses, Graves, and Sinclair 2004, 62) participated in military operations: 3,500, according to Veterans Affairs (Summerby 2005, 5), and more than 4,000, according to Winegard (2012). This does not include the unknown number of Metis and non-status Indians who participated in military operations during the First World War, 300 of whom died in combat while hundreds of others were wounded (Gaffen 1985, 20). According to Talbot (2011) the majority of Aboriginal groups on reserves in the south of the country or located near urban centres did not want to participate in the war (for reasons that will be addressed further on). However, many Aboriginal chiefs encouraged members of their communities to enlist. The chiefs' calls were so well heard that, on several reserves, almost all men of age left for combat. A number of Metis and non-status Indians volunteered also.

The voluntary participation of Aboriginal Canadians attests to the loyalty of First Nations towards the British Crown. Talbot also sees this involvement as a desire on the part of Aboriginal Canadians "to achieve greater recognition for their people" (Talbot 2011, 94). The First World War, however, brutally revealed that the nature of their relationship had changed since the historic treaties had been signed and made them realize that Canada, which was progressively emancipating itself from the British Crown, no longer considered them to be members of allied nations but as simple subjects. The first indication of this shift could be seen in the recruitment process. While, in previous conflicts, Aboriginal warriors would join the fighting without having their military value or linguistic competencies evaluated by the army, from the First World War on the Canadian Forces would treat Aboriginal persons as regular soldiers who were required to correspond to the same recruitment criteria as other Canadian combatants (Moses, Graves, and Sinclair 2004). Thus, from 1914 on, Aboriginal volunteers who were ill, illiterate, or insufficiently skilled in English were systematically sent home.[5] The Canadian government no longer came to terms with partner nations, but rather made terms with individuals whose merit it evaluated.

This changing position can also be seen in the government's refusal to recognize the neutrality of the League of Six Nations. During the conflicts of the preceding century, notably during the wars with the United States, the Iroquois Confederacy had remained officially neutral, leaving each member nation with the choice to support whatever side that it wished. When the Great War erupted, the Six Nations Confederacy Council on the Grand River Territory wanted its neutrality recognized. Ottawa refused, arguing that status Indians would have to enrol like other Canadians (Gaffen 1985, 20). Chief Thunderwater also opposed conscription, accusing the government of wanting to enrol the First Nations to "steal their lands while the quarrel was going on" (Lackenbauer 2007a, 69). As well, "some band councils refused to help the Allied war effort unless Great Britain acknowledged their bands' status as independent nations" (Summerby 2005, 6). This recognition was refused, however, compelling these groups to yield to government regulations concerning military participation. The effect of this government attitude was to reveal to Aboriginal leaders that the era of alliance had ended.

However, it was the Military Service Act of 1917, bringing mandatory military service for all British subjects in Canada, which muddied the waters of voluntary service for Aboriginal peoples. Falling in line with the Indian Act of 1876, and through the reassurances of the Deputy Superintendent of Indian Affairs Duncan Campbell Scott, the Military Service Act of 1917 included First Nations people in its definition of who was considered a British subject (Habkirk 2010, 87–88). To counter the ruling that they were Canadians like any other, and defining themselves first and foremost as members of autonomous nations, First Nations people across Canada protested, sending petitions and delegations to politicians, the Governor General, and even members of the Royal family (GWCA 2014). Through this protest, they won their case against their mandatory enrolment in January 1918. Their exemption from the Act, however, was based on the fact they did not have the right to vote in federal elections (a right they would not obtain until 1960) and therefore were considered wards of the Crown, and not separate nations. Nevertheless, few were able to actually take advantage of this exception because Duncan Campbell Scott manipulated the regulation, by making the registration of Aboriginal people a Department of Indian Affairs census and by not making it known to members of First Nations that they could be released from their military service. Furthermore, those who wished to exercise this right had to register with the Department of Indian Affairs and agree to become wards of the Crown (Habkirk 2010, 92).[6] The First World War therefore accelerated the marginalization of Aboriginal Canadians, especially status Indians, bringing them from a status of equal and independent to one of unequal and dependent.

Despite this, Aboriginal Canadians' faithfulness towards England brought them to ignore the impudence of the Canadian government, and they continued to feel a certain obligation toward the British Crown. According to Winegard (2012), statistically status Indians enlisted voluntarily to the same extent as other Canadians. However, this is contested by Talbot, who estimates that "the simple fact remains that First Nations men did not serve with the same frequency as their non-Aboriginal counterparts" (2011, 114). Talbot provides different examples of communities that strongly opposed conscription, such as Kanesatake, which "openly supported desertion to the point that many of the defaulters felt safe enough to continue living on their reserve in plain sight of government officials" (Talbot 2011, 105). According to him, although numerous Aboriginal Canadians had shown their support in the war efforts, both by enlisting and by making donations to the Red Cross and various other patriotic funds, "most First Nations did not support the Canadian war effort to any significant degree for a litany of reasons. Some had outstanding grievances with the Canadian state, others were ambivalent towards the imperialistic rhetoric of the day, and a great many more determined that direct involvement would not serve their interests" (Talbot 2011, 92–93). In fact, Talbot's reasoning for this weak "enthusiasm" for supporting the British Crown could be debated, notably because of the remote location of some reserves, which could have influenced the translation of this "enthusiasm" into concrete actions. In addition, on numerous occasions, status Indians were not accepted because they could not write. Discrimination also played a role in not accepting them into the army, as Poulin notes (2007, 6): "Racism reared its ugly head when Whites in British Columbia strongly objected in 1917 to amalgamation of Indians into their units." There is not enough space, and it is outside the objectives of this essay, to enter into arguments concerning the objective or subjective, quantitative or qualitative extent of Aboriginal participation in the war effort. However, the different examples Talbot offers, which establish dominant and minority Aboriginal attitudes, are interesting to keep in mind, since both the arguments of those opposed to the war and those who voluntarily enlisted are at the heart of affirmations made by the political organizations created after the war by its veterans, as we will see further on.

The large number of Aboriginal Canadians who responded to the call during the First World War meant that two battalions, the 114th and the 107th, were composed mostly of First Nations and Metis. Their bravery in combat and their contribution to the great battles won the respect of the other Canadian soldiers (Morton 2008, 49). In fact, although the Aboriginal Canadians would be subject to different kinds of discrimination, mainly during recruitment or during their initial training, most Aboriginal soldiers felt respected and treated as equals by their comrades in arms (Summerby 2005, 12; Poulin 2007, 6). That said, few among them, aside from a few Mohawk soldiers, held command positions (Morton 2008, 40). This demonstrates a form of institutional racism that Aboriginal veterans were either unaware of, or unwilling or unable to denounce. It could be argued, though, that their participation earned them the respect of the Canadian state, since enlisted Aboriginals obtained the right to vote (Dempsey 2006) while at war. However, the treatment that awaited them upon their return from the battlefield was a shock for many among them and made them realize the near-equal treatment they had enjoyed as part of the armed forces was only circumstantial.

After the war, veterans were the responsibility of the new Department of Soldiers' Civil Re-establishment, whose objective was to encourage demobilized military personnel to return to civil life by giving them land (160 acres per soldier). Since little land was available, the federal government decided to turn to the reserves and expropriated or obtained the cession of 85,000 acres of reserve land. Despite their opposition, band chiefs could do nothing to stop it; a series of modifications to the Indian Act permitting the sale and expropriation of land had been put in place in anticipation of the reintegration of veterans (RCAP 1996, 12). The injustice and discrimination did not stop there, as it was decided that status Indian veterans were not admissible to the re-establishment program since they were the responsibility of Indian Affairs (Dempsey 1989; Morton 2008). In most cases, agents from the Department of Soldiers' Civil Re-establishment also denied requests for land made by Aboriginals of other statuses (Metis and non-status Indians), who actually had the right to access this private property. It was rare that Aboriginal veterans of any status obtained the possibility of buying or leasing land, as the report of the Royal Commission on Aboriginal Peoples concludes: "In practice, almost no free land off-reserve was ever granted to a prairie Indian veteran. Neither treaty nor non-treaty Indians were able to homestead in Manitoba, Saskatchewan, Alberta or the North (the Territories)" (RCAP 1996, 13). Moreover, several years later, during the Great Depression that followed the crash of 1929, veterans received assistance from the federal government. It was decided, however, that Aboriginal veterans were not eligible for this special assistance (Morton 2008, 48). It was not until 1936 that this measure was finally rescinded (Gaffen 1985, 37).

This succession of discriminatory policies and practices (forced enrolment in the army, confiscation of reserve lands, non-allocation of subsidies, and refusal to allow Aboriginal veterans the possibility of setting up as farmers) was interpreted by some members of Aboriginal nations as a desire to deny them equal standing and to refuse to see the relationship as one between friends and allies. This was all the more disappointing since, upon returning to their communities, some veterans believed that their war efforts would help integrate them into society. Many even believed that the right to vote would be granted to all Aboriginal Canadians (Dempsey 2006). Consciousness of this prompted some veterans to initiate political movements: some radical and nationalist (Whiteside 1973), others more moderate and seeking mainly to mount an opposition to the dispossession of land (Gaffen 1985). In this way, the first Aboriginal organizations with the goal of uniting local movements were founded. Historians who have studied this question (Moses, Graves, and Sinclair 2004; Gaffen 1985; Innes 2004) are in agreement that these movements and the organizations that structured them played a critical role in raising the political consciousness of Aboriginals, and it will be argued here that they contributed to it and the emergence of the idea that, beyond their differences, their diverse groupings shared a common destiny. As for Aboriginal veterans, they were present not only at the origins of this movement, but they also accompanied it for decades. Hence, some of the leaders who participated in the creation of the Union of Saskatchewan Indians in 1946 were veterans of the First World War (Innes 2004; Federation of Saskatchewan Indian Nations 2006) and in the 1960s, all the chiefs who were members of the Federation of Saskatchewan Indian Nations were former soldiers (ibid.). In fact, as noted by Mishibinijima (2007, 32), Aboriginal leadership evolved a great deal because of the war. The role of veterans in the evolution of leadership is important. Upon their return from the war, not all veterans became engaged in politics or protest, of course; some responded to the call of assimilation—note that Aboriginal enlistment was surely an acculturation tactic on the part of the Department of Indian Affairs (Morton 2008). Numerous veterans participated in projects to modernize their communities; for example, a Masteuhiah chief installed toilets and dug wells in his community, but was reproached for these actions, and this cost him his place as leader. Others, realizing the impossibility of being accepted by society, sought refuge in Aboriginal traditions. This was the case for one of the most renowned Aboriginal heroes, Francis Pegahmagabow. After returning to his community, with 375 kills to his name, he was elected chief and "set about promoting traditional beliefs and customs" (Morton 2008, 43).

Of all the veterans who contributed to the emergence of a pan-Canadian Aboriginal social movement, the Mohawk Lieutenant Fred Loft was without a doubt the most committed. Immediately after the

war, he created the League of Indians in order to oppose the minoriza-
tion of his "people." With this league, Loft sought to bring together
Aboriginal Canadians from across the country in order to form a united front against Ottawa. His project was underpinned by the unam-
biguous idea that Aboriginal Canadians constituted a people distinct
from other Canadians and the demand that they be "heard as a nation"
(cited in Kulchyski 1988, 101). Created in eastern Canada in 1918,
the League of Indians soon found adherents in Manitoba (1920), Saskatchewan (1921), and Alberta (1922). Here is how John Tootoosis,
founder of the League of Indians of Western Canada, speaks about
Loft and how Loft inspired him:

> People from the eastern provinces also went to war. A man
> from the Six Nations went; F.O. Loft was his name. He tried to
> speak for the Indians in England and he was told to go home
> and organize his people. "You alone cannot be heard," he was
> told by the Privy Council. He started a movement. He orga-
> nized a meeting in Ontario. The fourth meeting was at Elphin-
> stone in Manitoba. I saw it; this was in 1920. He wanted to
> organize the Indians across Canada. The next meeting was in
> 1921 at Thunderchild's Reserve. People held that at their own
> expense, they were so anxious to stand up for themselves and
> to be seen to speak with one voice. The seeds that were placed
> in their heads were beginning to ripen. They saw that the only
> method was to sit together and talk in order to achieve any-
> thing. (John Tootoosis 2006)

Loft's influence displeased the federal government, mainly because
members of the league opposed land expropriation and other assimila-
tive practices of the Department of Indian Affairs, including forced
enfranchisement and residential schools. Deputy Superintendent
Duncan Campbell Scott severely suppressed this germinal Aboriginal
movement and used a variety of stratagems to thwart the league. First,
he took on Loft himself, threatening him with enfranchisement,[7] then
putting him under surveillance and sending police officers to attend

meetings of the league. Finally, the Indian Act was modified in order to prohibit status Indians from raising funds to finance the prosecution of claims (RCAP 1996, 17; Dickason 2002).

The continuous pressure applied by Indian Affairs agents brought about the decline of the League of Indians (Titley 1986). Nevertheless, the creation of the league constitutes a turning point in the relationship between Aboriginal Canadians and the state. It marks a beginning, the forebear from which the great Aboriginal organizations and contemporary pan-Canadian emancipatory movements would be born—namely the League of Indians of Western Canada, which became the Protective Association for Indians and their Treaties in 1933, and then the Union of Saskatchewan Indians in 1946. The National Indian Brotherhood, which gave rise to the Assembly of First Nations, the most important Aboriginal political entity in Canada, also came out of the League of Indians. In brief, although the First World War accelerated the marginalization of Aboriginal people in Canadian society, many First Nations continued to believe and hold true to the original treaties and agreements they had made with the British Crown before the war. Simultaneously, the war contributed to the emergence of an Aboriginal social movement that was at the origin of the struggles in which they engaged throughout the twentieth century—struggles to have their rights as first inhabitants recognized and to have historical treaties respected.

The Second World War and the Political Formation of Aboriginal Claims

When the Second World War erupted, many Aboriginal Canadians volunteered for the same reasons as during the war of 1914–1918. However, their socio-economic situation had deteriorated to the point that they lost the capacity to fulfill their basic needs, largely due to the fact that they had been dispossessed of their lands. Many of them enlisted to escape their misery (as was the case for many Canadians), for the army offered its soldiers a salary and food (Moses, Graves, and Sinclair 2004; Sheffield 2004; Poulin 2007). A Metis soldier illustrates this sentiment: "I joined up to make money ... free cloth ... free room and board.... I could send my folks a few dollars because of their problems and what their conditions were" (cited in Poulin 2007, 10). Many women participated for similar reasons, as reported by these two women: "I can't remember my pay but whatever money we got I shared with my family"; "I did not go out very much. I sent half my wages" (cited in Poulin 2007, 35). In this respect, their motivation did not differ much from that of a number of Canadians. The reader will remember that it was partially for this reason that Eddy Weetaltuk joined the Canadian Armed Forces. The health of Aboriginal volunteers was so poor, however, that many of them were refused by the army, so much so that there were fewer Aboriginal participants in the Second World War than in the Great War. As with the First World War, opinions within the Canadian Forces varied regarding whether or not Aboriginal volunteers should be integrated into combat forces. A recruiting agent from Alert Bay, British Columbia, declared that "the Indian would best serve their country by being exempt from active service and kept home in the fishing industry" (cited in Sheffield 2004, 50). A rumour even circulated that the most discontented Aboriginal Canadians were susceptible to Nazi propaganda (Sheffield 2004, 72). Despite their reluctance, the overriding opinion of the government, particularly Indian Affairs, was that the integration of Aboriginal soldiers into the army was a good way to assimilate them and was thus to be encouraged (ibid., 48).

Over 3,000 status Indians, according to the files of Indian Affairs, served their country. It has been estimated that 500 Aboriginal participants, of which 200 were status Indians, lost their lives on the battlefield (RCAP 1996, 38). In addition, Aboriginal Canadians of all origins made generous financial contributions to the Red Cross and the Salvation Army, and bought war bonds to support their country's efforts (RCAP 1996, 19).

Aboriginal participation in the war was once again in the name of their alliance with the British Crown, as expressed by several leaders: "Every Indian in Canada will fight for King George" (Chief Walking Eagle, Rocky Mountain House); "To help our King and Queen and to bring about the downfall of the tyrant" (Joe Delisle, Six Nations) (cited in RCAP 1996, 18). Nevertheless, the Second World War was an occasion for Aboriginal Canadians to remind the Canadian government of the attachment to the British Crown that they had developed: "Indian loyalty to Canada and to the Empire shows the outlook of the Indian is purely Canadian in its nature and character" (Teddy Yellowfly of the Blackfoot Council, cited in RCAP 1996, 18).

This commitment to Canada would also lead Aboriginal Canadians to look upon themselves, fully and henceforth, as citizens: "It is our duty as patriotic citizens to put aside our personal claims or claims of our brotherhood and aid our country in this time of stress ... our country is at war so we the Native Brotherhood are at War" (Ambrose Reid, Native Brotherhood of British Columbia, cited in RCAP 1996, 18). Also, just as during the First World War, Aboriginal Canadians serving in the military formed many bonds of friendship with Canadian soldiers of all origins, leading them to feel as though they were part of the great Canadian family: "For many Aboriginal men and women, life in the armed forces was a new world in which they were truly equal" (RCAP 1996, 33). This was a feeling shared by the women who enlisted, as is shown in the accounts gathered by Poulin, who notes that most of the women said they had not been victims of harassment or discrimination while they were members of the Canadian Forces, contrary to what they endured in civil life before and even after service (Poulin 2007, 39).

The first injustice faced by Aboriginal soldiers upon their return from the Second World War came in the passing of the Veterans' Land Act. The term "Veterans Charter" was created by the Canadian government to encompass all legislation related to veterans of the Second World War. This legislation was not easy to develop, as there were more than one million veterans to reintegrate into society. It had to be flexible enough to fit the needs of a wide variety of situations while taking into account the different experiences of veterans—namely the number of years of service, particularly years spent on the front (Sheffield 2007, 80). While "scholars have branded the Charter a success that helped hundreds of thousands of Canadian veterans make a smooth transition into a civilian life" (Sheffield 2007, 83), it was far from providing benefits to Aboriginal veterans. According to Sheffield (2007), the fact that the Charter was less beneficial to Aboriginal veterans than to their non-Aboriginal counterparts was not purely the result of conscious and systematic discrimination, but was due to the fact that Aboriginal veterans were more likely "to slip through the cracks in the system" (Sheffield 2007, 94). In fact, "the tremendous divergence in the postwar trajectory between Aboriginal and non-Aboriginal veterans had as much (or more) to do with their relative starting place after the war. Not only was the Veterans Charter insufficient to close that gap, it may well have made it wider" (Sheffield 2007, 95). The Veterans Charter includes the Veterans' Land Act,[8] and even before the end of the war, it was already being asked how much land could be secured for distribution to veterans. Not surprisingly, reserve lands were the subject of many of these conversations, as much between First Nations as between civil servants. Nevertheless, contrary to the First World War, the confiscation of reserve lands was not planned, even if the government accepted in certain cases—in breach of its fiduciary role towards Indians—to sell the best land on some reserves to non-Aboriginal veterans. However, even if the Veterans' Land Act did not lead to a massive dispossession of reserve lands, it was still the cause of another misappropriation that would incite the anger of many Aboriginal Canadians.

This act, much like the one put forth by the Department of Soldiers' Civil Re-establishment after the First World War, had the objective of helping veterans reintegrate into civilian life by becoming farmers. But in contrast to the policy put in place by the Department of Soldiers' Civil Re-establishment, which consisted in the allocation of land to demobilized soldiers, the new policy offered a loan to each veteran toward the personal acquisition of land, livestock, or equipment. This financial aid of up to $6,000 consisted in a $2,320 grant and $3,680 loan, repayable over a twenty-five-year period at a low interest rate of 3.5 percent. The state remained owner of the land so long as the non-forgivable portion of the loan was not repaid. This last provision posed a problem for Indian Affairs agents. In effect, given that Crown land is inalienable, it could not serve as security for a loan. They therefore did not know how to handle the requests of status Indians who wished to start a farm on their reserve land. In 1942, the law was amended in order to resolve this problem. The solution was simply to refuse the loan to any veteran starting up a farm on Crown land (in other words, reserves). Status Indians would thereby only have a right to a direct grant, corresponding to the forgivable portion of the loan available to other veterans, of $2,320 (RCAP 1996).

Not only was this solution disadvantageous to veterans who were establishing themselves on reserve land, but it also would affect Aboriginal veterans who were settling off-reserve. In fact, some Indian Affairs agents decided to interpret the law liberally and refused to grant the remaining loan portion of $3,680 to status Indians who were starting a farm off-reserve, and other "Indian [a]gents appear to have dissuaded veterans from this route" (Sheffield 2007, 92). Other agents told off-reserve status Indians that they would have to seek enfranchisement in order to obtain the promised aid (Gaffen 1985). A descendant of an Aboriginal veteran from the First World War reported such an experience. It should be added that if the promised aid was not enough to begin a viable farming operation, Aboriginal veterans could not obtain a bank loan, unlike non-Aboriginal veterans (on this topic, see Sweeny 1979; Innes 2000; Sheffield 2007). In other words, this modification of the Veterans' Land Act permitted Indian Affairs agents to increase their control over members of First Nations and to decide arbitrarily what they could justifiably be accorded. This unequal treatment was one of the grievances of Aboriginal Canadians heard by the RCAP, which motivated the government to establish the National Round Table on First Nations Veterans Issues. Following the submission of the round table report written by Sheffield (2001), the Canadian government apologized and offered compensation to veterans who were members of the First Nations. While many Aboriginal veterans refused the compensation, others welcomed the government's recognition of past errors. However, Metis veterans were excluded from this agreement, which brings to light the difficulty Aboriginal Canadians face when negotiating with the state and in having their rights as descendants of the First Peoples acknowledged.

This unjust distribution of land followed another instance of discrimination of a similar nature that took place during the war. Soldiers who were married or who had children had a right, in addition to their service pay, to a dependants' allowance. This allowance was administered by the Dependants' Allowance Board of the Department of National Defence. The allowance in 1939 was thirty-five dollars for a spouse and twelve dollars each for up to two children; a lump sum of two weeks' salary (a minimum of twenty dollars) was added to this. Indian Affairs officials quickly found that the amount paid was "a great deal more than they [the families of status Indians] actually need" (Inspector Robertson, cited in RCAP 1996, 41). Some even justified their refusal to give the entirety of the allowance under the pretext that "Indian women are the prey of all kinds of crooks and deadbeats... they are also preyed upon by other Indians who find their homes good places to get free meals" (RCAP 1996, 42).

In fact, administrators of Indian Affairs wanted dependants' allowances meant for families of status Indians to be made payable to their department so that they could manage the funds. The Dependants' Allowance Board resisted in the beginning and stipulated that the allowances had to be paid directly to the dependants of the soldiers. Then, accepting Indian Affairs' argument that those living on reserve already had access to forms of assistance, the Board reduced the amount paid to spouses by half. Later, trusting again the reasoning of Indian Affairs agents (for whom Aboriginal wives were legally minors), the board changed its policy once again and decided that, in order to receive the allowance, spouses of status Indian soldiers would have to invest (with the help of Indian Affairs) a portion of the amount received (RCAP 1996).

Further along these lines, the Department of Indian Affairs continued to put measures in place that reduced the amount of allowance paid out. For example, in 1942, the department informed its agents that allowances for dependent children should no longer be paid if the children in question were placed in a residential school, or if they were residing in a sanatorium or hospital. Although the Dependants' Allowance Board tried to oppose the practices of the Indian Affairs agents, the latter continued; not only did certain families not receive the small amount of allowance that the new provisions would accord them, but certain sums that should have been invested in their name simply disappeared. The Royal Commission on Aboriginal Peoples concludes its analysis of these practices with these words: "There were some responsible agents, but others were quick to take advantage of the situation. There is little doubt that some funds vanished, whether through bad administration or fraud" (RCAP 1996, 43–44).

As a consequence, many Aboriginal veterans of the Second World War returned to their communities with the feeling that Canada had used them and then had forgotten them as soon as it no longer had any use for them. The life of Thomas George Prince, veteran of the Second World War and the Korean War, one of the most well-known Aboriginal veterans not only among his community but also by the general population (see Lackenbauer 2007b; Sealey and Van De Vyvere 1981), is an illustration of this treatment. His courage in combat had won the respect of many soldiers and even earned him the Silver Star, a medal awarded by the United States Armed Forces (Gaffen 1985, 56). Returning from duty, Prince believed, as his predecessors had in the Great War, that Aboriginal contribution to the defence of the country would allow relations with non-Aboriginal Canadians to be renewed. He would soon be disappointed and decide, before volunteering for the Korean War, to act: "My job is to unite the Indians of Canada so we can be as strong as possible when we go to the House of Commons" (cited in Lackenbauer 2007b, 41). All the same, Prince died forgotten and destitute (ibid.).

Having become aware of the process of assimilation and dispossession taking place, many Aboriginal veterans were involved, after 1945, in political movements whose aim was to have their rights as veterans recognized and to advance the rights of all Aboriginal Canadians, as well as to ensure compliance with the terms of the treaties signed in the nineteenth and early twentieth century. Several authors, notably Davison (1993), affirm that veterans were once again at the forefront of the struggle for the recognition of Aboriginal rights. According to Innes (2004) and Drees (1997), however, the veterans were not active in Aboriginal political organizations immediately after their return. Rather, they became involved a few years later. A variety of factors explain this lack of participation. Many Aboriginal veterans tried, once demobilized, to integrate into society by the same means (paid work or agriculture) as other veterans—such as Eddy Weetaltuk—attempted to do. It was only after several years of trying in vain and finding no other solution that some of them became militant. Aboriginal political leadership was not lacking, since the leagues were already led by traditional chiefs who were not ready to relinquish their titles (Innes 2000, 2004; Drees 1997) and by veterans from the First World War. Thomas Prince was approached by the Manitoba Indian Association to become their spokesperson based on his reputation and experience, but veterans (who were generally very young) were not immediately called upon by political organizations. It was not until they gained a position of influence within their communities, thanks to their army experience (Innes 2004, 711), that Aboriginal veterans began to play an important part in political organizations. Ultimately, their political participation was great enough during the 1960s that they would play a significant part, as Innes's analysis of Aboriginal leadership in Saskatchewan indicates: "During the 1950s Aboriginal veterans became a force within their Aboriginal communities in Saskatchewan.... By the 1960s veterans were in position of significant influence" (Innes 2004, 711–12).

The involvement of these veterans in politics was such that, during the 1960s, all the chiefs of the Federation of Saskatchewan Indian Nations were veterans of the Second World War. It was under this leadership that Aboriginal organizations, especially those of the Prairies, became involved in a variety of political tussles with the state in which the respect of Aboriginal rights was at stake.

It should be noted that the Second World War greatly contributed to a positive change in the public's opinion of Aboriginal Canadians. In fact, the members of the Canadian population who were aware of their contribution to the war efforts were troubled by their deplorable living conditions and the unequal treatment they received from Canadian institutions, particularly the Department of Indian Affairs and its agents, and had begun to question the agents' authority on an increasingly frequent basis (Sheffield 2004, 127). During the war, many chiefs, "sparked by outrage at being deemed liable to national registration, conscription, and unprecedented taxation ... had begun to organize themselves in earnest in many parts of the country despite administrative opposition" (Sheffield 2004, 139). The change in the public's attitude fed a discourse of Aboriginal victimization, which constituted "the philosophical foundations of support for Indian-policy reform ... broadly accepted in Canada" (Sheffield 2004, 99). This empathy permitted Aboriginal leaders to obtain some support for their claims, moral support at the very least, as indicated by an excerpt from a *Saturday Night* article in British Columbia: "They are simply good citizens, exercising their rights to be heard" (cited in Sheffield 2004, 96). It was the war and the desire to create a better Canada that accompanied victory, in line with the values for which they had fought, which clearly improved how Canadian society saw its Aboriginal members, but this had not "fundamentally altered the nature of the relationship between the dominant society and its original inhabitants" (Sheffield 2004, 107). Aboriginal organizations, in particular those located in the Prairies that were engaged in numerous tugs-of-war with the state on the key issue of ensuring the respect of Aboriginal rights, gained little from this support during the years that followed the Second World War.

However, the growing sympathy for Aboriginal claims, largely due to the media, convinced the federal government to put in place a Senate and House of Commons Special Joint Committee in 1946 to review policy related to Indian Affairs and develop recommendations for revision of the Indian Act. Despite its clear intentions for reform, the committee was influenced by the paternalistic approach still dominant in government; the slogan adopted clearly demonstrates the committee's intentions: "Help the Indians to help themselves" (Sheffield 2004, 141). It was far from the Royal Commission of Inquiry that English-Canadian lobbyists demanded; the committee the government conceded paled in comparison.

The committee heard hundreds of individuals: Indian Affairs agents and departmental heads, scholars, and representatives of civil society groups (unions, religious groups, charities, political organizations, etc.). Some members of the committee even visited reserves in western Quebec and the Maritimes to see the situation of the Aboriginal peoples first-hand. The committee also received a remarkable number of memoirs. However, other committee members objected to having Aboriginal Canadians themselves give testimony, as they did not want to have to hear the "Indian representatives plus their papooses and squaws coming down here and camping in Ottawa" (cited in Sheffield 2004, 151); thus, a motion was passed dismissing the direct participation of Aboriginal Canadians. Instead, it was decided that representatives would participate—Aboriginal representatives if possible—because the committee felt that "there should be someone to control them" (ibid.). This condescending attitude outraged certain committee members and they denounced it publicly, resulting in severe criticism from the press: "Given the tenor of the public debate on the Indian problem and the intellectual and cultural milieu of the immediate post-war years, it was unthinkable to conduct a review of the Indian Act except in consultation with First Nations people" (Sheffield 2004, 156). The adoption of the motion opposing direct consultation cast the committee in a negative light, which is why it spent a great deal of time hearing the representatives of Aboriginal Canadians.

In *Red Man's on the Warpath*, Sheffield (2004) presents an extremely pertinent analysis of the testimonies presented to the committee, as well as the debates that they generated. He shows that the members were, in the end, quite sensitive to the arguments of the representatives and truly wished to offer solutions that would improve life for Aboriginal Canadians. However, they paid more attention to arguments presented by Indian Affairs representatives, and the comments and recommendations of these representatives greatly influenced the final report submitted on 22 June 1948 (Sheffield 2004). The report's objective was to direct policy regarding Aboriginal Canadians, in particular the anticipated Indian Act reforms adopted on 20 June 1951. While the committee's recommendations were hardly revolutionary, they still had little impact on the amendments made to the Indian Act. Some of these amendments provided certain protection to Aboriginal Canadians and recognized the need to grant the band councils more autonomy, but they still did not give them full citizenship and the ultimate goal of the act remained the assimilation of Aboriginal peoples into the dominant culture. The power held by Indian Affairs was not really reduced. More fundamentally, Aboriginals had not succeeded in making their greatest desire known: to become Canadian citizens while keeping their culture in order to develop as a distinct society within Canada. Even members of the Senate and House of Commons Special Joint Committee, who had recommended granting full citizenship, could not understand why Aboriginal Canadians would want to retain their Indian status as well as their way of life instead of joining the ranks of modern Canadian society and enjoying the new rights that the committee proposed to grant them.

While Sheffield (2004) makes the link between Aboriginal contributions to war efforts and the support of the Canadian population clear, his analysis does not specifically note the important part played by veterans during the committee's meetings. Aboriginal veterans undoubtedly played a substantial part since many of them, due to their experience within Canadian society acquired during service, "qualified" to act as representatives able to "control the Aboriginal peoples" as certain commissioners wished. Prince, a hero from the First World War, was one of these representatives. His statements were contested by a witness from Indian Affairs, which shows the extent to which the testimony of these veterans was taken seriously by Indian Affairs management, who recognized the veterans' power to influence the committee. Another veteran, Brigadier Oliver Martin, gave testimony that was very well-received by committee members, who thanked him for his eloquence and honesty.

In this context, Aboriginal leaders refused Prime Minister Pierre Trudeau's project to abolish reserves and then later opposed the Meech Lake Accord. Of course, at the time of this last event, veterans no longer made up the majority of the new Aboriginal leadership (many of them being either too old or deceased). Members of this leadership, however, were cultivated and groomed in political organizations set up by veterans. It is therefore not surprising that the rhetoric that guided their claims included demands of reparations for the state's violations of the provisions of historical treaties. Many Canadians wondered outright, especially after the opposition to the plans of Prime Minister Trudeau, why First Nations were hanging on to the very instruments of their domination (Indian status, reserves, colonial treaties). One might believe that they had arrived at a point of no return and thus refused to be dispossessed of what little they still had.[9]

However, the defence of these colonial attributes—reserves and Indian status—was going to serve as a springboard for a global emancipatory project: the defence of Indian title, which would become the linchpin for the demand for recognition of a specific status for Aboriginal peoples of all origins (Metis, Inuit, status Indians, and non-status Indians). As for the refusal to abandon reserves, it became the symbol of a generalized political rights movement in which all Aboriginal groups participated and whose goal was to secure the restitution of ancestral territories and the right to self-determination. In many respects, Aboriginal veterans from the Second World War were, as those from the First World War had been before them, the catalysts of this movement (Moses, Graves, and Sinclair 2004). Those who had known equality on the battlefield and had fought in the name of democratic values to liberate subjugated peoples wanted nothing other than equality and a return to self-determination.

From the Korean War to the Inuit
Assumption of the Defence of the Arctic
From 1950 to 1953, 26,000 Canadian soldiers participated in the Korean War. Amongst them were numerous veterans of the Second World War, of which several dozen were Aboriginal. The Korean War has never had the same mystique, for reasons now well-known, as the two World Wars that preceded it. Veterans of the Korean War, Aboriginal or not, were therefore relegated to the dustbin of history. They would find their way out only in 1991, when the Canadian government finally decorated the remaining few who were still alive. After the war, the government treated Aboriginal veterans no better and no worse than the others. Nevertheless, Eddy Weetaltuk's text reveals that the major problem they faced was their reintegration into civilian life. Some attempted to find work in large urban centres, but had to endure the prejudice of the population. Others returned to their community,

where socio-economic conditions were deplorable. In short, the time spent fighting for their country made them anticipate equal treatment or dream of a world that was still inaccessible to them. But since they had acquired, thanks to their training in the army, the tools and the knowledge of Euro-Canadian society necessary to be able to change things, some of them became involved in Aboriginal movements such as the Native Council of Canada or the Métis National Council.[10] Eddy Weetaltuk was among them. Most notably, he participated in the back-to-roots movement with Inuit of Kuujjuarapik, who moved to Umiujaq at the end of the 1980s in order to build a more traditional community—closer to nature and farther from the negative influences of modernity (Martin 2003).

But what was the specific impact of war on Canadian Inuit? The answer might be somewhat surprising because, while there was no combat on Inuit territory, the wars of the twentieth century had important repercussions for Inuit communities. In fact, war disrupted their lives on several occasions. These intrusions took the form of military bases, radar stations, and even a rocket-launching facility in Churchill. Beginning with the Second World War, the effects of the militarization of the Arctic on Inuit communities were not without importance, since the number of military personnel in some villages reached several hundred. Indeed, sometimes the number of personnel would even count in the thousands, as was the case with Churchill where, during the Cold War, 4,500 military personnel and support staff were stationed (Fleming 1988).

Most of the time, the presence of these military bases created employment that, although only temporary, contributed to the improvement of economic conditions for the Inuit. Interaction between military personnel and the local population also gave Inuit the opportunity to meet young Canadians or young Americans who were not working for the same few institutions with which they were traditionally in contact (Royal Canadian Mounted Police, Indian and Northern Affairs Canada, trading companies, and missionaries). In the beginning, these relationships had such positive effects that, as Mélanie Gagnon (1999) suggests in her study of the American base at Frobisher Bay (Iqaluit), Inuit hold positive memories of that era. On the other hand, from a

structural point of view, this military presence had significant negative repercussions. According to Jenness (1964), this accelerated Inuit
alienation from traditional modes of economic production, thereby
increasing their dependence on money and on goods imported from
the South. To this, one can add the important social impact resulting
from the introduction of alcohol and illicit drugs into communities, as
was the case with Kuujjuarapik (Martin 2003a). Concerning the military base at Churchill, Inuit were moved from Kuujjuaq in order to
participate in the construction of military installations, but once the
Cold War was over the military base was dismantled and the jobs it
provided were lost. As for the Inuit of Kuujjuaq that were in Churchill,
some of them were not able to return home.[11]

Still, the most negative experiences were of forced relocations in
the Canadian Far North, which also took place during the Cold War.
As mentioned previously, relocations were catastrophic for Inuit who
were settled in locations so northern and remote that the fauna was insufficient to sustain a community (Marcus 1991; Tester and Kulchyski
1994). It is noteworthy that several reasons led the state to organize
such relocations. First, as Eddy Weetaltuk states, the goal was to find
new hunting grounds in order to relieve the pressure placed on the
ecosystem by Inuit hunters in the more southern zones of their territory. In effect, it was forecast by agents of the federal government that
the concentration and sedentarization of Inuit around a rather small
number of service centres would lead rapidly to the overexploitation of
resources. This would, in turn, increase their dependence on subsidies
from the state. It was thus decided to send some Inuit families and sea-
soned hunters to "colonize" new territories. There was another factor,
however, that played a role in the creation of this policy. With the tension rising between the Soviet Union and the United States, the Canadian government feared that these other countries might want to annex
the "uninhabited" islands of Canada's Far North (Marcus 1991). Inuit
relocation was considered a means of ensuring Canadian sovereignty.
In demonstrating that these islands were in fact inhabited by Canadian
citizens, the federal government was responding to the international
community's criteria concerning the minimal conditions for ensuring

a country's sovereignty (ibid.). This reason was certainly never made public, but was confirmed by a confidential report written for the Department of Northern Affairs and National Resources by C.M. Bolger in 1960: "This community [Resolute Bay] also serves a distinctly useful purpose in confirming, in a tangible manner, Canada's sovereignty over this vast region of the Arctic" (cited in Marcus 1991, 64).

Thus, without even being made aware, the Inuit were mobilized to contribute to the defence of Canadian territory. The Cold War had, in its own way, landed on Inuit soil. However, contrary to these events, which left them with the sense that Canada's wars could indirectly affect their destiny, another aspect of Arctic militarization would give them occasion to contribute directly to the defence of their territory and of Canada—the creation of the Canadian Rangers in 1947. Little known to the larger public, the Rangers, today numbering more than 5,000, are enrolled as reservists in the Canadian Armed Forces. Of the 168 Ranger patrols situated in and managed by northern communities and coastal communities from Newfoundland to Nunavik and including Vancouver Island, 60 percent of members are Aboriginal Canadians (Lackenbauer 2007). In Nunavut, almost all reservists are Inuit. The Rangers represent a way to ensure, at a very low cost, an active military presence in the isolated regions of the Canadian North (essentially north of the 50th parallel). Their implementation also provided a way to circumvent strong Inuit opposition to the militarization of the Arctic, to which the government responded by listing the socio-political benefits that the Rangers would provide to Inuit communities (Lackenbauer 2007, 102). Their primary mandate is to conduct surveillance patrols in Arctic territory, and "if the unthinkable comes to pass to delay enemies using guerilla tactics" (Lackenbauer 2007, 101). They also play an important role in rescue missions. They provided assistance to victims of the 1 January 1999 avalanche in Kangiqsualujjuaq (Nunavik), which left nine dead and seventy wounded (Moses, Graves, and Sinclair 2004, 84).

What is particular about the Rangers is their considerable autonomy within the Canadian Armed Forces. This is most evident in the fact that they are organized by community and that they elect their own patrol leaders. They are therefore not conventional military units that group individuals together haphazardly, but rather are modern transpositions of traditionally minded communities. This traditional component is in addition to the fact that elders play a central role in the Rangers. They offer guidance if problems are encountered and they also pass on to young Rangers the knowledge relating to nature and the land that they need to perform their duties. This integration of traditional knowledge and modernity helps to reinforce the conviction of the Inuit that their knowledge and heritage still have an important role to play in contemporary society.

Their autonomy within the Armed Forces also applies to technical aspects, since they receive little material support and have to furnish the necessary clothing and equipment themselves, as the army only provides them with a uniform consisting of: "A red hooded sweatshirt, a T-shirt, a baseball cap, a brassard and a vest. They are equipped with a No. 4 Lee Enfield rifle, and each patrol group has a first aid kit, GPS (Global Positioning System), a compass, and a short-wave radio. The Rangers are responsible for providing all other equipment, such as snowmobiles and boats" (Moses, Graves, and Sinclair 2004, 83).

Because they play a role as guardians of the Arctic, Inuit do not feel dependent on the rest of Canada for their security. On the contrary, they have the assurance of providing their own protection, all the while participating in the affirmation of national sovereignty. One might certainly believe that surveillance of the Arctic has become an entirely symbolic task since the end of the Cold War. This is not at all the case, however, because the Arctic is now facing a new threat: climate change. Once again, then, Inuit have been called on to contribute to the defence of national interests. They are, in a way, the watchmen of climate change, since the observations they make serve regularly to bolster the arguments of Canadian scientists involved in international forums.[12] Moreover, as is now known, global warming is soon going to liberate the Northwest Passage from its ice, thereby making it the fastest maritime route connecting Asia to Europe. Already several governments, the United States and Russia among them, have made their position known: Arctic waters must be considered international waters. Of course, Canada is opposed to this and, once again, it can count on the collaboration of Inuit Rangers who continue to conduct surveillance of the territory and who, in patrolling it, establish *de facto* Canada's sovereignty over this immense region.

Because they participate of their own free will in the defence of Canadian sovereignty, Inuit feel engaged in an equal relationship with Canada. Thus, during the address that he gave at the inaugural ceremony of Nunavut, Paul Okalik, premier of the new territory, declared that the Inuit people were proud to join Canadian Confederation. He thereby signified that Inuit had never abdicated their sovereignty and that they were a free people choosing to ally themselves to Canada's destiny, just as the First Nations had engaged in alliances with the Europeans before them.

The state of Aboriginality is therefore less a fact *of nature* (anteriority on the land and ethnicity) or of *culture* (distinct way of life), than the result of a historical process of differentiation and unfavourable social stratification—one that we have called "marginalization." In fact, the term "Aboriginal" comes from a categorization imposed from outside. It is based on ethnicity, as the Indian Act categorizes members of the First Nations by blood. The reduction of Aboriginal Canadians to a state of inequality—that of minority—was for a long time legitimated by two principles. First of all, ethnicity: the Indian Act categorizes members of First Nations by blood. Second, by culture: to be Aboriginal is to have a distinct way of life. One must hunt or fish and maintain a *traditional* relationship with nature than a *modern* one. It is not surprising that these two criteria (ethnic membership and culture) form the basis of two current racist discourses to which Aboriginal Canadians and other minorities fall victim: conventional racism, which consists in disparaging the Other because of biological inferiority, and a racism that can be classified as neo-Darwinian, in which the Other is disparaged as a member of an inferior culture. If racism was at the heart of First Nations' marginalization, it also contributed to the essentialization of Aboriginality by imprisoning it in "ready-to-wear" constructs (the savage and the "noble savage"). If Aboriginal persons lose their cultural characteristics, or if they want to free themselves from them by urbanizing (going into business or commercial forestry, for example), their authenticity, even their status, is questioned.

This reduction of the Aboriginal person to these biological and cultural attributes has taken place progressively. In effect, at the time of first contact, Europeans and Indigenous peoples were engaged in a relationship of equals—even if it was often characterized by conflict— which explains why the latter were not classified as Aboriginal, but rather as Innu, Anishinabe, Wendat, Dene, Mohawk, Nisga'a, and so on. They defined themselves not as intrinsically distinct from Europeans, but more as a function of their "position" in alliances with the Europeans and other Aboriginal nations. It was the end of this equality that created the category of Aboriginal. Their participation in war efforts made them aware of how the state had reduced their status to that of minors and minorities. Of course, war was only one of several causes of this awareness. Residential schools, like some other assimilationist colonial projects, also played an important role. Nevertheless, war's contribution to Aboriginal comprehension of their marginalization is unique. In essence, war allowed them to experience, on the battlefield, equality as Canadian society defined it, only to realize that it had been refused them in other societal domains. At the same time, their participation in conflicts made them realize that the equality and freedom they were fighting for did not apply to them outside of the army. In addition, war was also instrumental to the emergence and the empowerment of a pan-Canadian Aboriginal social movement, since it was war that cultivated the first opponents—the veterans—to the state's project of accelerating their dispossession and assimilation.

Most of all, Aboriginal veterans' specific claims and the way they were expressed are largely at the origins of Aboriginal identity formation, political projects, and legal struggles as they are being played out today. Indeed, the first to stand against the state could have demanded equality in terms of identity status, or even treatment, but the conditions they returned to after the war made them realize that they had been refused this republican equality. This is why they would end up choosing another path, preferring rather to demand equality in difference, insisting on the preservation of reserves, Indian status, and the respect of rights and distinct treatment that results directly or indirectly from it. Some may be surprised or even irritated (Simard 2003) by the fact that the difference being claimed is one originally constructed to marginalize Aboriginal peoples. What is interesting from a sociological point of view is that the twentieth century saw Aboriginal Canadians become aware of the ethnic and cultural difference that the state used to justify their marginalization. But rather than deny it, they internalized it and fashioned from it the instrument of their emancipation. This process, whereby Aboriginal Canadians appropriated this difference for themselves in order to make a *distinction*, can be termed Aboriginalization.

Although Eddy Weetaltuk's text is, in my opinion, more of a literary creation than a historical narrative, as Bernadette Rigal-Cellard's analysis demonstrates, it nevertheless remains very important from a historico-anthropological standpoint, because it constitutes the first known Inuit perspective on war. The publication of this book is therefore unique, because it allows us to become aware of the existence of an Inuit narration of war. I began this text by emphasizing that history is not an objective fact experienced in an identical fashion by all concerned parties, but a construction of parallel realities. In order to understand the difficulties experienced by Aboriginal Canadians during Canadian wars, and to grasp how these oriented their history and helped to shape their present, one must adopt an *understanding* approach. That is to say, one must listen to the accounts that Aboriginal Canadians relate. This book that Eddy Weetaltuk has offered us represents a rare opportunity to stop telling, in their name, the history of Aboriginal Canadians. Rather, we can finally let them speak.

NOTES

1. I would like to acknowlege Evan Habkirk's additional research and revisions to prepare this text for publication. I would also like to thank John Moses for the information and the lines of reflection that he suggested. I wish to extend my thanks to friends and colleagues who helped with this final work.

2. Other examples could also be offered. One can simply look at the role that the French Resistance plays in the history written by the French, as opposed to the importance accorded it by historians of other nations. In this same vein, one could

examine the Battle of Stalingrad and the role it played in the "grand narrative" of the Second World War told by Russians just as much during the Soviet era as today.

3. Indeed, I am fully conscious that it is impossible to really understand the "Other," because when we speak of "Him," it is always in relation to a "We." Nevertheless, engaging in such a process allows us to free ourselves from the ethnocentrism that causes us to see the "Other" as a simple, inverse reflection of ourselves.

4. For example, several agreements signed with the Iroquois nations were complemented with the making of wampum.

5. Moses, Graves, and Sinclair (2004, 63) estimate that the more French or English speakers a band had, the higher the proportional enrollment.

6. During the Second World War, the Canadian government would again enact conscription, this time through the National Resources Mobilization Act of 1940. For more on how First Nations people fought their compulsory military service in the Second World War, see R. Scott Sheffield and Hamar Foster, "Fighting the King's War: Harris Smallfence, Verbal Treaty Promises and the Conscription of Indian Men, 1944," *University of British Columbia Law Review* 33 (1): 53–74.

7. Enfranchisement was generally voluntary and consisted in the renunciation of one's Indian status in order to be able to fill a position that had otherwise been prohibited. Certain forms of enfranchisement were, on the other hand, automatic. In the beginning of the twentieth century, all status Indians who graduated from a college or university were enfranchised. In addition, until 1985, women who married a non-status man lost their Indian status, as did their children. Conversely, Indian status would neither be lost to a man nor his children if he married a non-status woman. During the 1920s and '30s, the Department of Indian Affairs also began a program of forced enfranchisement in which they, without the consent of the individual about to be enfranchised, would select people they deemed ready to take on the responsibility of Canadian citizenship. This program was used for the enfranchisement of many veterans, including Loft, as their military service proved their readiness for Canadian citizenship. This also shows that the category of "Indian," as it was imposed upon First Nations by the state, was founded both on ethnicity and on cultural terms (an Indian being considered as having a lifestyle necessarily incompatible with a classical education). Today, some of these discriminatory provisions have been removed from the Indian Act. Nevertheless, Indian status still remains founded on ethnicity and is lost when one's genetic inheritance is insufficiently "Indian," according to the terms of the legislation.

8. This act is still in force and was last modified on 25 August 2013.

9. This attitude was not exclusive to Aboriginal Canadians, but rather was generalized amongst Aboriginal North Americans, as the words of Sherman J. Alexie Jr, an Aboriginal author from the United States, indicate: "So much has been taken from us that we hold on to the smallest things with all the strength we have left" (cited in Rigal-Cellard 2004, 14).

10. Information collected from Metis veterans interviewed in Manitoba in 2004.

11. Information given by Inuit in Nunavik and confirmed by residents of Churchill.

12. Of course, this question is much more complex, since Canada is itself one of the largest producers of greenhouse gases. That said, this has not prevented the federal government from using, on several occasions, the argument that climate change threatens the way of life of the Inuit (see Martin 2004).

REFERENCES

Alexie, Sherman. 2000. "The Unauthorized Autobiography of Me." In *Here First: Autobiographical Essays by Native American Writers*, edited by Arnold Krupat and Brian Swan, 3–14. New York: The Modern Library.

Balesi, Charles John. 1979. *From Adversaries to Comrades-In-Arms: West Africans and the French Military, 1885–1918*. Waltham, MA: Crossroads Press.

Basile, Suzy. 2001. "Diplomates autochtones au 18ᵉ siècle." *Innuvelle* 4 (6): 10.

Brownlie, Robin. 1998. "Work Hard and Be Grateful: Native Soldier Settlers in Ontario After the First World War." In *On the Case: Explorations in Social History*, edited by Franca Iacovetta, 181–203. Toronto: University of Toronto Press.

Canada. National Defence. 2005. "National Defence and the Canadian Armed Forces." http://www.forces.gc.ca/en/index.page (accessed 1 May 2005).

——. 2006. "Section Chefs des réserves et cadets." http://www.rangers.forces.gc.ca/pubs/rangers/overview/stats_f.asp (accessed 1 April 2006).

Canadian Encyclopaedia. 2006. "Fondation Historica du Canada." http://www.thecanadianencyclopedia.com/ (accessed 1 April 2006).

Chafer, Tony. 2008. "Forgotten Soldiers." *History Today* 58 (11): 35–37.

Davison, Janet. 1983. "We Shall Remember: Canada's Indians and World War Two." MA thesis, Trent University.

Delâge, Denys. 1985. *Le pays renversé: Amérindiens et Européens en Amérique du Nord-Est 1600–1664*. Montreal: Boréal. Translated by Jane Brierly as *Bitter Feast: Amerindians and Europeans in Northeastern North America, 1600–64*. Vancouver: UBC Press, 1993.

Dempsey, L. James. 1983. "The Indians and World War One." *Alberta History* 31 (3): 1–8.

——. 1989. "Problems of Western Canadian Indian War Veterans after World War One." *Native Studies Review* 5 (2): 1–18.

——. 1999. *Warriors of the King: Prairie Indians in World War I*. Regina: Canadian Plains Research Center.

——. 2006. "Aboriginal Soldiers in the First World War." Ottawa: Library and Archives Canada. http://www.collectionscanada.gc.ca/aboriginal-heritage/020016-4001-e.html (accessed 5 May 2016).

Dickason, Olive Patricia. 2002. *Canada's First Nations: A History of Founding Peoples From Earlier Times*. 3rd ed. Don Mills, ON: Oxford University Press.

Drees, Laurie Meijer. 1997. "A History of the Indian Association of Alberta." PhD diss., University of Calgary.

Federation of Saskatchewan Indian Nations. 2006. "Federation of Saskatchewan Indian Nations." http://www.fsin.com/ (accessed 1 April 2006).

Fleming, Mark. 1988. *Churchill: Polar Bear Capital of the World*. Winnipeg: Hyperion Press.

Frideres, James S., and René R. Gadacz. 2001. *Aboriginal Peoples in Canada: Contemporary Conflicts*. 6th ed. Toronto: Prentice Hall.

Gaffen, Fred. 1985. *Forgotten Soldiers*. Penticton, BC: Theytus Books.

Gagnon, Mélanie. 1999. "Les militaires américains à Crystal 2 (Frobisher Bay), dans les années 1940: perspectives Inuit." MA thesis, Laval University.

Goodwill, Jean and Norma Sluman. 1992. *John Tootoosis*. Winnipeg: Pemmican Publications.

GWCA (Great War Centenary Association). 2014. "Six Nations Conscription." http://doingourbit.ca/six-nations-conscription (accessed 25 November 2015).

Habkirk, Evan J. 2010. "Militarism, Sovereignty, and Nationalism: Six Nations and the First World War." MA thesis, Trent University.

Harrison, Julia D. 1985. *Metis: People between Two Worlds*. Vancouver: Glenbow-Alberta Institute and Douglas and McIntyre.

Innes, Robert Alexander. 1997. *Indian Veterans: Honouring the Experience* (Report for Chief Poundmaker Historical Centre Archival Research Project). Saskatoon: Department of Native Studies, University of Saskatchewan.

———. 1999. *Oral History Methods in Native Studies: Saskatchewan Aboriginal World War Two Veterans*. Vol. 19–20. Oral History Forum. http://www.oralhistoryforum. ca (accessed 5 May 2016).

———. 2000. "The Socio-Political Influence of the Second World War Saskatchewan Aboriginal Veterans, 1945–1960." MA thesis, University of Saskatchewan.

———. 2004. "'I'm On Home Ground Now. I'm Safe': Saskatchewan Aboriginal Veterans in the Immediate Postwar Years 1945–1946." *American Indian Quarterly* 28 (2–3): 685–715.

———. 2009. "'Wait a Second. Who Are You Anyways?' The Insider/Outsider Debate and American Indian Studies." *American Indian Quarterly* 33 (4): 440–61.

Ives, Don. 1999. "The Veterans Charter: 'The Compensation Principle and Principle of Recognition for Service.'" In *The Veterans Charter and Post-World War II Canada*, edited by Peter Neary and J. L. Granatstein, 85–94. Montreal: McGill-Queen's University Press.

Jenness, Diamond. 1964. "War Ferment." In *Eskimo Administration: II. Canada*. Technical Paper no. 14: 72–77. Montreal: Arctic Institute of America.

Krouse, Susan Applegate, and Joseph K. Dixon. 2007. *North American Indians in the Great War*. Lincoln: University of Nebraska Press.

Kulchyski, Peter. 1988. "A Considerable Unrest: F.O. Loft and the League of Indians." *Native Studies Review* 4 (1–2): 95–107.

Lackenbauer, P. Whitney. 2004. "The Irony and the Tragedy of Negotiated Space: A Case Study on Narrative Form and Aboriginal-Government Relations during the Second World War." *Journal of the Canadian Historical Association* 15 (1): 177–206.

———. 2007a. *Battle Grounds: The Canadian Military and Aboriginal Lands*. Vancouver: University of British Columbia Press.

———. 2007b. "'A Hell of a Warrior': Sergeant Thomas George Prince." *Journal of Historical Biography* 1 (1): 27–78.

Lackenbauer, P. Whitney, and Craig Leslie Mantle. 2007. *Aboriginal Peoples and the Canadian Military: Historical Perspectives*. Winnipeg: Canadian Defence Academy Press.

Lackenbauer, P. Whitney, R. Scott Sheffield, and Craig Leslie Mantle. 2007. *Aboriginal Peoples and Military Participation: Canadian and International Perspectives*. Winnipeg: Canadian Defence Academy Press.

Marcus, Alan R. 1991. "Out in the Cold: Canada's Experimental Inuit Relocation to Grise Fjord and Resolute Bay." *Polar Record* 27 (163): 283–96.

Martin, Thibault. 2002. "Rivalités franco-anglaises en hudsonie (1904–1926), à l'origine de la structuration du territoire." *Recherches Amérindiennes au Québec* 32 (2): 71–82.

———. 2003a. *De la banquise au congélateur: Mondialisation et culture.* Paris and Quebec: UNESCO and Presses de l'Université Laval.

———. 2003b. "From Documentary to Social Sciences: How the Issue of Representing the Other Emerges." In *Screening Culture: Constructing Image and Identity,* edited by Heather Norris Nicholson, 191–205. London: Lexington Books.

———. 2004. "Le changement climatique, un problème global." *Accès International* (November): 23–35.

Mishibinijima, Jaime. 2007. "Aboriginal Identity, Leadership and Values in the Profession of Arms." *In Aboriginal Peoples and Military Participation: Canadian and International Perspectives,* edited by P. Whitney Lackenbauer, R. Scott Sheffield, and Craig Leslie Mantle, 17–34. Kingston: Canadian Defence Academy Press.

Morton, Desmond. 2008. "Les canadiens indigènes engagés dans la première guerre mondiale." *Guerres Mondiales et Conflits Contemporains* 230 (June): 37–49.

———. 2008. "From Mashantucket to Appomattox: The Native American Veterans of Connecticut's Volunteer Regiments and the Union Navy." *New England Quarterly* 81 (4): 596–635.

Moses, John, Donald Graves, and Warren Sinclair. 2004. *A Sketch Account of Aboriginal Peoples in the Canadian Military.* Ottawa: Minister of National Defence. http://publications.gc.ca/collections/Collection/D61-16-2004E.pdf.

Poulin, Grace. 2007. *Invisible Women: Aboriginal Servicewomen in Canada's WWII Military.* Thunder Bay: Grace Poulin.

RCAP (Royal Commission on Aboriginal Peoples). 1996. *Royal Commission Report on Aboriginal Peoples.* Ottawa: Canada Communication Group Publishing. http://www.ainc-inac.gc.ca/ (accessed 1 January 2006).

Rigal-Cellard, Bernadette. 2004. *Le mythe et la plume: la littérature indienne contemporaine en Amérique du Nord.* Monaco: Éditions du Rocher.

———. 2009. "From the Tundra to the Trenches d'Eddy Weetaltuk ou les lettres persanes r evisitées: quand un Inuk découvre la sauvagerie de l'Occident." In *La fabrique du sauvage dans la culture Nord-Américaine,* edited by Lionel Larré and Véronique Béghain, 61–72. Pessac: Presses universitaires de Bordeaux.

Saskatchewan Indian Veterans Association. 1999. *We Were There: Saskatchewan Indian Veterans.* Saskatoon: Federation of Saskatchewan Indian Nation.

Sealey, D. Bruce, and Peter Van de Vyvere. 1981. *Manitobans in Profile: Thomas George Prince.* Winnipeg: Peguis.

Sheffield, R. Scott. 1996. "'Of Pure European Descent and of White Race': Recruitment Policy and Aboriginal Canadians, 1939–1945." *Canadian Military History* 5 (1): 8–15.

———. 2001. *A Search for Equity: A Study of the Treatment Accorded to First Nations Veterans and Dependents of the Second World War and the Korean Conflict.* Ottawa: Department of National Defence.

———. 2004. *The Red Man's on the Warpath: The Image of the "Indian" and the Second World War*. Vancouver: UBC Press.

———. 2005. "Rehabilitating the Indigene: Post-War Reconstruction and the Image of the Indigenous Other in Anglo-Canada and New Zealand, 1943–48." In *Rediscovering the British World*, edited by Phillip Buckner and R. Douglas Francis, 341–60. Calgary: University of Calgary Press.

———. 2007. "Canadian Aboriginal Veterans and the Veterans' Charter After the Second World War." In *Aboriginal Peoples and Military Service: Canadian and International Perspectives*, edited by Whitney Lackenbauer, R. Scott Sheffield, and Craig Mantle. Kingston: Canadian Defence Academy Press.

Sheffield, R. Scott, and Hamar Foster. 1999. "Fighting the King's War: Harris Smallfence, Verbal Treaty Promises and the Conscription of Indian Men, 1944." *University of British Columbia Law Review* 33 (1): 53–74.

Simard, Jean-Jacques. 2003. *La réduction: l'autochtone inventé et les amérindiens d'aujourd'hui*. Sillery: Septentrion.

Sioui, George. 1992. *For an Amerindian Autohistory: An Essay on the Foundations of a Social Ethic*. Montreal: McGill-Queen's University Press.

Stanley, G.F. 1985. "The Significance of the Six Nations Participation in the War of 1812," *Ontario History* 40 (4): 215–21.

Steckley, John L., and Bryan D. Cummins. 2010. *Full Circle: Canada's First Nations*, 2nd ed. Toronto: Prentice-Hall.

Stevenson, Michael D. 1996. "The Mobilisation of Native Canadians During the Second World War." *Journal of the Canadian Historical Association* 7 (1): 205–26.

Summerby, Janice. 2005. *Native Soldiers—Foreign Battlefields*. Ottawa: Veterans Affairs Canada. http://www.veterans.gc.ca (accessed 5 May 2016).

Sweeny, Alastair. 1979. *Government Policy and Saskatchewan Indian Veterans: A Brief History of the Canadian Government's Treatment of Indian Veterans of the Two Wars*. Ottawa: Tyler, Wright, and Daniel.

Talbot, Robert J. 2011. "'It Would Be Best to Leave Us Alone': First Nations Responses to the Canadian War Effort, 1914–18." *Journal of Canadian Studies* 45 (1): 90–120.

Tester, Frank, and Peter Kulchyski. 1994. *Tammarniut (Mistakes): Inuit and Relocation in the Eastern Arctic, 1939–1963*. Vancouver: UBC Press.

Titley, E. Brian. 1986. *Narrow Vision: Duncan Campbell Scott and the Administration of Indian Affairs in Canada*. Vancouver: UBC Press.

Tootoosis, John. 2006. "Federation of Saskatchewan Indian Nations History." Federation of Saskatchewan Indian Nations. http://www.sicc.sk.ca/archive/heritage/ethnography/fsin/fsin_history_jt.html (accessed 1 April 2006).

Whiteside, Don. 1973. *Historical Development of Aboriginal Political Associations in Canada: Documentation, Reference Aids, Indexes*. Ottawa: National Indian Brotherhood.

Winegard, Timothy C. 2012. *For King and Kanata: Canadian Indians and the First World War*. Winnipeg: University of Manitoba Press.